Leadership in Sport

Effective leadership is essential in any sports organisation, both in the boardroom and on the training pitch. *Leadership in Sport* is the first textbook to examine sports leadership in the world, across both management and coaching environments. It includes a section dedicated to underpinning core leadership theories, and employs a number of case studies throughout to show how best practice is applied in real world settings.

Drawing on expertise from some of the leading academics and practitioners throughout the world, and from both disciplines, the book covers various leadership issues including:

- facilitative leadership
- strategic leadership
- leading effective change
- diversity in leadership
- communication and empathy
- motivation and performance.

Key conceptual questions – the nature of leadership, its role in sport, styles of leadership, what constitutes ineffective leadership – and other contemporary issues are also explored to give students and practitioners the most complete and clear picture of contemporary leadership in sport. With useful features in every chapter, such as key terms and review questions, this is an essential text for sport management or coaching degree courses.

Ian O'Boyle is with the School of Management in the UniSA Business School, Australia. He is an expert in the fields of sport governance and leadership. His work appears in the leading sport management journals including *European Sport Management Quarterly, International Journal of Sport Management* and *Sport Management Review* and also within traditional business and management based journals such as *Journal of Career Development* and *Organization Development Journal*. Dr O'Boyle's passion and interest within sport management research is fuelled from his previous experiences as an NCAA athlete in the United States and member of the Irish national basketball team.

Duncan Murray is also with the School of Management in the UniSA Business School, Australia. He has published in a range of academic journals in areas including: leadership, globalisation, celebrity endorsement in sport, customer behaviour in recreation and sport settings, tourism, appearance and attractiveness, and the management of sport and recreation. He is an editorial board member for *Sport, Business, Management: An International Journal*. He is also a reviewer of academic papers for a number of leisure, recreation and sport academic journals, including the *Journal of Leisure Research, Managing Leisure* and *Annals of Leisure Research*.

Paul Cummins is an expert in leadership within sport coaching having gained his PhD at the University of Ulster School of Psychology, UK. He is a lecturer in performance psychology and has numerous research publications within the field. His research interests include various aspects of leadership in sport, athlete transitions, culture change and social identity, particularly as they apply within the sport coaching context. Within the applied sports setting, Paul is a qualified sport psychologist who has worked with Olympic level athletes and top coaches seeking to increase their leadership and overall coaching performance.

Foundations of Sport Management

Series Editors:
David Hassan, University of Ulster at Jordanstown, UK

Foundations of Sport Management is a discipline-defining series of texts on core and cutting-edge topics in sport management. Featuring some of the best known and most influential sport management scholars from around the world, each volume represents an authoritative, engaging and self-contained introduction to a key functional area or issue within contemporary sport management. Packed with useful features to aid teaching and learning, the series aims to bridge the gap between management theory and practice and to encourage critical thinking and reflection among students, academics and practitioners.

Also available in this series

Managing Sport Business: An Introduction
David Hassan and Linda Trenberth

Managing Sport: Social and Cultural Perspectives
David Hassan and Jim Lusted

Managing High Performance Sport
Popi Sotiriadou and Veerle De Bosscher

Routledge Handbook of Sport and Corporate Social Responsibility
Kathy Babiak, Juan Luis Paramio-Salcines and Geoff Walters

Sport Governance: International Case Studies
Ian O'Boyle and Trish Bradbury

Research Methods for Sport Management
James Skinner, Allan Edwards and Ben Corbett

Leadership in Sport
Ian O'Boyle, Duncan Murray and Paul Cummins

Leadership in Sport

**Edited by
Ian O'Boyle,
Duncan Murray
and Paul Cummins**

 Routledge
Taylor & Francis Group

LONDON AND NEW YORK

First published 2015
by Routledge
2 Park Square, Milton Park, Abingdon, Oxon OX14 4RN

and by Routledge
711 Third Avenue, New York, NY 10017

Routledge is an imprint of the Taylor and Francis Group, an informa business

© 2015 I. O'Boyle, D. Murray and P. Cummins

British Library Cataloguing-in-Publication Data
A catalogue record for this book is available from the British Library

Library of Congress Cataloging in Publication Data
Leadership in sport/edited by Ian O'Boyle, Duncan Murray and Paul Cummins.
    pages cm. – (Foundations of Sport Management)
    Includes bibliographical references and index.
    1. Coaching (Athletics) 2. Leadership. 3. Teamwork (Sports) I. O'Boyle, Ian.
    GV711.L42 2015
    796.07'7 – dc23
    2014048171

ISBN: 978-1-138-81824-8 (hbk)
ISBN: 978-1-138-81825-5 (pbk)
ISBN: 978-1-315-74537-4 (ebk)

Typeset in Perpetua and Bell Gothic
by Florence Production Ltd, Stoodleigh, Devon, UK

Contents

Illustrations

FIGURES

TABLES

Editors' biographies

Ian O'Boyle, PhD, is with the School of Management in the UniSA Business School. He is an expert in the fields of sport governance and leadership. His work appears in the leading sport management journals including *European Sport Management Quarterly*, *International Journal of Sport Management* and *Sport Management Review*, and also within traditional business and management based journals such as *Journal of Career Development* and *Organization Development Journal*. Dr O'Boyle's passion and interest within sport management research is fuelled from his previous experiences as an NCAA athlete in the United States and member of the Irish national basketball team.

Duncan Murray, PhD, is also with the School of Management in the UniSA Business School. He has published in a range of academic journals in areas including: leadership, globalisation, celebrity endorsement in sport, customer behaviour in recreation and sport settings, tourism, appearance and attractiveness, and the management of sport and recreation. He is an editorial board member for *Sport, Business, Management: An International Journal*. He is also a reviewer of academic papers for a number of leisure, recreation and sport academic journals, including the *Journal of Leisure Research*, *Managing Leisure* and *Annals of Leisure Research*.

Paul Cummins, PhD, is an expert in leadership within sport coaching, having gained his PhD at the University of Ulster School of Psychology. He is a lecturer in performance psychology and has numerous research publications within the field. His research interests include various aspects of leadership in sport, athlete transitions, culture change and social identity, particularly as they apply within the sport coaching context. Within the applied sports setting, Paul is a qualified sport psychologist who has worked with Olympic level athletes and top coaches seeking to increase their leadership and overall coaching performance.

Contributors

Chris Bond – University of Roehampton (United Kingdom)
Laura Burton – University of Connecticut (United States)
Tony Cassidy – University of Ulster (United Kingdom)
Sarah Chua – University of South Australia (Australia)
Dave Collins – University of Central Lancashire (United Kingdom)
Andrew Cruickshank – University of Edinburgh (United Kingdom)
Ljiljana Erakovic – University of Auckland (New Zealand)
Lesley Ferkins – AUT University (New Zealand)
Andrea N. Geurin-Eagleman – Griffith University (Australia)
E. Kevin Kelloway – Saint Mary's University (Canada)
Sarah Leberman – Massey University (New Zealand)
Laura Gail Lunsford – University of Arizona (United States)
James McCalman – University of Portsmouth (United Kingdom)
Tadhg MacIntyre – University of Limerick (Ireland)
Judith McMorland – CO-LEARNZ Ltd (New Zealand)
Damian O'Keefe – Saint Mary's University (Canada)
Art Padilla – North Carolina State University (United States)
Samantha A. Penney – Indiana State University (United States)
David Shilbury – Deakin University (Australia)
Jarrod Spencer – Mind of the Athlete (United States)
Nick Takos – University of South Australia (Australia)
Robert Vaughan – University of Birmingham (United Kingdom)

Abbreviations

AFL	Australian Football League
ALQ	authentic leadership questionnaire
ASCQ	Autonomy-Supportive Coaching Questionnaire
ASQ	athlete satisfaction questionnaire
BA	Bowls Australia
BALCO	Bay Area Laboratory Cooperative
CBAS	Coaching Behaviour Assessment System
CFQ	coaching feedback questionnaire
CGO	Common Good Organisation
CRT	Cognitive Resource Theory
EEO	equal employment opportunities
GEQ	group environment questionnaire
GSO	global sport organisation
ICC	International Cricket Council
IM	intrinsic motivation
IMI	intrinsic motivation inventory
IOC	International Olympic Committee
IPA	interaction process analysis
LMX	Leader–Member Exchange
LSS	Leadership Scale for Sports
MO	member organisation
NCAA	National Collegiate Athletics Association
NSO	national sport organisation
NZRU	New Zealand Rugby Union
OMSAT-3	Ottawa mental skills assessment tool-3
OCB	organisational citizenship behaviour
PEDs	performance-enhancing drugs
PJDM	professional judgement and decision making
RLSS	Revised Leadership Scale for Sport
RSLP-S	revised servant leadership profile for sport
SDT	self-determination theory

SLOC	Salt Lake City Organizing Committee
SLT	situational leadership theory
SSCM	Strategic Sport Communication Model
SWOT	strengths, weaknesses, opportunities and threats
UCI	Union Cycliste Internationale
USADA	United States Anti-Doping Agency
USPS	United States Postal Service
VDL	Vertical Dyad Linkage
W/O	work and organisational

Chapter 1

Framing leadership in sport

Ian O'Boyle, Paul Cummins and Duncan Murray

LEADERSHIP IN THE CONTEMPORARY WORLD

The days of the leader as hero appear to be over. The day of the leader as humble facilitator appears to be beginning.

One of the notable features of leadership has been the changes that have occurred in both the academic exploration of leadership as a construct, as well as the social environment and what we, as people, perceive as good leadership. In 100 years we have moved from a view of leadership as one of authoritative control to one of the leader as facilitator, guide and mentor. Leadership is now often considered a concept that is shared — we have leadership groups in sports teams, cyclical leadership positions in some organisations — and the leader as a monolithic titan, immutable, absolute and eternal, has perhaps become as relevant to contemporary society as the typewriter is to the modern office. The few such leaders of this type that remain, for example the North Korean leader Kim Jong Un, are treated more as objects of scorn, ridicule and amusement, rather than as admired figureheads of state.

This doesn't mean that everything we knew about leadership up to the turn of the century should be cast aside and ignored as antiquated and irrelevant. Far from it. Leadership is a dynamic, fluid concept, and it is one of the most interesting reflections of its contemporary social environment and context. How it has changed, how it continues to change, is of general interest, and of critical importance to the sporting world in particular.

The first section of this text focuses on leadership as a general construct, exploring how leadership is defined, the trait and styles theories of leadership, as well as how leaders work within teams and what happens when it goes horribly wrong — the destructive side of leadership. While this section of the text focuses on introducing and exploring these ideas as concepts in their own right, many pertinent and relevant sport-based examples are also used throughout to highlight the applicability of these concepts to the sporting world, to sport management, and to coaching and training.

When we were collating the first section of the text, we were initially a bit perplexed at how similar some of the themes were that kept emerging from apparently disparate areas, such as trait theories of leadership, leadership styles and destructive leadership. We'd like to explore these themes a little, as they are not overtly stated as distinct points or ideas in this text.

First, leadership is about relationships. A leader exists solely because of the fact followers will acknowledge and legitimise their leadership. This can only happen if the leader can influence the follower – if they can convince them of the legitimacy of their ideas, their approach, their behaviour and vision. In this sense, many of the disparate concepts of leadership – transformational leadership styles, relational leadership, leader–member exchange, authentic leadership, servant leadership – clearly coalesce into a consistent idea.

Second, leadership is not always and completely positive. We can have bad leaders. These leaders can be bad for the organisation, or bad for the individuals within that organisation. We are increasingly aware in modern society of concepts such as bullying in the workplace, of harassment, of misconduct and professional impropriety by our leaders. Silvio Berlusconi's fall from grace as Italian Prime Minister is a clear example of this. And this concept of bad or destructive leadership is not limited solely to the corporate or political world. The sporting world is replete with examples of leaders who may be considered destructive, whether coaches of East German athletes in the 1970s and their systematic use of anabolic steroids and other performance-enhancing substances, or more recently scandals such as the Penn State scandal, with allegations of sexual abuse and cover-ups.

What emerges in our mind from this first section of the text is that leadership and what it means to be a leader is anything but simple. As a construct it is complex in meaning. It has multiple facets and subtleties. It is a constant and yet ever-changing construct, and that makes it one of the most relevant and interesting areas of sport management and sport coaching to explore.

LEADERSHIP IN SPORT MANAGEMENT

There has been a growing appreciation for the importance of effective leadership within sport management as the industry continues to professionalise and develop a more commercial ethos within many aspects of sport. The leadership styles, models and theories outlined previously are all important frameworks within which to examine leadership within any setting including this new sport management environment. Leadership and management in general have long been associated with each other. Soucie (1994) suggested that leadership pervades all the managerial activities of the sport administrator. We can see this from everyday practical examples within the sport industry where leaders are required to plan, organise, control, delegate and empower others to achieve organisational objectives as effectively and efficiently as possible.

Although it is clear that leadership and management go 'hand in hand', it also must be acknowledged that leadership and management are ultimately different. An effective leader does not necessarily require effective management skills; however, a manager who does not possess the ability to lead their organisation and the people within it may find it difficult to ensure the organisation is performing at the required level. In fact, according to Chelladurai (1992), the relevance of effective leadership is high for skill-related, excellence-related and sustenance-related service organisations in sport.

The section of 'leadership in sport management' within this text outlines a number of practical examples where leadership plays a key role in defining the success or failure of an organisation's ability to provide a high level service to its stakeholders. This section of the text covers topics such as the applicability of being a facilitative leader in sport management, communication in sport management, strategic leadership, leading organisational change and addressing the issue of diversity within the leadership space in the sport management industry. The importance of each of these elements of leadership and their specific relevance to the sport management setting are briefly outlined below.

The federated model of non-profit sport management that has evolved within nations such as Australia, New Zealand, Canada, UK and a number of other European countries has resulted in autonomous bodies operating at a state or regional level being affiliated with a national governing body. The relationships that exist within these systems can often be strained and underpinned by high levels of conflict and distrust. The contemporary leader of such national governing bodies, normally being the CEO or board members, are often required to enact facilitative leadership to ensure there is cohesion and shared understanding within these networks in an attempt to unify the direction of the sport they are charged with leading.

One of the key requirements of the facilitative leader is the capability to communicate with a diverse group of stakeholders. Pedersen *et al.* (2007) defined sport leadership communication style as 'the way a leader behaves toward and interacts and communicates with followers' (p. 139). It is important to understand the communication styles exhibited by leaders, as these have direct implications for the entire organisation and its culture. The emergence of 'new media' such as Facebook, Twitter and Instagram has also required leaders to adapt their communication strategies in response to the growth within this form of communication where stakeholders expect almost instant, accurate and up-to-date information to be constantly forthcoming.

Complementary to facilitative leadership and being an effective communicator is the ability to undergo a robust strategic planning process that engages stakeholders from all areas of the sport and in particular those autonomous bodies that comprise the sporting network. Strategic leadership has emerged as a core requisite of the contemporary leader within sport management. Leaders, through strategic leadership, bring to life the direction setting function through strategic planning. Leaders can empower others and invite them to contribute to the direction setting function, as well as invite them to share the vision generated through the strategic planning process.

The constant rate of change that is now unfolding within the sport industry has resulted in the need for leaders to be proactive, and to have the ability to lead organisational change in a dynamic industry that can be impacted by a range of external and internal factors. The uncertainty surrounding levels of government funding, developments in technology, increasing rates of sedentary lifestyles, and a more competitive environment requires sport leaders such as CEOs and board members to have an intimate knowledge of the organisational change process and capabilities to overcome resistance to change from stakeholders within their organisations.

Finally, an important issue that is beginning to receive an increase in attention from both scholars and practitioners is the under-representation of diverse groups within leadership positions in the sport industry. Gender diversity in leadership positions in particular has been shown to have positive impacts for organisational performance, yet the sport industry is still very much a male dominated environment where a 'glass ceiling' appears to exist for the progression of females into CEO and board member roles. The importance of diversity in

3

leadership within the sport industry is further exemplified when one examines the demographics of participation in sport and draws contrast to leader demographics within the industry where clearly there is little correlation.

The 'leadership in sport management' section of this text covers each of these topics in in-depth detail to illuminate some of the key issues related to each of these areas. Of course there are other areas of leadership within the sport management domain that can impact on an organisation's overall performance and reputation but the authors believe that the topics covered in this section are currently the most pertinent facing the contemporary sport industry, and aspects of leadership that are critical to ensure a sustainable, vibrant, and equality driven sector can thrive moving forward.

LEADERSHIP IN SPORT COACHING

Within the sport coaching literature, an important area of contemporary research is recognising what makes an effective coach. Researchers have drawn on the field of leadership and endeavoured to apply a range of leadership theories and perspectives to an analysis of coaching behaviour and coaching style, with varying success.

Previous research in sport coaching and leadership suggests that coaches have a significant role in influencing their athletes, in particular youth athletes, mainly through the attitudes, values and beliefs they emphasise; the behaviours and actions they model; the goals and targets they set for their players; and the overall environment and culture they seek to create. Research on coaching behaviours emerged over 30 years ago with a specific focus on coach–athlete interactions within sports participation and subsequent athletic psychosocial development. Scholarly works have investigated coaching behaviours and the frequency and timing of coaching behaviours mainly through observational methods; delivering instruction, punishment and praise.

Sport is an excellent setting in which one can research the behaviours of leaders and the dimensions of leadership. This may be because sport performance (successes and failures) are accurately measurable, sports teams provide a neat sample size that can provide both scope and depth of investigation, and leadership behaviours are critical and widely relied upon within sport at every level. The majority of leadership research brings light to the fact that when we think of the concept of leadership, we have been automatically led towards thinking in terms of the individual, and specifically the characteristics that individual possesses within their personality which enables them to influence and lead others in achieving a goal. This popular concept of leadership, which predominantly hinges on an individual's unique qualities – ability to motivate, natural charisma, desire to succeed, willingness to delay gratification, stubbornness to gain results and devotion to inspire – has gained huge attention and distribution of resources in the western world, particularly within an organisational setting. Despite the saturation of individual-based leadership, recent leadership research has focused more on 'we' than 'I' and has begun to mount a challenge against the established leadership credo (i.e. the social identity approach). The 'leadership in sport coaching' section of the text explores five themes that present an overview of leadership in the sport coaching domain.

This section opens with an overview of coaching in participation and performance settings. Second, models of the coaching process are described with a particular focus on the coach's underpinning knowledge. Based on the multitude of factors involved, as well as the complexity of the environment, the merits of a professional judgement and decision-making approach for coaching research and practice are then discussed. In particular, how choices and chains of decisions can be supported by a form of planning and execution termed 'nested thinking' are considered. The concluding element of the opening chapter in this section addresses how multi-directionality; emotional intelligence; socio-political awareness and micro-political literacy; context manipulation; and a broad behavioural repertoire can all help to make nested coaching work.

An exploration of extant sport leadership models within four main overarching leadership approaches (e.g. relational, athlete-centred, group-centred and coaching effectiveness) follows the opening chapter in this section. In addition, the chapter highlights the most significant leadership in sport coaching models used both previously and currently (e.g. multidimensional, cognitive-mediational, servant, authentic and transformational models) that link with excellence in sport coaching.

An overview of the more established methods of measuring leadership in sport follows this chapter. The Mediational Model of Leadership and the Multidimensional Model of Leadership are outlined with their respective measures: the Coaching Behaviour Assessment System and the Leadership Scale for Sports respectively (Smoll and Smith, 1989; Chelladurai, 1993). This chapter also highlights specific issues regarding measurement of the scales (i.e. psychometrics). An explanation of the methods used to assess a scale's psychometrics is also provided throughout, therefore enhancing the usability of the chapter for practitioners with an interest in measuring leadership. The reliability and validity of the instruments are discussed with reference to scales development and later empirical research assessing the utility of the measures. Furthermore, recommendations and summaries of current directions along with alternative measures are proposed.

Following this chapter and scaffolding on the topics discussed in the previous section, the lessons that can be learned from leadership in organisational management and that may be applicable to the sport coaching environment are explored. The psychological study of leadership is historically located in the field of organisational psychology and tells a story of moving from a focus on the leader to a focus on a social interaction between leader and followers. On that journey some misleading deviations occurred in failing to distinguish early on between management and leadership. The focus gradually moved from the elevated great man to the leader as servant to the group in which the decisions of followers are equally as important as decisions of leaders in determining performance. This chapter attempts to show that what was learned can usefully be applied to any group or team situation, therefore having important implications for the sport coaching environment.

The penultimate chapter in the text first highlights the potential implications of conflict in coach–athlete relationships. Next, the traditional account of relationships in sport from a social psychology perspective is explored. New perspectives focusing on the role of empathy in sport are then proposed which provide a pathway for understanding coach–athlete relationships. Two case studies are presented to illustrate how empathy can operate both between rivals and across a team. The chapter then summarises the complex nature of the processes and the key take-home message for our understanding of leadership and coaching.

Finally, Chapter 17 outlines the future trends and challenges surrounding leadership within the sporting environment. This chapter provides a summary of the topics covered within the text while also addressing practical implications for leaders within the sport management and coaching environments. A consideration of extensions for future leadership in sport research is provided along with a discussion of the emerging trends within both management and coaching disciplines that relate to both effective and contemporary leadership.

REFERENCES

Chelladurai, P. (1992). A classification of sport and physical activity services: Implications for sport management. *Journal of Sport Management*, 6, 38–51.

Chelladurai, P. (1993). Leadership. In R. Singer, M. Murphey, and L. K. Tennant (eds), *Handbook of research on sport psychology* (pp. 647–671). New York: Macmillan.

Pedersen, P. M., Miloch, K. S., and Laucella, P. C. (2007). *Strategic sport communication*, Champaign, IL: Human Kinetics.

Smoll, F. L., and Smith, R. E. (1989). Leadership behaviors in sport: A theoretical model and research paradigm. *Journal of Applied Social Psychology*, 19, 1522–1551.

Soucie, D. (1994). Effective managerial leadership in sport organization. *Journal of Sport Management*, 4, 211–223.

Part A

Leadership theories applicable to the sport environment

Chapter 2

What is leadership?

Duncan Murray and Sarah Chua

CHAPTER OBJECTIVES

This chapter concentrates on providing a conceptual overview on the concept of leadership at the broader level. After completing this chapter you should be able to:

1   recognise that leadership is a social application of power;
2   be able to articulate the distinction between a leader and a manager;
3   understand that what we see as leadership is malleable, and changes over time and social context.

KEY TERMS

- leadership
- the bases of power
- influence
- management

WHAT IS A LEADER?

What is a leader? What does it take to be a leader? Is it strength? Resilience? Are some people 'born' leaders? Can we learn how to lead? The term leadership seems to inspire us with visions of mythical or legendary heros, perched atop their rearing steed and leading their followers into battle. When we think of the notable events of history, it is the leaders that feature. A discussion of the Second World War, for example, is difficult to contemplate without the names Hitler, Churchill, Stalin or Roosevelt prominently featuring. When we consider the business world we think of the corporate high flyers, the great names, such as Rockefeller, Gates, Jobs or Ford. Likewise, when we think of sports we think of the great players and leaders on the field. We think of Michael Jordan leading the Chicago Bulls to six NBA championship titles, of Diego Maradona leading Argentina to their 1986 World Cup triumph, of Sir Donald Bradman leading Australia to victory over England in the Ashes.

We seem fascinated by the concept of the 'leader' and imbue them with qualities and traits that seem to make them more than human. But is this view changing? With the spate of corporate collapses that followed the global financial crises, high flying celebrity CEOs became more vilified and shunned. Managers of sports teams began to move from a more traditional autocratic style of leadership to a more inclusive style. The concept of the 'leadership group' in professional sporting teams is becoming more and more common. Is our concept of leadership changing? If so, then what do we even mean by leadership?

In this chapter we explore the definitions of leadership and seek to unpack the essence of what leadership is. Of note is that we distinguish two points: first, that leadership is application of power in a social context and second, that leading and managing are not necessarily interchangeable concepts.

DEFINING LEADERSHIP

Defining leadership is somewhat like describing the taste of water. We all know the taste, but trying to articulate a specific description of that taste is almost impossible. So too with leadership. We all know what it is, but it is surprisingly difficult to precisely define it. For all the simplicity of the concept, there appears to almost be an intangible quality to it. There are myriad definitions of leadership. For example, Burns (1978, p. 18) states that, 'Leadership is exercised when persons . . . mobilize . . . institutional, political, psychological, and other resources so as to arouse, engage, and satisfy the motives of followers.' Likewise Drath and Palus (1994, p. 4.) define leadership as 'the process of making sense of what people are doing together so that people will understand and be committed'. However, what do these definitions really mean?

Bass (2008, p. 25) proposed an expanded definition of the concept of leadership, suggesting:

> Leadership is an interaction between two or more members of a group that often involves structuring or restructuring of the situation and the perceptions and expectations of the members. Leaders are agents of change, whose acts affect other people more than other people's acts affect them. Leadership occurs when one group member modifies the motivation or competencies of others in the group. Leadership can be conceived as directing the attention of other members to goals and the paths to achieve them.

Yukl (2002, p. 21) provided a synopsis of different leadership definitions. He summarised that the common features of the definitions were that they, 'reflect the assumption that it involves a process whereby intentional influence is exerted over other people to guide, structure, and facilitate activities and relationships in a group or organization'. Outside of this, Yukl notes that there appears to be little agreement or consistency among the definitions.

Leadership as influence

The central theme of influence being exerted over others is a core tenet of leadership. Social influence can be described as, 'a change in the belief, attitude, or behaviour of a person (the target of influence), which results from the action of another person (an influencing agent)' (Raven, 2008, p. 1). So, from a leadership perspective, social influence would involve a shift in the attitude or behaviour of the subordinates as a direct result of the actions of the leader. For example, a leader of a retail sales team who requires greater input from sales staff in attracting potential shoppers might encourage their staff to approach people in the store more frequently. The actions of the sales leader should result in higher staff and shopper engagement, indicating the social influence of the leader over the subordinates.

However, the assumption that influence is a top-down, one directional process is starting to change. Traditionally, 'influence' may have been seen as a directive from a leader to a subordinate. However, influence is increasingly being seen as multi-directional, with leaders influencing followers, just as followers may influence leaders, as well as each other. Nevertheless, the ability to influence others is still one of the hallmarks of a leader. It is this influence, this application of social power, that perhaps defines the leader.

So let us consider the concept of power, and how it is central to leadership. We start with considering the legitimacy of the leader, grounded in the notion of the bases of power.

THE BASES OF POWER

When one reads both the current and historical literature examining leadership, it is clear that dynamics and interactions between leaders and followers may be heavily influenced by the perceived power the leader yields. For example, how does the coach of a basketball team get their team to train and to train effectively? How do military generals and leaders such as Alexander the Great exert their power that may provoke unyielding confidence or belief in their abilities? And finally, just how do leaders increase their subordinates', or followers', satisfaction, productivity and effectiveness? Just what power does their position of leadership legitimise that allows leaders to influence change?

A key component of a leader's social power centres on the tactics they use to influence, and how effective and motivating these tactics are on a follower's behaviours and attitudes. Different types of power used by leaders may result in different social influences. Let's distinguish between the different types of power as these are indicative of the different ways in which leaders may influence organisational and follower change (Atwater and Yammarino, 1996).

The bases of social power were originally developed by John French and Bertram Raven (1959), who initially suggested that there were five sources of social influence or power as they referred to it. The original five bases of power comprised: *reward*, *coercion*, *legitimate*, *expertise* and *referent* power (French and Raven, 1959). *Informational* power was added later as the sixth source of power (Raven, 2008). The fundamental feature of these forms of power is that they differ in the way that social change can be applied as well as the permanency of such change (Raven, 2008). We expand on each of those forms below, and they are articulated diagrammatically in Figure 2.1.

11

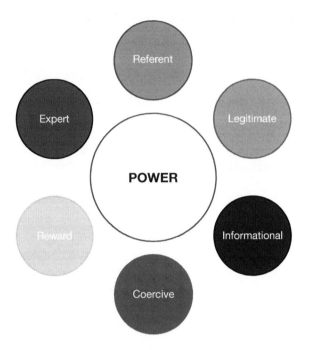

Figure 2.1 *The six bases of power.*

Source: adapted from Raven (2008).

Reward power

Reward power is based on the leader's ability to provide followers with rewards (French and Raven, 1959). It depends on the leader's capacity to offer positive reinforcements while also limiting the chance of negative ones. Likewise, followers' compliance is dependent on the perceived likelihood that the leader will deliver these desirable outcomes. Consider factory workers on a production line. If a manager wants to increase employee productivity they may offer pay rises or a productivity bonus at the end of the month. Of notable importance is the dependence of follower compliance and conformity on the probability of receiving the rewards. Reward power only influences changes in follower behaviour and attitudes if the leader actually delivers rewards and positive valences (Raven, 2008).

Coercive power

In many ways coercive power shares common elements with reward power. Coercive power describes the leader's actions of bringing about change by the threat of punishment and negative consequences if their wishes are not fulfilled (French and Raven, 1959). To be a little more specific, the leader might try and cause follower change by threatening pay cuts, de-motion or even job losses if the follower does not conform to the leader's wishes. Let's return to our hypothetical production line for an example. If a worker on the line falls below expected productivity targets, or fails to meet new performance or output standards, then their job or wages may then be under threat. Although based on punishment rather than reward, coercive power, like reward power, is dependent on the follower's perceived knowledge of the leader following through with the threat of punishment. For example, 'I only did it because if I didn't I would lose my job'. The degree of follower conformity and thus the effectiveness of the social influence of coercive power relies on the leader's duress of negative consequences.

In addition to follower change depending on either the promise of reward or the threat of punishment, the effectiveness of both reward and coercive power requires leaders and organisations to monitor employees' behaviour (Raven, 2008). Meaning if the leader solely relies on either reward or coercive power as the only bases of social influence, the follower may then only obey if they perceive that their behaviour is being consistently scrutinised and observed by the leader.

Legitimate power

In contrast to the ongoing surveillance and scrutiny that reward and coercive power require, legitimate power, expert power and referent power do not require the same level of leader observation (Pierro *et al.*, 2008). Initially, legitimate, referent and expert power can be considered as socially dependent on the leader. However, the effectiveness of these influencing tactics are not solely determined by the rigorous monitoring of follower behaviour and outcomes.

Legitimate power stems from the leader's position as an authority figure, and one who has the perceived right to enforce change and influence behaviour (Raven, 2008). This type of power is based on social norms whereby the individual on the receiving end of power, in this case the follower, is required to conform because of the perceived position held by the influencing agent, in this case the leader (Raven, 2008). An example of the use of legitimate power could be a manager of a high profile sporting team, such as an NBA side, or a professional European football team such as Manchester United. The manager decides that during season all players must volunteer for a selected charity at least once a fortnight. While adding this into their busy schedules may be tricky, players would most likely comply because they feel obliged to and that they should do it. Often legitimate power follows the line of, 'I'm going to do it because I'm required to, and after all they are my leader'. In many ways legitimate power is founded on seminal studies of legitimacy of authority focused on by sociologist Max Weber (1947).

Expert power

Expert power translates the attribution of knowledge and expertise to the leader from the follower (French and Raven, 1959). Essentially this type of power is the perception by the follower that the leader possesses insight and wisdom within that particular field (Raven, 2008). Raven (2008) describes that target individuals of expert power hold faith in the influencing agent's superior knowledge and accordingly adjust their behaviour and attitudes. A key example would be in the form of an individual accepting the expert advice of a lawyer and allowing their influence to change their behaviour (French and Raven, 1959). From a leadership view-point, expert power could be in the form of a professional swimming coach advising their

13

athlete on their stroke technique. The swimmer would adjust their technique based on the expert influence of their coach. Expert power translates into statements such as, 'I will listen to my coaches' suggestion because they have experience and knowledge of these things, and they're probably right'. Raven (2008) suggests that the key distinguishing component of expert power compared to informational power is that followers or employees do not need to know or understand the reason behind the leader's decisions in order for them to conform to the outcomes.

Referent power

The final power source of the original five bases of power is referent power, based on the foundation of a follower identifying with their leader (French and Raven, 1959). French and Raven (1959) define identification as a desire for an individual to want to emulate the influencing person's identity or behaviour. The leader becomes a person that the follower models their behaviour on because they are perhaps highly attracted to that individual and/or they wish to be associated with them (Raven, 2008). Under referent power, followers may also derive a feeling of membership from their leader. This power source is based on the personality of the follower and how strongly they identify with their leader; for example, a leader may not even be aware of the strength of their referent power over followers (French and Raven, 1959). An example of referent power could be a teacher in training. Young teachers may model and identify strongly with their mentor teachers and subsequently mould their teaching styles based on their mentor's behaviour. Referent power can be summated in the statement, 'I really admire my mentor teacher and I want to teach and behave like they do'.

To reiterate, the leader or person in the position of power may be unaware of the referent power they yield. However, the stronger the follower identification, the stronger the referent power will be.

Informational power

Finally, let us consider informational power. This is the sixth power source and was not originally included in the French and Raven (1959) power base typology. Informational power can be defined as the leader clearly communicating to the follower how the task should be undertaken (Raven, 2008). It is persuasive communication by the leader of how the job should be done in order for it to be more effective and better for the follower. It centres on the strength of the communication, information and position of the leader to influence a change in the follower's behaviour. Likewise, followers need to understand the leader's reasons behind wanting to change certain tasks and outcomes and accept these into practice (Raven, 2008). An example of this type of power could be the head of a website design company wanting to change internet browsers to increase productivity. Followers would need to understand why the new browser would be more efficient and how it could increase productivity in order for them to adopt it into their workplace habits. This adoption of new practices would result in cognitive change in the followers, resulting in them accepting the new methods as more effective. This results in the change becoming socially independent of the leader.

MODERN LEADERSHIP IN CONTEMPORARY SOCIETY

When we turn on the television, or the radio, what appears to be a constant is that things are changing. We live in a world in which the speed of change is exponential. Twenty years ago the internet was only just beginning to make an appearance in homes around the world. Now, imagining a disconnected world is almost impossible. Ten years ago Facebook was being created in dorm rooms in Harvard University. It now has a stock value in the billions of dollars, and if it was a country, it would be the most populous on Earth. Organisations face rapid change. Outsourcing of staff, deregulation of markets, global economies – all are examples of how we live in a dynamic, not a static world. The best leaders are the ones who can operate effectively in a world of turbulent change. It appears that trying to maintain the status quo is the fast track to ruin.

Leadership itself therefore has had to adapt. Old views on leadership – as a directive, stable controlling force – are largely antiquated and ineffective in our dynamic changing, turbulent contemporary society. Let's compare the old views on leadership, and how it has needed to change.

Leadership as control or collaboration?

Traditionally, leaders were seen as the people who controlled others. Via the five (or six) bases of power, leaders controlled and subordinates did. Rigid lines of command were the norm. Consider factories in the 1950s. The worker reported to the supervisor, who reported to the manager, who reported to the managing director, who reported to the CEO, who reported to the Board. This rigid structure made the power differential between the leaders and the subordinates clear. When automated manufacturing was the dominant employer, and made up the majority of jobs, this may have been effective. However, today organisations need to maximise the talent within. Leaders therefore are seen as facilitators and guides, empowering employees and devolving control.

Interestingly, from the perspective of this text, one of the areas we first see acceptance of change as positive and being embraced by leaders is in sport. Athletes and coaches have always been searching for competitive advantage. This search ushered in a slew of new training techniques, a boom in sports science and the understanding of biomechanics, new tactics in team sports such as football that progressed the development of the sport and made existing tactics obsolete. While we are not suggesting that such pressures were solely limited to the sporting arena (consider the development of the automobile throughout the twentieth century for example) we do suggest that a 'changing playing field' was generally more accepted in sport than in business in general.

THE LEADER AND THE MANAGER

> Leadership begins where management ends, where the systems, rewards and punishments, control and scrutiny, give way to innovation, individual character, and the courage of convictions.
>
> (Kouzes and Posner, 1987, p. 32)

15

Part of the conceptual confusion when we consider the concept of leadership comes from the fact that the terms leadership and management are often used interchangeably. However, the concepts are clearly distinct. We have defined the key feature of leadership earlier in this chapter as influence over others. In contrast, management can be considered as the attainment of organisational outcomes or goals through planning, organising, staffing, directing and controlling resources within the organisation. Clearly what is apparent is that the key focus of the two concepts is different. While leadership focuses on influencing others, the focus of management is on the attainment of organisational goals. The concepts may overlap, but they are not the same.

We can have leaders who do not manage. For example, leaders who arise informally do not tend to manage people. For example, pro-democracy protests in Hong Kong were widespread following the decision by the central Chinese government to appoint a new Governor of Hong Kong. These protests had a number of leaders behind them, but no one was formally managing the protestors, and these leaders seemed to informally appear rather than be leaders of a pre-existing political group. Likewise we can have managers who do not lead. A manager of a transport company who is efficient and effective at meeting organisational targets such as delivery schedules may have no demonstrable leadership qualities at all.

Where a clear distinction between leaders and managers appears is in their approach to change. John Kotter (1996) suggests that leaders need to cope with change, whereas managers need to cope with complexity. The nature of a contemporary leader is to embrace change, to understand its inevitability as well as the potential opportunities that may exist beyond the horizon, and to articulate this to their followers. In contrast, managers seek consistency and

Leadership Produces change and movement	Management Produces order and consistency
1 Establishes direction • Creates a vision • Clarifies the big picture • Sets strategies	1 Planning and budgeting • Establishes agendas • Sets timetables • Allocates resources
2 Aligns people • Communicates goals • Seeks commitment • Builds teams, coalitions and alliances	2 Organizing and staffing • Provides structure • Makes job placements • Establishes rules and procedures
3 Motivates and inspires • Energizes • Empowers subordinates and colleagues • Satisfies unmet needs	3 Controlling and problem solving • Develops incentives • Generates creative solutions • Takes corrective action

Figure 2.2 *The distinction between management and leadership.*

Source: Peter G. Northouse, *Leadership: Theory and Practice* (2007).

16

continuity as it assists in coping with complex situations and environments. This distinction is articulated in Figure 2.2.

What is important to note is that with all the focus on leadership, management is still important. Organisations need both good leadership and good management to flourish. Likewise, while the concepts are distinct, they are not necessarily mutually exclusive. Someone can be a good leader and a good manager. Being one does not automatically restrict being the other.

SUMMARY

In this chapter we have introduced the concept of leadership, discussing that for all its inherent attraction, it is surprisingly difficult to define. We identify that influence appears to be a critical component of being a leader, the ability to influence others. This social influence is articulated via different forms of power, whether coercive or rewarding, based on expert knowledge, or personal attraction or information. We acknowledged that in the twenty-first century the leadership paradigm is changing. The traditional directive form of leadership, the 'leader as boss' approach, is being replaced by a 'leader as facilitator' mindset. Change is a constant and the best leaders understand the need to embrace change and to see the opportunities on the horizon, rather than mark time and eventually decline into slow but inevitable stagnation. Finally, we identified that, while not mutually exclusive, the concepts of manager and leader are distinct, that a leader is focused on dealing with change and a manager on dealing with logistical complexity.

At first glance these concepts and ideas may seem to not relate to sport and sport management. However, sport is one context where such issues as power, and how the best leaders embrace change, clearly shine through. As this section of the book progresses we will explore some of the theories around leadership. We will look at the traits of effective leaders, the styles that are considered to be effective as well as the other side of leadership – when leaders are destructive.

REVIEW QUESTIONS

1   What is the central feature of definitions of leadership? Does this feature seem consistent with your experiences of leaders, or your experiences as a leader yourself?

2   What are the six bases of power? Briefly outline the key features of each.

3   How has leadership and the concept of leadership changed?

4   Outline the key distinctions between leadership and management.

REFERENCES

Atwater, L. E. and Yammarino, F. J. (1996). Bases of power in relation to leader behavior: A field investigation. *Journal of Business and Psychology. 11* (1), 3–22.

Bass, B. M. (2008). *The Bass handbook of leadership: Theory, research and managerial applications.* New York: Simon & Schuster.

Burns, J. (1978). *Leadership.* New York: Harper & Row.

Drath, W. H. and Palus, C. J. (1994). *Making common sense: Leadership as meaning-making in a community of practice.* Greensbro, NC: Center for Creative Leadership.

French Jr, J. R. and Raven, B. (1959). The bases of social power. In *Studies in social power;* 150–167, Cartwright, D., ed. Oxford: Oxford University Press.

Kotter, J. P. (1996). *Leading change.* Boston, MA: Harvard Business School Press.

Kouzes, J. M. and Posner, B. Z. (1987). *The leadership challenge: How to get extraordinary things done in organisations.* San Francisco, CA: Jossey-Bass.

Northouse, P. G. (2007). *Leadership: Theory and practice* (4th edn). Thousand Oaks, CA: Sage.

Pierro, A., Cicero, L. and Raven, B. H. (2008). Motivated compliance with bases of social power. *Journal of Applied Social Psychology. 38* (7), 1921–1944.

Raven, B. H. (2008). The bases of power and the power/interaction model of interpersonal influence. *Analyses of Social Issues and Public Policy. 8* (1), 1–22.

Weber, M. (1947). *The theory of social and economic organization.* Translated by Henderson, A. M. and Parsons, T. New York: Free Press.

Yukl, G. (2002). *Leadership in organizations* (5th edn). Upper Saddle River, NJ: Prentice Hall.

Chapter 3

Trait theories of leadership

Samantha A. Penney, E. Kevin Kelloway and
Damian O'Keefe

CHAPTER OBJECTIVES

After completing this chapter you should be able to:

1   discuss the history of trait theories of leadership;
2   explain how positive and negative traits can influence leadership emergence and
    effectiveness;
3   describe how the trait approach relates to transformational leadership theory;
4   identify the implications of the trait approach for organizations.

KEY TERMS

■   trait theory
■   traits
■   leadership
■   personality
■   Big 5
■   Dark Triad

TRAIT THEORIES OF LEADERSHIP

Leadership is arguably one of the most studied topics in organisational behaviour (Barling
et al., 2011). This is not surprising, given that leadership is said to be the most important
factor in organisational success, and is associated with numerous positive organisational
outcomes (Barling, 2014), as well as employee well-being (Kelloway and Barling, 2010).

Given the importance of the topic for individuals and organisations, it is not surprising that a great deal of research attention has been focused on the definition, and prediction, of leadership.

Perhaps the earliest approach to understanding leadership was to study the lives of 'great men [sic]'[1] (Carlyle, 1907) with the belief that the history of the world was shaped by great men. Through studying the biographies and life stories of leaders such as Napoleon, or Alexander the Great, Carlyle (1907) and others believed that we would be able to identify the personal characteristics that led to great leadership. This 'great man' approach to understanding leadership led directly to what are now known as the trait theories of leadership.

Traits are relatively enduring and stable characteristics of an individual and may comprise both physical (e.g. height) and psychological (e.g. personality) characteristics. The attempt to identify traits that differentiated 'leaders' from 'non-leaders' was one of the earliest scientific approaches to studying leadership (House and Aditya, 1997). Most of this research was published between 1930 and 1950, after which it was gradually supplanted by a focus on leadership behaviours (Barling et al., 2011). However more recently, leader traits have again become a notable focus of research.

Evidence regarding the relationship between individual traits and leadership has been mixed. Some reviewers have argued that there are typically few universal traits associated with leadership (Mann 1959; Stogdill 1948), while others have concluded that there are consistencies across traits that are associated with leadership emergence or effectiveness (Judge et al., 2002; Lord et al., 1986; Zaccaro et al., 2004).

Two early reviews (Mann, 1959; Stogdill, 1948) in part led to the initial demise of the trait approach as they concluded a lack of association between traits and leadership. Stogdill reviewed studies from 1904 to 1947 while Mann later updated this review and incorporated studies up until 1957. Re-appraisals of these early reviews reversed this conclusion, suggesting that, although the findings within each review were variable, both demonstrated trends between personality and leadership indices, even though methodological and statistical issues were evident (Lord et al., 1986; Zaccaro, 2012).

The lack of more encouraging findings from these early studies on trait theories of leadership can be attributable to several factors. First, Stogdill's (1948) review consisted of numerous studies that were based on adolescents and children (House and Aditya, 1997). When these studies were excluded from Stogdill's (1948) review, more consistent patterns emerged (House and Baetz, 1979). Second, both reviews focused on leader emergence perceptions and personality and did not examine leadership performance or objective measures, thus limiting the scope and inferences that could be made from such reviews. Third, these reviews were based on average and medium correlations between traits and leadership, which likely attenuated the results. The introduction of meta-analytic strategies has allowed researchers to correct for these issues (Lord et al., 1986). Lastly, it has been argued that the early research the reviews were based upon lacked an organised framework of personality measures (House and Aditya, 1997; Judge et al., 2002). This lack of framework resulted in numerous traits being examined under different names, operationalised differently, with few traits being examined across studies. Thus, even if relationships did exist, they were near impossible to identify across the disparate studies (Kenny and Zaccaro, 1983).

New developments in the field such as meta-analyses and a scientifically accepted organizing framework (i.e. the Big Five model of personality; Costa and McCrae, 1992) have allowed researchers to correct for some early methodological issues (Lord *et al.*, 1986) and provided structure in describing personality and how it is related to leadership. Accordingly, although researchers shied away from the trait approach following some less than promising early reviews, these developments have resulted in a renewed interest in the ability of traits to predict leader emergence and effectiveness (Zaccaro, 2012), and consequently research on individual differences and leadership has continued (Hogan *et al.*, 1994).

The question of whether or not there are specific traits linked to leadership is closely related to the more fundamental question of whether leaders are 'born or made'. The trait approach suggests that leaders are born, not made. Behavioural genetic research has provided support for this assertion, at least to some extent that leadership is genetically influenced. Studies examining identical twins reared apart have further supported such a claim through the large number of similarities they share. For example, Arvey and colleagues (Arvey *et al.*, 2006), using a sample of 426 twins (238 identical and 188 fraternal) found that 30 per cent of the variance in leader role occupancy was attributable to genetic factors. These genetic findings are similar to early research by Kenny and Zaccaro (1983), which suggested that 48 to 82 per cent of the variance in leader emergence could be attributable to personality traits and was quite stable across situations. Hence, there is evidence that, at least to some extent, individuals are born with some genetic predispositions to emerge as a leader (Ilies *et al.*, 2004). On the other hand, other variables (e.g. situation, culture) may also partially influence whether one emerges as a leader but these variables are not components of the trait approach or the focus of this chapter.

DEFINITIONS

Before considering what traits might be related to leadership, we first need to understand what we mean by 'traits' in the context of leadership. What constitutes a trait has sometimes been unclear in the literature. Zaccaro *et al.* (2004, p. 104) identified leader traits as:

> Relatively stable and coherent integrations of personality characteristics that foster a consistent pattern of leadership performance across a variety of group and organizational situations. These characteristics reflect a range of stable individual differences, including personality, temperament, motives, cognitive abilities, skills, and expertise.

Therefore, a person's behaviour is related to the traits they possess and traits explain why people act similarly across situations. Individuals that have traits that are associated with indices of leadership may be more likely to emerge as a leader, and accordingly be an effective leader in comparison to individuals lacking such traits.

The study of leadership in the trait literature is often broken down into two distinct constructs: *leader emergence* and *leader effectiveness* (Lord *et al.*, 1986). Leader emergence refers to the degree that an individual is perceived to be leader-like and have leadership qualities more than others, and consequently assumes a leadership role (Hogan *et al.*, 1994; Judge *et al.*, 2002).

On the other hand, leader effectiveness refers to a leader's actual performance as a leader and ability to influence subordinates towards achieving their goals. One concern is the perceived reliability of measures or ratings of leader effectiveness. Are they reliable indicators of how effective a leader actually is? Typically, assessments of leader effectiveness are often subjective ratings from subordinates of supervisors' perceived leader effectiveness and are not objective measures (Judge *et al.*, 2002). Furthermore, one's assessment of leader effectiveness likely depends on what they perceive an effective leader to be. Nonetheless, Hogan and colleagues (Hogan *et al.*, 1994) found that ratings of leader effectiveness and more objective measures of leader effectiveness or performance are positively associated. Therefore there is support for the use of leader effectiveness ratings as a valid and reliable reflection of actual leadership effectiveness.

TRAITS AND LEADERSHIP: EARLY FINDINGS

Early reviews and meta-analyses (i.e. Lord *et al.*, 1986; Mann, 1959; Stogdill, 1948; 1974) on trait theories of leadership focused on individual physical and psychological traits that differentiated leaders and non-leaders. Some of the physical traits found to steadily differentiate leaders and non-leaders were: height, weight, appearance and gender.

Physical traits

Height and weight

It has been suggested that height is related to leader emergence (Hensley and Cooper, 1987; Stogdill, 1948). Stogdill (1948) found an average correlation of .30 across 14 studies. A recent meta-analysis by Judge and Cable (2004) further supported this finding with results indicating one's height was significantly positively associated with both leader emergence and performance, with corrected correlations of .24 and .18 respectively. Similar to physical height, Stogdill (1948) also found a low average correlation of .23 between weight and leadership, with most studies reporting leaders to be heavier. Thus, being taller and/or heavier than others in a group may assist in emerging as a leader (Bass, 2008). Clearly the suggestion is that physical size conveys an impression of dominance in social interactions.

Physical appearance

One's physical appearance (e.g. attractiveness, dress) was positively associated with leadership in most of the studies examined in Stogdill's reviews (1948; 1974). Recent studies have supported comparable findings. Specifically, Goktepe and Schneier (1989) demonstrated that leaders received higher physical attractiveness ratings than non-leaders within groups. Similarly, Cherulnik and colleagues (Cherulnik *et al.*, 1990; Cherulnik, 1995) demonstrated that some characteristics of physical appearance (i.e. physical attractiveness and facial maturity) were also positively related to leader emergence. Therefore, it appears that stereotypes surrounding physical appearance may influence leadership emergence.

Gender

Early research by Mann (1959) and Lord *et al.* (1986) focused on the masculinity–femininity dimension, with masculinity being positively correlated with leadership perceptions. More recent meta-analyses have examined the influence of gender on both leader emergence and effectiveness. In particular, Eagly and Karau's (1991) meta-analysis on leader emergence in leaderless groups indicated that men emerged as leaders more often than women. However, when broken down into different types of leadership roles, men were more likely to emerge in task-oriented and unspecified leadership roles, whereas women were more likely to emerge in social-oriented leadership roles. A later meta-analysis by Eagly and colleagues (Eagly, Karau, and Makhijani, 1995) indicated the male and female leaders did not significantly differ in overall leader effectiveness. However, when broken down into roles, males were seen as more effective than women in more 'masculine roles' and women were seen as more effective than men in more 'feminine roles'. These results suggest that the negative bias continues to persist against female leaders, but that signs are evident that it appears to be improving.

Psychological traits

Numerous psychological traits, including self-confidence, sociability, dominance and intelligence, have also been found to differentiate leaders and non-leaders (i.e., Lord *et al.*, 1986; Mann, 1959; Stogdill, 1948; 1974).

Self-confidence

Self-confidence is one's ability to be certain about their skills and competencies (Northouse, 2013). It is considered a general term that encompasses related constructs such as self-efficacy and self-esteem (Yukl, 2010). Stogdill's reviews (1948; 1974) reported that almost all studies examined reported positive correlations between self-confidence and leadership, with leaders reporting higher self-confidence and self-esteem than followers. Accordingly, leaders with high self-confidence are more likely to try to influence followers, and be successful at influencing them. They are also more likely to be confident in their ability to accomplish difficult tasks and make decisions, which can increase followers' trust in the leader and their decisions.

SOCIABILITY

Sociability refers to one's inclination to seek out social situations and relationships. Stogdill's reviews (1948; 1974) were among the first to identify sociability as a trait associated with leadership. Of the 14 studies examined in Stogdill's initial review, 13 studies demonstrated positive correlations. Stogdill's (1974) follow-up review consisted of 35 studies that had positive correlations between leadership and sociability. Since individuals high in sociability are more likely to be outgoing, friendly, genuinely interested in seeking a relationship with others and concerned for their well-being, they may be perceived as more effective leaders than individuals with lower sociability.

23

Dominance

Dominance is characterised by one's tendency to be assertive, persistent and independent. Most of the studies reviewed by Stogdill (1948) indicated that there was a positive relationship between dominance and leadership but the results were somewhat contradictory. Mann's (1959) examination of dominance and leadership across 12 studies revealed positive associations between dominance and leadership in 73 per cent of the relationships examined. More recent meta-analyses have found similar results. In particular, Lord *et al.*'s (1986) meta-analysis showed a positive relationship between dominance and leader emergence with Judge *et al.*'s (2002) meta-analysis also indicating a strong relationship between dominance and overall leadership (both emergence and effectiveness). Thus, the qualities associated with dominance have resulted in a relatively consistent positive association between dominance and leadership.

Intelligence

Although sometimes considered more an ability than a trait, intelligence has consistently been studied as a leadership attribute. Various reviews have linked intelligence to indices of leadership as well as deemed it the most critical characteristic for a leader to be successful (Judge, Colbert and Ilies, 2004; Lord *et al.*, 1986). Stogdill's (1948) and Mann's (1959) reviews were the first to link general intelligence to leadership. Being intelligent appears to be related to emerging as a leader and being an effective leader. This is reasonable given the complexity associated with leadership positions, whether it be integrating a large amount of information, solving problems, or monitoring others. On the other hand, it has also been suggested that a leader's intelligence should not significantly exceed their followers as it could pose a disadvantage (Bass, 1981; Stogdill, 1948). Thus, leaders generally exhibit above average intelligence in comparison to non-leaders, but they don't have to necessarily be exceedingly above average in their intelligence (Kirkpatrick and Locke, 1991).

Although this brief discussion of physical and psychological traits has focused on certain characteristics, it should be noted that it is not inclusive of all traits that have been shown to be related to leadership in early research, with the ones identified being the more common ones (for reviews see Lord *et al.*, 1986; Mann, 1959; Stogdill, 1948; 1974).

MODERN TRAIT THEORIES

There are inconsistencies in the early literature regarding personality and leadership. Nonetheless one thing researchers can agree on is that numerous traits have consistently been examined under different terminology and operationalised differently across studies for decades. One explanation for this is the lack of a consistent organisational framework for traits, mentioned previously. Modern trait theories have typically adopted one of two organising frameworks for characterising traits; the Big Five model of personality (Costa and McCrae, 1992) and the Dark Triad model of personality (Paulhus and Williams, 2002).

The Big Five

Since the development of the Big Five model of personality (Costa and McCrae, 1992), it has been used as the superior organising framework for personnel psychology research (e.g. sociability falls under extraversion) and has resulted in the identification of stronger relationships between personality and leadership than have studies that do not use the Big Five (Ilies *et al.*, 2004).

The Big Five model of personality encompasses five personality dimensions: *Neuroticism (emotional stability), Extraversion, Agreeableness, Openness to Experience* and *Conscientiousness* (Costa and McCrae, 1992). Each of these dimensions contain six traits or facets. Although the Big Five framework didn't exist when early reviews were conducted, the variables that were examined can still be adapted and organised into this framework. For example, the variables examined by Mann (1959) and Stogdill (1948; 1974) fit into the Big Five organising framework as follows: extraversion (i.e. dominance, assertiveness, energy or activity level and speech fluency), conscientiousness (i.e. responsibility, ambition and initiative), agreeableness (i.e. cooperativeness), neuroticism (i.e. self-confidence and adjustment) and openness to experience (i.e. originality). Although the early reviews didn't organise their results this way, more recent studies have tended to follow this approach (e.g. Judge and Bono, 2000; Judge *et al.*, 2002).

Neuroticism

Neuroticism is the extent to which a person experiences distress, worry, fear, sadness, anxiousness, insecurities and inability to control impulses (Costa and McCrae, 1992). Individuals high on neuroticism tend to be irrational, easily angered, hostile and find it challenging to cope with stress. Thus, individuals high on neuroticism may be less likely to emerge as a leader or be an effective leader for a couple of reasons. First, their tendency to exhibit hostility or anger towards others (Colbert, Judge, Choi and Wang, 2012) might cause others to fear them. Second, the unpredictability of their behaviour and emotions might make it difficult for others to trust them and perceive them as a potential or effective leader (Colbert *et al.*, 2012). In line with the theoretical associations between neuroticism and leadership, Judge *et al.*'s (2002) meta-analysis on leadership and the Big Five, to date the most inclusive, indicated that neuroticism and leadership were negatively correlated. An examination of the facets of neuroticism examined in this study revealed weaker relationships, in particular self-esteem had a correlation of .19 whereas locus of control had a correlation of .13 (but the confidence intervals contained zero).

Extraversion

Extraversion is the extent to which a person is assertive, outgoing, energetic optimistic and gregarious (Costa and McCrae, 1992). Since extraverted individuals are more likely to dominate social situations, and social dominance is associated with ratings of leadership (Kalma *et al.*, 1993), individuals high on extraversion are more likely to be perceived as a

25

leader. Based on theory and previous empirical research, it is not surprising that reviews and meta-analyses have shown extraversion to be related to leader emergence and leader effectiveness. Judge and colleagues' (Judge et al., 2002) meta-analysis indicated extraversion and leadership were positively correlated, and when extraversion was broken down into facets of extraversion, sociability and dominance correlated particularly strongly with leadership.

Openness to experience

Openness to experience is the extent to which a person is curious, imaginative and aesthetically sensitive (Costa and McCrae, 1992). Individuals high on openness to experience are also highly receptive of novel situations, given their tolerance and ability to adjust (Judge et al., 1999). Therefore, individuals high on openness to experiences tend to think outside the box and be creative, which has been linked to effective leadership (Bass, 1990a). Consistent with theoretical associations, Judge et al.'s (2002) meta-analytic results indicated openness to experience and leadership were positively correlated.

Agreeableness

Agreeableness is the extent to which a person is sympathetic, altruistic, cooperative, trusting and warm (Costa and McCrae, 1992). Individual's high on agreeableness are likely to assist others and believe others will do the same for them. Although agreeable individuals tend to be caring and warm, which are perceived as positive leader traits (Bass, 1990b), these same traits could potentially prevent them from emerging as a leader in a group setting (Colbert et al., 2012). Thus, of the Big Five personality traits, based on the lack of theoretical evidence, agreeableness is often seen as the trait that has the smallest relationship with leadership. Empirical evidence reveals corresponding findings in which a meta-analysis by Judge et al. (2002) demonstrated that agreeableness and leadership had a negligible correlation. In comparison, the other dimensions of the Big Five demonstrated much higher correlations.

Conscientiousness

Lastly, conscientiousness is the extent to which a person is responsible, organised, dependable and achievement-oriented (Costa and McCrae, 1992). Individuals high on conscientiousness tend to thoroughly plan out tasks and carry them out. Thus, their determination and tendency to strive for goals may increase their chance of being perceived as leader-like. Judge and colleagues (Judge et al., 2002) found a positive association between leadership and conscientiousness. Notably, conscientiousness was more strongly related to leader emergence than effectiveness, possibly because of the persistence and determination of conscientious people to achieve their goals.

Summary: the Big Five

Accordingly, extraversion, conscientiousness and openness to experience were positively related to leadership emergence and effectiveness, whereas neuroticism was negatively correlated with leadership. Of the Big Five traits, agreeableness has the smallest relationship with leadership. In addition to the above mentioned correlations between the Big Five factors, Judge et al.'s (2002) comprehensive meta-analysis revealed strong multiple correlations between the Big Five and overall leadership, leader effectiveness and leader emergence.

The Dark Triad

An emerging area of research on personality traits is the dark side of personality. Among dark traits, three non-pathological personalities: narcissism, Machiavellianism and psychopathy have been the most studied and termed the 'The Dark Triad' of personality (Paulhus and Williams, 2002). Although these socially aversive personality traits are conceptually different, they are moderately related. Individuals with these traits tend to be malevolent in their interpersonal behaviour, displaying coldness, selfishness and aggression (Paulhus and Williams 2002). Consequently, leaders with these socially undesirable personality traits might not always be perceived as the most effective leaders. At the same time, these same traits may result in individuals advancing in organisations resulting in them occupying leadership positions in disproportionate numbers (Babiak and Hare, 2006).

Narcissism

Narcissism encompasses arrogance, self-absorption, grandiosity and hostility (Rosenthal and Pittinsky, 2006). Narcissists lack empathy and perceive others to be inferior to themselves (Judge et al., 2009). Individuals high on narcissism often act in an insensitive or hostile manner towards others (Judge et al., 2009), and won't resist the chance to exploit others' work (Brunell et al., 2008).

Narcissism is associated with numerous negative organisational consequences such as lower contextual performance and higher counterproductive work behaviours (Judge et al., 2006; O'Boyle et al., 2012; Penney and Spector, 2002). Narcissists can also be hostile or aggressive when they feel their ego is being threatened (Bushman et al., 2009). Narcissistic leaders tend to make decisions with a self-serving bias and based on how such decisions may affect them (Judge et al., 2009). Although narcissists view themselves as exceptional leaders, research indicates that others don't always have the same perception. For example, Judge et al. (2006) reported that narcissism level positively predicted self-ratings of leadership but negatively predicted others' perceptions of leadership. While there are many negative qualities associated with being a narcissistic leader, it isn't all negative; their chance of succeeding as a leader increases when their goals align with the organisation and followers (Rosenthal and Pittinsky 2006).

Machiavellianism

Machiavellianism is characterised by a person's ability to be cunning and manipulative in order to achieve their own ends and power (Judge et al., 2009; Kessler et al., 2010). The term comes from the classic work *The Prince* written by Niccolo Machiavelli in the fifteenth century. In the book, Machiavelli advises the Prince on the art of politics and how to achieve his goals by manipulating others. Individuals high on Machiavellianism are more likely to engage in counterproductive work behaviours such as stealing, violating supervisor trust, verbally abusing co-workers and damaging property (Dahling et al., 2008; Fehr et al., 1992; Harrell and Hartnagel, 1976; O'Boyle et al., 2012). Machiavellianism is also associated with reduced organisational, supervisor and team commitment (Zettler et al., 2011).

Although little research on Machiavellian leaders has been conducted to date, the research that has been examined demonstrates some patterns. In particular, Machiavellian leaders tend to abuse their power in order to influence people into doing things for their own benefit. They are more likely to forego policies and procedures in order to increase their own power (Judge et al., 2009), and although they don't always engage in extreme forms of antisocial behaviour, they are more likely to cheat, lie, betray others (Jones and Paulhus, 2009) and engage in unethical behaviour (Kish-Gephart et al., 2010). Hence, Machiavellian leaders tend to be more successful when they work in unstructured work environments (O'Boyle et al., 2012).

Psychopathy

Psychopathy encompasses impulsiveness, manipulation, callousness and antisocial tendencies. Psychopaths lack empathy, loyalty and feelings of guilt and remorse (Babiak and Hare, 2006). Of the three Dark Triad personality traits, psychopathy is considered to be the most destructive (Williams et al., 2010). Psychopathy has a prevalence rate of 1 to 3 per cent in the general population (Hare, 2006) and is estimated to be closer to 3.5 per cent in top executives (Babiak and Hare, 2006). Individuals high on psychopathy are more likely to engage in counter-productive work behaviours and have lower job performance (O'Boyle et al., 2012).

Psychopaths seek out short cuts to achieving their own selfish ends, whether it be through cheating, bullying or manipulating others to do their work for them. Since they do not care about the rights of other people they are quick to blame others instead of taking any sort of responsibility (Babiak and Hare, 2006). Hence, it is not surprising that perceived psychopathy traits in leaders are negatively associated with employee job satisfaction (Mathieu et al., 2014). Psychopathy is also associated with various forms of criminality (Babiak and Hare, 2006). Although a psychopath's behaviour would typically go against social norms, they may prosper in some organisations, especially if they are required to take risks, even at the expense of others, and exhibit no emotion in doing so (O'Boyle et al., 2012).

So, if leaders possess these dark personality traits, how do they become leaders? Somewhat ironically, individuals with these traits often exhibit behaviours that are associated with attaining leadership positions (Rosenthal and Pittinsky, 2006). One reason for this is that, despite the negative connotations associated with these personality traits, they are difficult to screen for and assess in interviews because they often coincide with other positive traits such as good social skills (Hogan *et al.*, 1994). Let's use narcissism as an example. Because narcissism is associated with extraversion and overconfidence, narcissistic individuals are more likely to be confident in themselves and communicate their opinion in a more powerful way. This in turn may cause people to perceive them as a confident, and potentially effective, leader (Brunell *et al.*, 2008). Narcissistic individuals are also more likely to self-promote even though they might not be qualified (Hogan *et al.*, 1990). Likewise individuals high in Machiavellianism and psychopathy may be able to use their charm and social skills to their advantage, camouflaging their intentions and manipulating and persuading others and situations to their favour (Babiak and Hare, 2006; O'Boyle *et al.*, 2012). It typically is only once these individuals are in the leadership position that the negative side of these personality traits tend to come through and they are no longer perceived as effective (Hughes *et al.*, 2009). As mentioned above, there are specific environments where leaders high on these maladaptive personality traits may thrive, but for the most part they are not valuable traits for leaders to possess.

PERSONALITY AND LEADERSHIP: CONCLUSION

Overall, a review of the literature on personality and leadership indicates that personality is important when examining leader emergence and leadership effectiveness. And although no universal combination of traits will predict who does and does not become a leader, we are aware that certain traits or a combination of such traits increase the chances, whereas other traits might decrease the chances of either emerging as a leader or being perceived as an effective leader.

PRACTICAL IMPLICATIONS OF A TRAIT APPROACH TO LEADERSHIP

Although early reviews rejected the idea that traits could influence leadership, more recent studies confirm that leaders do differ from non-leaders on a number of traits. This conclusion comes from developments in the field such as the Big Five organising framework and methodological techniques that resulted in a re-emergence and reassessment of previous conclusions regarding trait theories of leadership. Although it is clear that there are no universal traits that differentiate leaders and non-leaders, the possession of certain traits can increase the likelihood that one will emerge as a leader and be an effective leader. Understanding the influence good and bad traits can have on leader emergence and effectiveness is therefore of critical importance.

Perhaps most importantly a trait approach to leadership lends itself to the selection, as opposed to the development, of leaders. Leadership theories that focus on leader behaviours and styles, such as transformational leadership, are useful for leadership development as they identify the behaviours that comprise effective leadership and therefore can be learned (e.g. Barling *et al.*, 1996; Kelloway *et al.*, 2000; Mullen and Kelloway, 2009). However, there is little in transformational leadership that would allow organisations to identify who might become a transformational leader or who might benefit most from leadership development. In contrast, trait theories focus on relatively stable and enduring characteristics of an individual. Identifying traits that are reliably associated with leadership effectiveness provides a basis for developing selection systems to identify potential leaders.

29

SUMMARY

Although early trait theories of leadership research received harsh criticisms, advances in the field have led to a reappearance of the approach, supported by an abundance of recent empirical research. Inferences from these reviews support the initial notion that leaders differ from non-leaders on various traits and that most of these traits, at least to some extent, are heritable. The development of the Big Five has contributed significantly to the trait approach and has acted as an organising framework for the copious amount of traits that have been examined in conjunction with leadership. Of the Big Five personality traits, extraversion, conscientiousness and openness to experience are positively related to indices of leadership, whereas neuroticism is negatively related. Likewise, an examination of the Dark Triad traits – narcissism, Machiavellianism and psychopathy – suggests that although they may be effective in specific situations, for the most part they are not considered valuable traits for leaders to possess. In conclusion, given how important good leaders are to organisational outcomes and organisational success, understanding how traits can influence leadership emergence and effectiveness is essential.

REVIEW QUESTIONS

1   Are leaders born or made? Why or why not?

2   Of the Big Five personality traits, which traits are the most strongly associated with leadership?

3   Can the possession of certain personality traits negatively influence leadership? If so, why?

4   What are the practical implications of trait theories of leadership?

NOTE

1   Historically, a strong gender bias excluded the consideration of 'great women', although a great deal of research now speaks to the leadership effectiveness of both men and women in organisations.

REFERENCES

Arvey, R. D., Rotundo, M., Johnson, W., Zhang, Z. and McGue, M. (2006). The determinants of leadership role occupancy: Genetic and personality factors. *The Leadership Quarterly, 17*(1), 1–20.
Babiak, P. and Hare, R. D. (2006). *Snakes in suits: When psychopaths go to work.* New York: HarperCollins Publishers.

Barling, A. J. (2014). *The science of leadership: Lessons from research for organizational leaders.* New York: Oxford University Press.

Barling, A. J., Weber, T. and Kelloway, E. K. (1996). Effects of transformational leadership training on attitudinal and financial outcomes: A field experiment. *Journal of Applied Psychology, 81*(6), 827–832.

Barling, A. J., Christie, A. and Hoption, C. (2011). Leadership. In S. Zedick (ed.), *Handbook of industrial and organizational psychology.* Washington, DC: American Psychological Association, pp. 183–238.

Bass, B. M. (1981). *Stogdill's handbook of leadership: A survey of theory and research.* New York: Free Press.

Bass, B. M. (1990a). From transactional to transformational leadership: Learning to share the vision. *Organizational Dynamics, 18*(3), 19–36.

Bass, B. M. (1990b). *Bass and Stogdill's handbook of leadership.* New York: Free Press.

Bass, B. M. (2008). *The Bass handbook of leadership: Theory, research and managerial applications.* New York: Simon & Schuster.

Bono, J. E. and Judge, T. A. (2004). Personality and transformational and transactional leadership: A meta-analysis. *Journal of Applied Psychology, 89*(5), 901–910.

Brunell, A. B., Gentry, W. A., Campbell, W. K., Hoffman, B. J., Kuhnert, K. W. and DeMarree, K. G. (2008). Leader emergence: The case of the narcissistic leader. *Personality and Social Psychology Bulletin, 34*(12), 1663–1676.

Bushman, B. J., Baumeister, R. F., Thomaes, S., Ryu, E., Begeer, S. and West, S. G. (2009). Looking again, and harder, for a link between low self-esteem and aggression. *Journal of Personality, 77*(2), 427–446.

Carlyle, T. (1907). *Heroes and hero worship.* Boston, MA: Houghton Mifflin.

Cherulnik, P. D. (1995). Physical appearance, social skill, and performance as a leadership candidate, *Basic and Applied Social Psychology, 75*(3), 287–295.

Cherulnik, P. D., Turns, L. C. and Wilderman, S. K. (1990). Physical appearance and leadership: Exploring the role of appearance-based attribution in leader emergence. *Journal of Applied Social Psychology, 20*(18), 1530–1539.

Colbert, A. E., Judge, T. A., Choi, D. and Wang, G. (2012). Assessing the trait theory of leadership using self and observer ratings of personality: The mediating role of contributions to group success. *The Leadership Quarterly, 23*(4), 670–685.

Costa, P. and McCrae, R. (1992). *Revised neo personality inventory (neo pi-r) and neo five-factor inventory (neo-ffi).* Odessa, FL: Psychlogical Assessment Resources.

Dahling, J. J., Whitaker, B. G. and Levy, P. E. (2008). The development and validation of a new Machiavellianism scale. *Journal of Management, 35*(2), 219–257.

Eagly, A. H. and Karau, S. J. (1991). Gender and the emergence of leaders: A meta-analysis. *Journal of Personality and Social Psychology, 60*(5), 685–710.

Eagly, A. H., Karau, S. J. and Makhijani, M. G. (1995). Gender and the effectiveness of leaders: A meta-analysis. *Psychological Bulletin, 117*(1), 125–145.

Fehr, B., Samson, D. and Paulhus, D. L. (1992). The construct of Machiavellianism: Twenty years later. In C. Spielberger and J. Butcher (eds), *Advances in personality assessment Vol. 9.* Hillsdale, NJ: Lawrence Erlbaum, pp. 77–116.

Goktepe, J. R. and Schneier, C. E. (1989). Role of sex, gender roles, and attraction in predicting emergent leaders. *Journal of Applied Psychology, 74*(1), 165–167.

Hare, R. D. (2006). Psychopathy: A clinical and forensic overview. *Psychiatric Clinics of North America, 29*(3), 709–724.

Harrell, W. and Hartnagel, T. (1976). The impact of Machiavellianism and the trustfulness of the victim on laboratory theft. *Sociometry, 39*(2), 157–165.

Hensley, W. and Cooper, R. (1987). Height and occupational success: A review and critique, *Psychological Reports, 60*(3), 843–849.

31

Hogan, R., Raskin, R. and Fazzini, D. (1990). The dark side of charisma. In K. E. Clark and M. B. Clark (eds), *Measures of leadership*. West Orange, NJ: Leadership Library of America, pp. 343–354.

Hogan, R., Curphy, G. and Hogan, J. (1994). What we know about leadership: Effectiveness and personality. *American Psychologist, 49*(6), 493–504.

House, R. J. and Baetz, M. L. (1979). Leadership: Some empirical generalizations and new research directions. In B. Staw (ed.), *Research in organizational behavior*. Greenwich, CT: JAI Press.

House, R. J. and Aditya, R. N. (1997). The social scientific study of leadership: Quo vadis? *Journal of Management, 23*(3), 409–473.

House, R. J. and Javidan, M. (2004). Overview of GLOBE. In R. J. House, P. J. Hanges, M. Javidan, P. W. Dorfman and V. Gupta (eds), *Culture, leadership, and organizations: The GLOBE study of 62 societies*. Thousand Oaks, CA: Sage, pp. 19–28.

Hughes, R. L., Ginnett, R. C. and Curphy, G. J. (2009). *Leadership: Enhancing the lessons of experience*. New York: McGraw-Hill Higher Education.

Ilies, R., Gerhardt, M. W. and Le, H. (2004). Individual differences in leadership emergence: Integrating meta-analytic findings and behavioral genetics estimates, *International Journal of Selection and Assessment, 12*(3), 207–219.

Jones, D. N. and Paulhus, D. L. (2009). Machiavellianism. In M. R. Learly and R. H. Hoyle (eds), *Handbook of individual differences in social behavior*. New York: The Guilford Press, pp. 93–108.

Judge, T. A and Bono, J. E. (2000). Five-factor model of personality and transformational leadership. *Journal of Applied Psychology, 85*(5), 751–765.

Judge, T. A. and Cable, D. M. (2004). The effect of physical height on workplace success and income: Preliminary test of a theoretical model. *Journal of Applied Psychology, 89*(3), 428–441.

Judge, T. A., Colbert, A. E. and Ilies, R. (2004). Intelligence and leadership: A quantitative review and test of theoretical propositions. *Journal of Applied Psychology, 89*(3), 542–552.

Judge, T. A., Piccolo, R. F. and Kosalka, T. (2009). The bright and dark sides of leader traits: A review and theoretical extension of the leader trait paradigm. *The Leadership Quarterly, 20*(6), 855–875.

Judge, T. A., Thoresen, C. J., Pucik, V. and Welbourne, T. M. (1999). Managerial coping with organizational change: A dispositional perspective. *Journal of Applied Psychology, 84*(1), 107–122.

Judge, T. A, Bono, J. E., Ilies, R. and Gerhardt, M. W. (2002). Personality and leadership: A qualitative and quantitative review. *Journal of Applied Psychology, 87*(4), 765–780.

Kalma, A. P., Visser, L. and Peeters, A. (1993). Sociable and aggressive dominance: Personality differences in leadership style? *The Leadership Quarterly, 4*(1), 45–64.

Kelloway, E. K. and Barling, J. (2010). Leadership development as an intervention in occupational health psychology. *Work and Stress, 24*(3), 260–279.

Kelloway, E., Barling, J. and Helleur, J. (2000). Enhancing transformational leadership: The roles of training and feedback. *Leadership and Organization Development Journal, 21*(3), 145–149.

Kenny, D. A. and Zaccaro, S. J. (1983). An estimate of variance due to traits in leadership. *Journal of Applied Psychology, 68*(4), 678–685.

Kessler, S. R., Bandelli, A. C., Spector, P. E., Borman, W. C., Nelson, C. E. and Penney, L. M. (2010). Re-examining Machiavelli: A three-dimensional model of Machiavellianism in the workplace. *Journal of Applied Social Psychology, 40*(8), pp. 1868–1896.

Kirkpatrick, S. A. and Locke, E. A. 1991. Leadership: Do traits matter? *The Executive, 5*, 48–60.

Kish-Gephart, J. J., Harrison, D. A. and Trevin, L. K. (2010). Bad apples, bad cases, and bad barrels: Meta-analytic evidence about sources of unethical decisions at work. *Journal of Applied Psychology, 95*(1), 1–31.

Lord, R. G., de Vader, C. L. and Alliger, G. M. (1986). A meta-analysis of the relation between personality traits and leadership perceptions: An application of validity generalization procedures. *Journal of Applied Psychology, 71*(3), 402–410.

Mann, D. R. (1959). A review of the relationships between personality and performance in small groups. *Psychological Bulletin, 56*(4), 241–270.

Mathieu, C., Neumann, C. S., Hare, R. D. and Babiak, P. (2014). A dark side of leadership: Corporate psychopathy and its influence on employee well-being and job satisfaction. *Personality and Individual Differences, 59*, 83–88.

Mullen, J. E. and Kelloway, E. K. (2009). Safety leadership: A longitudinal study of the effects of transformational leadership on safety outcomes. *Journal of Occupational and Organizational Psychology, 82*(2), 253–272.

Northouse, P. G. (2013). *Leadership: Theory and practice.* Thousand Oaks, CA: Sage.

O'Boyle, E. H., Forsyth, D. R., Banks, G. C. and McDaniel, M. A. (2012). A meta-analysis of the Dark Triad and work behavior: A social exchange perspective. *Journal of Applied Psychology, 97*(3), 557–579.

Paulhus, D. L. and Williams, K. M. (2002). The Dark Triad of personality: Narcissism, Machiavellianism, and psychopathy. *Journal of Research in Personality, 36*(6), 556–563.

Penney, L. and Spector, P. (2002). Narcissism and counterproductive work behavior: Do bigger egos mean bigger problems? *International Journal of Selection and Assessment, 10*(1/2), 126–134.

Rosenthal, S. A. and Pittinsky, T. L. (2006). Narcissistic leadership. *The Leadership Quarterly, 17*(6), 617–633.

Stogdill, M. R. (1948). Personal factors associated with leadership: A survey of the literature. *The Journal of Psychology, 25*(1), 35–71.

Stogdill, M. R. (1974). *Handbook of leadership: A survey of theory and research.* New York: Free Press.

Williams, K. M., Nathanson, C. and Paulhus, D. L. (2010). Identifying and profiling scholastic cheaters: Their personality, cognitive ability, and motivation. *Journal of Experimental Psychology: Applied, 16*(3), 293–307.

Yukl, G. A. (2010). *Leadership in organizations.* Upper Saddle River, NJ: Prentice Hall.

Zaccaro, S. J. (2012). Individual differences and leadership: Contributions to a third tipping point. *The Leadership Quarterly, 23*(4), 718–728.

Zaccaro, S. J., Kemp, C. and Bader, P. (2004). Leader traits and attributes. In J. Antonakis, A. T. Cianciolo and R. J. Sternberg (eds), *The nature of leadership.* Thousand Oaks, CA, Sage, pp. 101–124.

Zettler, I., Friedrich, N. and Hilbig, B. E. (2011). Dissecting work commitment: The role of Machiavellianism. *Career Development International, 16*(1), 20–35.

Chapter 4

Leadership styles

Chris Bond

CHAPTER OBJECTIVES

This chapter concentrates on reviewing the literature and research related to leadership styles. After completing this chapter you should be able to:

1   identify and explain the early theories and research that have contributed to our understanding of leadership styles;

2   discuss and review contemporary approaches to debates and discussions about leadership styles;

3   recognise the strengths and limitations of research approaches to leadership that are largely based on behaviourism or ideology and place too much emphasis on leaders' styles.

KEY TERMS

■   transactional
■   transformational
■   autocratic
■   democratic
■   laissez-faire
■   charismatic
■   servant

INTRODUCTION

Psychologists and management scholars have had a fascination with leadership styles and there are numerous management textbooks and autobiographies of famous entrepreneurs and political leaders that discuss various styles and approaches to leadership. In this chapter we will first review the origin of research into leadership styles and its place in the wider discussion about leadership and management. The chapter will then focus on a number of classical studies related to leadership style such as those by Lewin *et al.* (1939), Tannenbaum and Schmidt (1973) and Blake and Mouton (1964). The chapter then reviews more contemporary models and research into leadership styles, exploring concepts such as charismatic, transformational, transactional and servant leadership. Finally the chapter concludes by reviewing a conceptual model developed by Bond and Seneque (2013) that reviews coaching as a leadership style in contrast to other approaches commonly used in organisational and team-based contexts.

THE ORIGIN AND EVOLUTION OF LEADERSHIP STYLES THEORY

As a reaction to the perceived limitations of theories of leadership based on the trait approach, psychologists and management scholars became interested in exploring leadership theory in relation to leadership styles. This approach recognised that leaders could be made as well as born. The literature that informs thinking about leadership styles is often labelled behaviourist theories as it concentrates on the behaviour and approach exhibited by various leaders. These theories of leadership often focus on what leaders actually do and how they behave in relationship to exercising power over others rather than personal characteristics or qualities which is the main focus of the trait approach.

CLASSIC APPROACHES TO LEADERSHIP STYLE

One of the earliest research based studies into leadership styles was conducted by Kurt Lewin and colleagues (1939). He identified three main types of leadership style which he labelled as *authoritarian*, *democratic* and *laissez-faire*.

Authoritarian

Authoritarian leaders adopt a very directive style and provide a very clear set of expectations and structure for what they require those whom they are leading to achieve. This normally involves setting very clear objectives and expectations of what needs to be done, when it should be done and often how it should be done as well. There is a very clear division of leadership responsibility in this style or approach where the leader often makes decisions independently with little input or participation from other members of the group. These decisions are then communicated to the other members in the form of orders, instructions and clear guidelines on what is expected.

While authoritarian leadership is often perceived as very controlling, allowing little room for freedom or creativity, there are situations where it may be appropriate to adopt this style. In crisis or emergency situations there is often a need for decisive and firm leadership where

35

an individual who has the appropriate knowledge, skills and experience takes charge and directs other members of the team or group. Consider, for example, a building catches fire – in such a situation when the emergency services arrive it is important that there is decisive and clearly directed leadership so that the fire can be tackled without risk to life and that those involved in tackling this emergency all understand the role that they need to play to achieve a successful outcome.

Democratic

The second style that Lewin identified was labelled *democratic leadership*, also sometimes referred to as *participative leadership*. This is generally considered to be the most effective form of leadership. In this approach leaders still maintain control but involve other group members in helping to solve problems or challenges and often listen to opinions and ideas from others. Approaches to leadership based on this style often result in more creative solutions being found than when simply using the authoritarian style. Most contemporary organisations and groups use approaches to leadership and management based on a democratic approach. Interestingly, in Lewin's original study of leadership he found that while democratic approaches produced work of a higher quality the group members were less productive than those managed through an autocratic or authoritarian approach.

Laissez-faire

The third style that Lewin identified was termed *laissez-faire*, and is also sometimes referred to as *delegative leadership*. These leaders offer little or no guidance to the group and often leave decision making to those involved in carrying out the task. This approach to leadership can be highly effective where the group members are highly qualified, work quite autonomously and have considerable expertise. It can, however, lead to poorly defined roles and a lack of co-ordination between various group members. In Lewin's study the group that were led by this style were the least productive of all the three groups, found it challenging to work collaboratively and made many more demands on the leader.

Lewin's work on identifying three primary leadership styles is supported by work undertaken by Hersey–Blanchard's (1969) theory of Situational Leadership. Their research identified that it was important to use different leadership styles depending on the maturity of the team or group members that are being led. Thus they claim that when working with inexperienced individuals a more directing approach is needed, whereas with more experienced individuals a more participative or delegating leadership style is appropriate.

According to Hersey and Blanchard, there are four rather than three main leadership styles; these are summarised below:

Telling (S1) – leaders tell their people what to do and how to do it.
Selling (S2) – leaders provide information and direction, however, there's more
    communication with followers. Leaders 'sell' their message to get people on board.
Participating (S3) – leaders focus more on the relationship and less on direction. The
    leader works with the team, and shares decision-making responsibilities.

Delegating (S4) – leaders pass most of the responsibility on to the follower or group. The leaders still monitor progress, but they're less involved in decisions.

Styles S1 and S2 are focused on getting the task done. Styles S3 and S4 are more concerned with developing team members' abilities to work independently and collaboratively as appropriate.

In practice, managers and leaders in contemporary organisations and groups will use a blended approach to leadership that draws on a range of styles from autocratic, democratic and laissez-faire, dependent on the context and situation. The skilful leader is able to judge when a more controlling or autocratic approach is required or where an approach that is more democratic or delegative might be appropriate.

MOVING TOWARDS A CONTINUUM OF STYLES

Robert Tannenbaum and Warren Schmidt (1973) also focused their work on leadership styles. They developed a continuum of styles that identified seven different approaches or styles that leaders could use (see Figure 4.1). In developing their model of leadership they gave primary consideration to two factors that exerted an influence on leadership behaviour and helped to determine the most appropriate style for a leader to use. The first related to the degree of authority that the leader had and the second the degree of freedom available to those being led. The leader's actions described on the left characterise the manager who maintains a high degree of control, while those on the right describe a manager who delegates authority. Tannenbaum and Schmidt felt that a leader should not choose one style and adhere to it strictly but should be flexible and adapt their style to the situation.

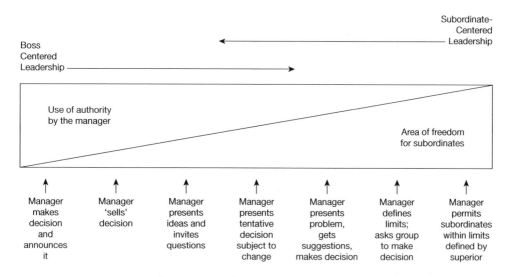

Figure 4.1 The Tannenbaum and Schmidt continuum of leadership behaviour.

Source: Tannenbaum and Schmidt (1973).

37

The model developed by Tannenbaum and Schmidt goes further than the work of Lewin or Hersey and Blanchard and identifies seven distinct leadership styles that can be deployed by leaders. These different styles are:

Tells: When using this style the leader is very directive and makes decisions, communicates them to team or group members and expects them to follow the orders or instructions that have been given. Members of the team have little or no involvement in decision making. Once again this can be an appropriate style to use in crisis situations or where a leader has considerable expertise and is working with a team that has little experience or expertise. The leader retains a strong degree of control and little trust is placed in team members. While this approach is appropriate in some situations, continued use of this style can lead to a lack of motivation in team members and tends to develop a dependency on the leader.

Sells: When using this approach the leader still makes a decision but provides a justification or rationale for this to team members. The leader aims to gain buy-in from team members and while decision making still resides with the leader, members may ask questions or seek clarification. In selling ideas or actions to team members, leaders may make appeals based on facts and research or emotion and opinion. Sometimes selling an idea might require a mix of appeals to objective facts and subjective emotions.

Suggests: When using this style of leadership the leader may propose several possible solutions or courses of action and will usually recommend the course that they feel most appropriate. They will often outline the course of action that they are recommending and offer a justification for this. While the decision is already made, this style helps the team understand why, so team members don't feel so much that the decision is forced on them. According to Tannenbaum and Schmidt, because people have the opportunity to discuss the decision, they feel that they have participated in it, and they accept it more readily.

Consults: When using this style of leadership the leader often suggests a solution or proposes a decision and then allows discussion and suggestion of alternatives to ensure that the best solution has been found. In this respect the team or group members are able to influence the final outcome and participate in the decision-making process. By using an approach of this nature the leader recognises that team members have expertise and experience and that their opinions are valued. This style of leadership values the ideas and opinions of others, helps to build trust and develop cohesive teams that can work collaboratively. It also tends to increase motivation among team members when implementing solutions as they feel they have been part of the process in determining the problem and possible solutions.

Joins: This approach to leadership is even more participatory and sees leaders and team members working fully collaboratively to diagnose problems or challenges and search together for possible solutions. The team works together and, while the leader retains ultimate responsibility for decision making and action, members of the team can exert a significant influence over the way decisions are made and acted upon. This style of leadership places significant trust in and between team members and recognises the individual strengths, expertise and contributions that team members can make.

Delegates: When using this approach leaders often give considerable scope and freedom to members of the team. The leader will normally reach agreement with the team on objectives but leaves considerable freedom for team members to decide which is the best way to approach the problem or challenge that they are facing. The leader, however, still remains accountable for the ultimate outcome so effective delegation is often carried out within clearly defined parameters and guidelines. For the leader this helps to minimise risk and ensure that decisions and actions are in line with the overall objectives and ways of working acceptable to the organisation or group.

Abdicates: The leader asks the team to define the problem, develop options and make a decision. The team is free to do what's necessary to solve a problem while still working under reasonable limits, given organisational needs and objectives. Although the level of freedom is very high, the leader is still accountable for the decision and therefore must make sure the team is ready for this level of responsibility and self-control.

THE MANAGERIAL GRID: BLAKE AND MOUTON

The Managerial Grid was developed by Robert Blake and Jane Mouton and identifies five main leadership styles that can be used in leading and managing others. The grid sought to identify which style was most appropriate in different situations and contexts where leadership or management needed to be exercised. The authors of the grid suggest that there are two main factors that influence the type of leadership style that might be used; these are:

a) *Level of concern for results* – how much does the leader need to be task oriented and focus their energy and leadership activity on achieving specific results, delivering to schedule and within cost at the appropriate quality etc. All of these factors focus on the task that needs to be accomplished.
b) *Level of concern for people* – how much does the leader need to be process oriented and focus their energy and leadership activity on social processes that recognise individual and group contributions, promote good social relations, ensure that those who you are leading are satisfied and content.

When these two factors are plotted on a grid as shown in Figure 4.2 it suggests that there are five main styles that may be used by a leader/manager, dependent on which factors are most important in the particular situation. So, if there is a very high concern for results but little concern for people's needs, a style termed Authority Obedience is best used, whereas if there is both a high concern for the task and for people, then an approach termed Team Management is best employed.

The following gives a brief overview and description of the five leadership styles that Blake and Mouton identify:

Impoverished leadership: This style of leadership manifests itself when there is a low concern for results coupled with a low concern for people. The leader is largely ineffective and has little regard for creating systems or motivating the team members for whom they are

39

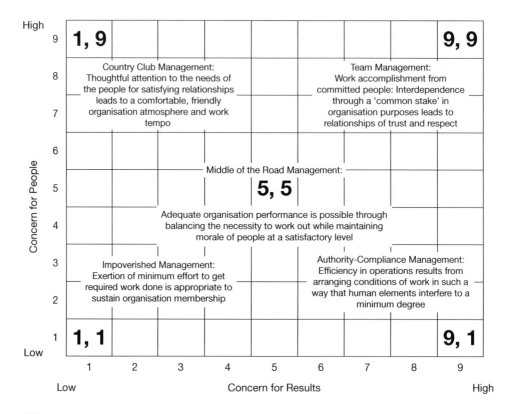

Figure 4.2 *The Blake Mouton Grid.*

Source: Reproduced from Blake and Moulton (1964).

responsible. This often results in poor quality work and high levels of dissatisfaction among team members. Working environments are often chaotic and disorganised and there can be high levels of conflict among team members and poor levels of trust with the leader.

Country club leadership: This style of leadership can often be observed where there is a high concern for people and low concern for results. A leader that adopts this approach has as their primary concern the happiness, needs and feelings of members of their team. The underlying assumption is not that dissimilar to McGregor's Theory Y, in that if members of the team are content they are more likely to be motivated and thus work harder. The resulting work environment tends to be relaxed and relationships are generally good; while this can be an advantage, the lack of attention to concern for the task can result in deadlines often being missed or poor quality work being produced.

Authority/compliance leadership: This style of leadership is most often apparent when there is a high concern for results and a low level of concern for people. It is not that dissimilar to earlier autocratic models of leadership that Lewin and Tannenbaum and Schmidt identified.

In this type of environment human resources (people) are merely another commodity, often expendable and easily replaced. These environments often have very strict rules and can be very target driven. Others have termed this style *'impoverished management'*. The lack of attention to individuals' or teams' needs can lead to team members feeling alienated from the organisation and its leaders, and often leads to highly stressful work environments with considerable burn out and disengagement from team members.

Middle-of-the-road leadership: This type of leadership style is often seen in contexts or situations where there is a medium concern for results and a medium concern for people. Leaders adopting this approach try to balance the requirements for production with the needs of members of their team. As an approach it is largely based on compromise and adaptation, which inevitably means that in some cases either production or people's needs go unmet. Leaders who use this style settle for average performance and often believe that this is the most anyone can expect.

Team leadership: This leadership approach is more often adopted where there is a high concern for both people and results. Blake and Mouton advocate this as the ideal leadership style. Leaders who adopt this approach are concerned with both production requirements and team members' needs equally. This style seeks to balance these needs but without making significant sacrifices in terms of quality or emotional/relational needs of members. Leaders who adopt this approach are able to gain commitment from their team members to organisational goals and purposes; thus, this often creates a team-based environment based on trust and respect that results in high levels of motivation and satisfaction as well as high quality production.

While many may think that a people-centred approach is always the best approach to use, in particular circumstances an approach based on authority obedience can be the most appropriate, particularly in crisis or emergency situations. This type of approach can be seen in a battlefield situation or if a group of firefighters arrive to tackle an industrial blaze. In these contexts control and command leadership become essential to ensure that the desired outcome – in these cases, winning the battle or extinguishing the blaze – is achieved.

CONTEMPORARY APPROACHES TO LEADERSHIP STYLES

So far within this chapter we have reviewed a number of historical but important studies that have had a significant effect on thinking about leadership and management styles. While those concerned with leadership and management have more recently started to understand that leadership is a complex social process, there stills remains a strong interest among scholars and practitioners in research that relates to leadership styles. The next section of this chapter reviews some more contemporary perspectives on leadership styles that have become popular in recent years. While many of the earlier studies may seem dated, they were often grounded in large-scale research studies. Many of the more contemporary approaches to thinking about leadership styles are more ideologically than empirically derived. This means they are based on values and ideas but whether they exist or work in practice has not necessarily been as well explored through in-depth research studies.

Transformational leadership

The evolution of the concept of transformational leadership is often attributed to work undertaken by James Burns, an American historian and presidential scientist. Burns (1978) shifted the focus from defined leadership traits and style solely of the leader to a focus on the interaction between leaders and their followers. He was particularly interested in how this relationship could be used to advance to higher levels of morality and motivation. Transformational leaders use their strong personalities, sense of values and strength of vision to inspire others for the good of the wider group, organisation and society. Transformational leadership is often associated with large-scale change programmes and seeking to bring about a new order and new ways of working and operating.

Bass (1985) developed these original ideas further to what is often referred to as Bass' 'Transformational Leadership Theory'. He suggests that transformational leadership is defined by the effect that leaders have on their followers and is based on gaining trust and respect from them.

Bass and Riggio (2006, p. 4) stated:

> Transformational leaders . . . are those who stimulate and inspire followers to both achieve extraordinary outcomes and, in the process, develop their own leadership capacity. Transformational leaders help followers grow and develop into leaders by responding to individual followers' needs by empowering them and by aligning the objectives and goals of the individual followers, the leader, the group, and the larger organization.

Bass claimed that there are four characteristics of leadership often associated with the exercising of a transformational leadership approach; these are:

1   *Intellectual stimulation*: Transformational leaders have a tendency both to challenge the current situation or dominant paradigm and to encourage creativity and problem solving attitudes with their followers.
2   *Individualised consideration*: Transformational leadership fosters cultures that are supportive and encourage contributions from individual members of the team. Team members are actively encouraged to share ideas and the contributions of individuals in the team are recognised by the leader and other members.
3   *Inspirational motivation*: Transformational leaders offer a clear vision and are able to communicate this effectively to their followers.
4   *Idealised influence*: Transformational leaders model their values and principles in their exercise of leadership; in this way they act as a role model for their followers and gain respect and trust from their followers who seek to align their values and practice with that of the leaders.

Transformational leaders are very self-aware and have high levels of integrity and emotional intelligence, and are very driven. They inspire and motivate members of their team by setting clear goals and high expectations, and developing cultures and environments where all members of the team can participate and feel that they are making a contribution to the overall vision.

Yukl (2002, pp. 290–291) draws some tips for effective transformational leadership:

1   Develop a challenging and attractive vision, together with the employees.
2   Tie the vision to a strategy for its achievement.
3   Develop the vision, specify and translate it to actions.
4   Express confidence, decisiveness and optimism about the vision and its implementation.
5   Realise the vision through small planned steps and small successes in the path for its full implementation.

Charismatic leadership

Approaches to leadership based on charisma are not that dissimilar to the notion of transformational leadership. Both approaches are based on styles that seek to inspire and motivate their team members or followers. The major difference relates to the leaders' motivation and intent. Transformational leaders tend to have a more external focus and a desire to change or transform their teams, organisations and on occasions wider society, whereas charismatic leaders often have a strong focus on their own ambitions and values and seek to persuade others to follow a path or course of action that they define. Charismatic leaders tend to exercise more control over their followers, allow for less dissent among team members and can lead through applying sanctions and punishment as well as offering incentives.

The notion of charismatic leadership was originally advanced by Weber (1947). Weber was a sociologist and thus much of his and other early advocates' views about charismatic leaders were based on sociological studies relating to significant political and religious leaders who were deemed to be charismatic. Weber argued that charismatic leaders emerge in times of social crisis, when their followers are facing serious threats and often suffering severe stress as a result. He claimed that effective leaders using this style articulate clear visions that are based on normative ideological values, seek innovative solutions to major social problems, promote radical approaches to change and are generally most effective in situations of crisis.

More recently, studies into the idea of charismatic leadership have been conducted from a psychological tradition and there has been a growing interest as well in the field of organisational behaviour. House and Shamir (1993) claim that charismatic leaders are differentiated from others by possessing an unusual capacity to experience passion, extraordinary self-confidence, persistence, determination and optimism. These characteristics are required as charismatic leaders are often proposing visions and solutions that are radical and challenge the current dominant values and paradigms that are in operation.

SERVANT LEADERSHIP

As society and leadership contexts have become more complex and challenging there has been increased interest in alternative models, approaches and leadership styles that can work with this complexity and recognise leadership as a social process rather than simply a set of characteristics exhibited in an individual.

One such approach that views leadership as more of a social process is the concept of servant leadership advocated by Greenleaf in his essay *The Servant as Leader* (1970 cited in Greenleaf, 1977). The concept of servant leadership is both a philosophy and a set of leadership practices. Servant leadership challenges the dominant perception that leadership must be exercised from the top and that effective leadership relies on the use and deployment of power and control by those in leadership roles. Rather, servant leadership involves the sharing of power and puts the needs of those being served first and above those of leader.

The idea of servant leadership is most closely associated with participative styles of leadership that seek to support, develop and empower followers to reach their full potential and abilities. This leads to highly collaborative leadership approaches where leadership processes are often distributed among the team members. The exercise of servant leadership requires leaders who are comfortable working in situations where they do not have overall control or exercise absolute authority; it also requires good skills of empathy (understanding and identifying with others' needs), an ability to actively listen and willingness to recognise the skills and expertise of others. Spears (2010) identifies ten characteristics of servant leaders. These are: listening, empathy, healing, awareness, persuasion, conceptualisation, foresight, stewardship, commitment to the growth of others, and building community.

Advocates of a style based on servant leadership claim that it offers a good model of leadership in a world where values and ethics are increasingly important and where servant leaders can command the respect and support of followers because they identify with these values and the integrity of the leader. However, others claim that the approach is too soft and fails to recognise the reality of competition, power and politics in most leadership contexts, thus often resulting in servant leaders being left behind or ignored.

COACHING AS A LEADERSHIP STYLE

Bond and Seneque (2012) through research with accredited organisational coaches in Australia in 2008 identified five main leadership approaches to promoting change being used in organisations at that time: *managing, consulting, mentoring, facilitating* and *coaching*. Through a series of focus groups and interviews they developed a conceptual framework that sought to identify the particular features or characteristics identified with each of these leadership approaches. These are presented in Table 4.1.

As a result of this study the authors claimed that coaching, when used as part of an organisation-wide strategy, can offer a framework for human resource development that is grounded in the 'here and now' and assist with balancing individual, team and organisational development needs. The outcome of this small-scale investigation supports the assertions of Cavanagh (2006) and others in seeing coaching as a systemic activity that seeks to foreground complexity, pluralist perspectives, unpredictability and contextual factors, and the search for achieving a balance between stability and instability as one of the major contributions that it can make to management intervention.

44

Table 4.1 *The managing–coaching continuum*

Managing	Consulting	Mentoring	Facilitating	Coaching
Controlling and directing (resources, people, processes and risk)	Advising (expertise)	Developing individual relationships	Encouraging and empowering	Goal orientation
Defining and drawing boundaries (roles, responsibilities, etc.)	Diagnosis	Developing competence and capacity	Challenging	Individual and team based Strong emphasis on self-reflection
Balancing strategic thinking with operational action	Bringing in outside perspectives/ other views	Promoting personal growth/ development	Guiding process	Building capacity to work relationally, socially and organisationally (holistic)
Planning and monitoring action	Supporting and developing	On-going and flexible time frame: normally long term	Developing frameworks for social interaction	Focus on situation/ context Focus on 'Here and Now'
Normally long-term relationship with organisation	Normally short-term focused intervention	Normally long-term relationship with individual	Medium-term relationship	Contracted relationship for fixed time
Achieving results through others	Promoting/ effecting change	Transfer of domain specific knowledge (exercising expertise giving)	Promoting reflection	Circumscribed/ deliverables to be achieved
Based on unequal power dynamics	Based on power dynamics where the consultant is seen to have technical or process expertise	Unequal power relationships	Ultimate power generally remains with the individual or group	Issues of power and influence are addressed and negotiated as part of the relational process

The findings from this study support recent research conducted by Hamlin *et al.* (2009), who suggest that effective managers and managerial leaders embed effective coaching at the core of their management practice. It also supports earlier research by Evered and Selman (1989) that contended that good coaching was at the heart of management.

SUMMARY

Within this chapter we have reviewed a number of theoretical and research based approaches to leadership styles. These have ranged from classical studies that develop models that offer a range of leadership styles that can be deployed in various situations and contexts to more contemporary approaches that advocate a dominant style, largely based on certain philosophies and values about what leaders are, should be and do. The earlier contributions to discussion about leadership styles often offer a menu driven approach to leadership and describe a broad range of leadership styles that can be used by leaders. Later contributions such as transformational or charismatic leadership tend to advocate a dominant approach and focus on the essential characteristics that underpin this style. We concluded this chapter by offering a comparative conception of contemporary leadership styles advocated by the author and a co-writer (Bond and Seneque, 2013) which contrasts a variety of leadership approaches currently being used in contemporary organisational contexts.

In recent times, debates about leadership styles have now largely been overtaken by a real concern for investigating and exploring leadership as a social process with an emphasis on how leadership operates in practice and exploring links between leadership and effective management. Nevertheless many leaders and managers still have a concern to develop a leadership style that suits their personal characteristics and meets the needs and culture of the organisations that they work for; thus, there still remains a legitimate interest in research into leadership styles.

REVIEW QUESTIONS

1   Think of a situation where you have experienced leadership. This may be where you were a leader or where you were being led by someone else. It could also be a formal situation such as a work place, a place of worship or a sports team that you belong to or it could be a more informal context such as a friendship group or a social group at university/college. What style of leadership do you think was used? Why do you think this style may have been used by yourself or others that were leading? How did you react to this approach to leadership?

2   Compare and contrast the two frameworks of leadership styles described above by Tannenbaum and Schmidt and Blake and Mouton. What do you think are the strengths and limitations of the two models? In each model, which would you identify as your preferred management style?

3   In the world of team sports to what extent do you think it would be desirable or possible for a team captain to adopt a servant leadership style in their approach? What do you think might be the advantages and disadvantages of a team captain adopting such an approach?

REFERENCES

Bass, B. (1985) *Leadership and performance*. New York: Free Press.

Bass, B. and Riggio, R. (2006) *Transformational leadership*. Mahwah, NJ: Lawrence Erlbaum Associates.

Blake, R. and Mouton, J. (1964). *The Managerial Grid: The key to leadership excellence*. Houston, TX: Gulf Publishing.

Bond, C. and Seneque, M. (2013). Conceptualizing coaching as an approach to management and organizational development, *Journal of Management Development, 32*(1), 57–72.

Burns, J. (1978). *Leadership*. New York: Harper & Row.

Cavanagh, M. (2006). Coaching from a systemic perspective: A complex adaptive approach. In D. Stober and A. Grant (eds), *Evidence-based coaching handbook*, 313–354. New York: Wiley.

Evered, R. and Selman J. (1989). Coaching and the art of management, *Organizational Dynamics, 8*(2), 16–32.

Greenleaf, R. (1977). *Servant-leadership: A journey into the nature of legitimate power and greatness*. Mahwah, NJ: Paulist Press.

Hamlin, R. G., Ellinger, A. D. and Beattie, R. S. (2009). Toward a profession of coaching? A definitional examination of 'coaching', 'organization development' and 'human resource development', *International Journal of Evidence-based Coaching and Mentoring, 7*(1), 13–38.

Hersey, P. and Blanchard, K. (1969). Life cycle theory of leadership: Is there a best style of leadership? *Training and Development Journal, 33*(6), 26–34.

House, R. and Shamir, B. (1993) Toward the integration of charismatic, transformational, inspirational and visionary theories of leadership. In M. Chemmers and R. Ayman (eds) *Leadership theory and research perspectives and directions*, 81–107. New York: Academic Press.

Lewin, K., Lippit, R. and White, R. K. (1939). Patterns of aggressive behavior in experimentally created social climates, *Journal of Social Psychology, 10*, 271–301.

Spears, L. (2010). Character and servant leadership: Ten characteristics of effective, caring leaders, *The Journal of Virtues* and *Leadership, 1*(1), 25–30.

Tannenbaum, R. and Schmidt, W. (1973). How to choose a leadership pattern, *Harvard Business Review*, May–June, 1–12.

Weber, M. (1947). *The theory of social and economic organization*. Translated by A. M. Henderson and T. Parsons. New York: Free Press.

Yukl, G. (2002). *Leadership in organizations*. Upper Saddle River, NJ: Prentice Hall.

Chapter 5

Leadership, teams and exchange

You're either in or you're out

James McCalman

CHAPTER OBJECTIVES

After completing this chapter you should be able to:

1   understand how leaders interact with different team members;
2   understand the notion of dyadic leader–member exchange and how this can establish in and out groups;
3   differentiate leadership from management in managing meaning;
4   be able to describe how Hill's team leadership model can help an individual lead and represent a sporting team;
5   understand the complexity of the leadership role and how this expands beyond the team itself. This contains notions of strategy, power, politics, vision, ego and people management.

KEY TERMS

■   leader–member exchange
■   team leadership
■   compliance

INTRODUCTION

Somewhat surprisingly I begin this chapter by stating that leadership isn't about leadership! It's actually about the nature of behaviour, power and control in organisations. The concept of power and control was introduced in Chapter 2. However, perhaps nowhere is the notion of power and control more clear than in the sporting arena. To understand leadership in sports we have to understand the nature of compliance. Why do some people follow others? One starting point is the notion of rewarded behaviour. Burrhus Frederick (B. F.) Skinner first introduced the notion of shaping behaviour in individuals by selectively reinforcing desired behaviour. His argument was that our behaviour is shaped by our experience within our environment and by the selective rewards and punishments we received. Reinforcement theory argues that control of behaviour can be achieved by manipulating the consequences of behaviour. So for example, in a sporting context, reinforcement theory would employ rewards for desirable behaviour by team members while punishing undesirable behaviour to help steer team members towards intended performance goals. Skinner classified this as operant conditioning. This process is illustrated in Figure 5.1.

So, in leadership terms, reinforcement theory allows us to begin to influence specific outcomes through the control of individuals or team behaviours. However, although operant conditioning is a powerful explanation for followers' behaviours, it doesn't explain how the leader may often treat individuals in the same team differently. One explanation for this differentiation is understood through Leader–Member Exchange (LMX) theory.

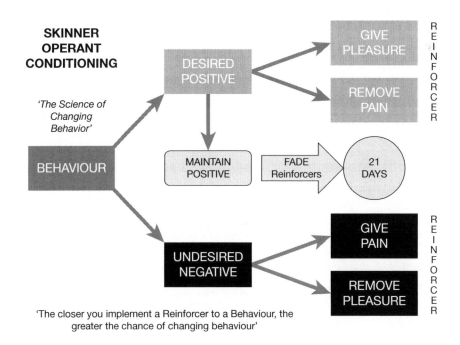

Figure 5.1 *Skinner's model of operant conditioning.*

Source: https://sites.google.com/a/adams12.org/harp-mrhs-home-v1/06-powerpoint-section/skinner-s-operant-conditioning.

LEADER–MEMBER EXCHANGE (LMX) THEORY

The origin of LMX theory is largely credited to Dansereau *et al.* (1975) although it has developed, metamorphosed and, in some views, has exploded over the last 40 years (Graen and Uhl-Bien, 1995). The core theory started life as an attempt at developing better leadership through relationship management and argued that leaders adapted and varied their style and behaviour with different individuals and thus by doing so influenced the quality and nature of the relationships. The crucial element of the subsequent development of work in relation to LMX is identification of domains – leader-based, relationship-based and follower-based. Similarly, this is important because it places LMX clearly within the relationships-based arena, 'effective leadership processes occur when leaders and followers are able to develop mature leadership relationships (partnerships) and thus gain access to the many benefits that these relationships bring' (Graen and Uhl Bien, 1995, p. 222). However, Graen and Uhl Bien (1995) argue that LMX has progressed beyond this in four stages to encompass social exchange theory.

Stage 1 involved what is termed Vertical Dyad Linkage (VDL) research investigating how leaders developed differentiated relationships with their direct reports (dyads within groups and the in-group or out-group notion). Stage 2 involved investigating the nature of these differentiated relationships and the implications of these for the organisation. Stage 3 examined, 'the utility of increasing proportions of high-quality relationships in organizations and described a process for accomplishing this through dyadic partnership building' (Graen and Uhl Bien, 1995, p. 225). Finally, Stage 4 explored how these dyads can be built into larger collectivities.

The reader might well ask what has any of this to do with leadership and teams? There is a certain truth that LMX has forged an academic 'industry' of duplication, replication and research that has somehow lost the plot. However, there are certainly interesting elements in each stage of development that are worthy of consideration.

As both Dansereau *et al.* (1975) and Graen and Uhl-Bien (1995) noted, many managerial processes in organisations were found not to occur at the overall level, as predicated by the Ohio State and Michigan, but rather on a dyadic basis, with managers developing differentiated relationships with different employees. This placed a focus on the leader–follower relationship with an emphasis very strongly in the leader domain. However, one of the main issues here is the direct association between supervisor, manager and leader, assuming that they are one and the same. As was noted in Chapter 2 of this text, not all managers are leaders! Subsequently, LMX began building a large body of quantitative research founded on studies of supervisory/management groups and their relationships within dyads.

By Stage 3, however, there appears to have been a shift in focus,

> [towards] an examination of leadership as *partnership* among dyadic members. The key difference in this stage of investigation is that rather than managers treating some employees more favourably than others . . . this stage states that managers should provide all employees access to the process of LMX by making the initial offer to develop LMX partnership to each subordinate.
>
> (Graen and Uhl-Bien, 1995, p. 133)

50

There appears here to be a recognition that the research is dealing with management as opposed to leadership, and that the nature of the leadership process, or what is termed as 'leadership making' is still very transactional or contractual. However, the authors make claim that subsequent developments of the theory by nurturing the notion of LMX as partnerships have moved it from transaction to transformational through the development of peer relationships. Nevertheless, perceiving LMX as an exchange-based approach does problematize the leader/management idea because,

> when material exchange is the basis for leadership, the process is not really leadership; it is closer to 'managership' or 'supervision' . . . LMX is both transactional and transformational. It is a dyadic social exchange process that begins with more limited social 'transactions', but for those who are able to generate the most effective LMX relationships, the type of leadership that results is transformational.
>
> (Graen and Uhl-Bien, 1995, p. 238)

What we can really take from LMX is the notion of in-groups and out-groups within sporting teams and the emphasis on social exchange theory as a means of determining effective leadership processes as opposed to management hierarchy.

There is a fundamental difference between the identity and the social processes associated with leadership and management. Managers can expect their direct subordinates to obey orders. This behaviour must not be misunderstood as constituting leadership. If a manager has to explore transformational strategies that involve changing culture at work, or request higher standards of performance that require extraordinary effort, this is an attempt at enacting a leadership identity (Burns, 1978; Schein, 2004). Most employees will accept an individual as a legitimate manager if that individual is appointed through normative processes. As long as the manager observes cultural protocols in the way they administrate their managerial office there should be reduced potential for staff relationship issues. Managers who operate within cultural convention can draw on official authority to expect some degree of conformity on the part of staff. However, leadership is far more intimate because followers determine their leaders; leaders do not determine their followers. It is a flawed assumption that all managers in organisations are also leaders because their job description says so. There may be expectancy on the part of the employer that managers will also fulfil the role of leaders (Kotter, 1990), but this expectancy should not be assumed to be a straightforward goal to achieve. Warner Burke (2011, p. 255) states:

> Leadership requires followers. A person may think that he or she is a leader, but if there is no one to follow, it does not matter what the person's self-concept may be: Without a follower, a person is not a leader. Thus leadership is about influence, but that influence is a reciprocal process. Leadership occurs when a potential follower exists and wants direction.

Managers and leaders are two very different social identities that both rely on very different emergent dynamics for their legitimacy and effectiveness as regards influencing others.

51

CASE STUDY

LEADERSHIP AND MEMBER EXCHANGE: THE SIR ALEX FERGUSON WAY

In 2013 Harvard Business School professor Anita Elberse in collaboration with Sir Alex Ferguson published a Harvard Business School article 'Ferguson's formula'. This wide-ranging review of Ferguson's playing and management career focused on the leadership lessons Ferguson took away from his years of coaching especially at Manchester United. I have taken some of these and attempted to adapt them to LMX theory below.

Start with the foundation

When Ferguson joined United, he refocused the club's programme for finding young players and began to very quickly nurture them and expose them to first team football. This led to the successful development of the club's mainstay performers during the 1990s – David Beckham, Ryan Giggs, Gary and Phil Neville, and Paul Scholes. Ferguson argues:

> I wanted to build right from the bottom. That was in order to create fluency and a continuity of supply to the first team. The players all grow up together, producing a bond that, in turn, creates a spirit. . . . Winning a game is only a short-term gain. . . . Building a club brings stability and consistency.

Q: What elements of LMX theory would this approach illustrate?

Dare to rebuild your team

In the article Ferguson discusses how on many occasions he cut players, including those he cared about. Focusing in his early coaching period on youth, he sold team members, more often at their peak, making money for the club. David Beckham was one. Ferguson sold him to Real Madrid 2003, after his public persona began to overshadow his playing career. There were exceptions, such as Dutch strikers Ruud van Nistelrooy and Robin van Persie, whom Ferguson bought for £19 and £24 million respectively. As Ferguson stresses:

> The goal was to evolve gradually, moving older players out and younger players in. It was mainly about two things: First, who did we have coming through and where did we see them in three years' time, and second, were there signs that exiting players were getting older?

Q: What elements of LMX theory would this approach illustrate?

Set high standards – and hold everyone to them

Ferguson looked for players who were 'bad losers'. On joining United he comments:

> I had to lift players' expectations. They should never give in. . . . I constantly told my squad that working hard all your life is a talent. But I expected even more from my star players. . . . Superstars with egos are not the problem some people may

> think. They need to be winners, because that massages their egos, so they will do what it takes to win.
>
> *Q: What elements of LMX theory do you believe this illustrates?*
>
> Source: 'Ferguson's formula' by Anita Elberse with Alex Ferguson (2013).

THE LEADERSHIP–MANAGEMENT PARADOX

As we saw in Chapter 2, managers maintain order and observe cultural traditions so that they may render the environment more predictable and manageable. Leaders, in contrast, seek to disrupt and change cultural norms that are the product of tradition when they interpret these as liabilities to the ongoing prosperity of the organisation at large (Schein, 2004).

Schein (2004, p. 11) distinguishes between management and leadership with some clarity when he states:

> If one wishes to distinguish leadership from management or administration, one can argue that leadership creates and changes cultures, while management and administration act within cultures. Culture is the result of a complex learning process that is only partially influenced by leadership behavior. But if the group's survival is threatened because elements of its culture have become maladapted, it is ultimately the function of leadership at all levels of the organization to recognize and do something about this situation.

[handwritten margin note: distinction @ ldrs vs mgrs + their role in culture]

Leadership and management operating in tandem are both unquestionably critical to successful teams. However, when we seek to examine the difference between how a sporting team gets better at doing the same thing – reproduction and maintenance – versus breaking the existing mould of performance – quantum change – we need to examine how managers trigger the leadership/follower life cycle in a creative tension that generates a mutually reinforcing relationship. Thus the identity of the leader is an outcome of what we could usefully call '*leadership becoming*' which is a process of social construction between people and managers that involves a metamorphosis into dynamic relations of followers and leaders. This process can be considered as the '*life cycle*' that involves four stages:

[handwritten margin note: in relation to sport]

1 *Being*: the process of becoming a leader that is mediated through contingent needs on the part of followers that may be framed and made active through meaning management on the part of potential leaders.
2 *Identity actualisation*: the active performance of leader or follower through the production and actualisation of follower/leadership processes that ratify both sets of identities.
3 *Leadership/Follower enactment*: the exchange of authority and compliance that transcends normative management/staff obligations and expectations.
4 *Demise*: the fading of the follower identity and the dilution of the leader's authority to lead that inevitably results in the fragmentation and demise of the servant leadership dynamic.

53

Leaders control a set of variables to achieve a certain end. One could argue that managers in the traditional conceptualisation of their role are fundamentally engaged with maintaining and policing the established cultural norms of the organisation (Kotter, 1990; Alvesson, 2002). It is not too much of a conceptual leap to appreciate that this interpretation of management is the antithesis to attempts at changing culture. Therefore, all managers by definition of their job titles and by what they actually do manage an established culture relatively unreflectively.

The main distinction between managers and leaders is that managers operate within culture and maintain cultural norms while leaders also work within cultures but they also can influence the modification and in some cases the transformation of culture in organisations and this becomes very interesting in sporting terms (Schein, 2004; Alvesson and Sveningsson, 2008).

The servant or the master?

The theme that this discussion has been following thus far is that a major source of contrast between leaders and managers is to be located within the nature of the relationship that exists between both groups and their main constituents. Managers have staff; they have direct reports while leaders have followers. The flow of power shifts from the manager to the staff member resulting in a social dynamic whereby the staff member submits to the legitimate authority of the senior manager. The expectations are that such submission is implicit in the employment contract and is further imbedded within the control mechanisms that characterise the hierarchical structure of the organisations.

In contrast, leaders exist to serve their constituents. If we accept the proposition that to be a leader one requires followers and that followers appoint and dispose of leaders, then the choice of leader will be contingent on the needs of followers and the needs of followers will vary (Alvesson, 2002). Leaders are required to 'serve' their followers and they are granted authority to lead on the basis that they actively apply their leadership authority, rights and privileges in the interests of their followers (Gramsci, 1971). For this reason, the concept of 'servant leadership' is useful (Greenleaf, 1977). Servant leadership advocates the principle that some individuals have a desire to serve through leadership processes the agenda of followers (Gill, 2006). Ken Melrose the CEO of the Toro Company quoted in Gill (2006, p. 40) states that, 'I came to understand that you best lead by serving the needs of your people. You don't do their jobs for them; you enable them to learn and progress on the job.' The extent to which sporting coaches/leaders enact these principles has a strong bearing on leader behaviours.

The men and women employed in the sporting arena as managers have to be able to switch identities and draw on internal social and intellectual resources to shift form to that of a leader which involves shifting the form of relationships to that of leader/follower dynamics. This is a very challenging idea to grasp and one that in reality demands considerable social and intellectual flexibility on the part of both parties. It is also potentially very confusing for those involved. Exactly how do managers shift from traditional management roles to the model of leadership we are advocating? The answer to this question is with some difficulty. Managers cannot realistically shape shift at will from orthodox management types to servant leaders.

Management, leadership and meaning

Leadership is the capacity to mobilise reflective thinking towards cultural themes and when to change such themes. Thus, leadership involves changing aspects of the meaning system and resulting beliefs of organisational members (Opler, 1945). Smircich and Morgan (1982, p. 258) argue that leadership as a process is fundamentally concerned with the management of meaning. Leaders emerge,

> because of their role in framing experience in a way that provides a viable basis for action, e.g., by mobilizing meaning, articulating and defining what has previously remained implicit or unsaid, by inventing images and meanings that provide a focus for new attention, and consolidating or confronting, or changing prevailing wisdom.

Leaders, through articulating meaning in their management processes establish the support required for a course of action in relation to the defined situation. For assumptions to change there has to be a shift in the structure and common interpretation of cultural themes. This shift has to be shared among enough people within a team to constitute a change in aspects of a local culture (Alvesson and Sveningsson, 2008). This is a leadership process. For example, Smircich and Morgan (1982, p. 257) claim: 'For, in leading, managers enact a particular form of social reality with far reaching, but often poorly understood and appreciated, consequences.'

Thus leadership is concerned with influencing the subjectivities of individuals and the inter-subjectivities of groups. This process is based on dialogical relations between followers and leaders (Dixon, 1998). While followers implicitly surrender their power to define social reality, this is based on a delicate process of symbolic negotiation. This ability is bestowed on the leader by their followers. It is not uncommon for emerging leaders to encounter different factions in their teams who may be building reality constructions and meaning systems that are in opposition to their intended interpretative schemes. A recent sporting example of this would be the succession of David Moyes as manager of Manchester United Football Club and his interaction with a senior group of players within the club. If the emerging leader cannot harmonise meaning systems through dialogical methods with their followers, then they cannot lead effective change.

Managers, in contrast with leaders, are engaged in meaning preservation of established cultural archetypes that are used to make sense of and maintain order within their domains. Managers who engage in the strategy of 'management by objectives' engage in 'meaning management recovery' as they aim to define the nature of a problem in ways that support traditional perspectives. They draw on historical sense making models that offer a stock of symbolic frameworks that are understood as legitimate and proven to help them define a problem as a management objective. People respond to these symbolic reference points and follow the guidance or instruction of the manager. This is a form of leadership that Smircich and Morgan refer to as *institutionalised leadership*. They state: 'Authority relationships legitimize the pattern of dependency relations that characterize the process of leadership, specifying who is to define social reality, and in what circumstances' (1982, p. 259).

55

HILL'S TEAM LEADERSHIP MODEL

Hill's Team Leadership model goes a long way in helping us bridge the realities between the meaning of management and institutionalised leadership (see Figure 5.2). Although based on a perspective that the team leader monitors the team in a functional sense and takes action where necessary to ensure team effectiveness, it also provides a highly relevant and simplified tool for analysis. However, key to the model is that Hill points out that the effective starting point is the leader's mental model of the situation. This mental model encompasses team problems and the external and organisational issues that define how the problem can be addressed. This also begins to draw us closer to a differentiation between management and leadership in terms of types of problems the leader can address versus those that are of a managerial concern. We shall return to this later.

Hill argues that there are four levels or steps in the model:

1   Effective team performance begins with the leader's mental model of the situation and then determining if the situation requires Action or just Monitoring?

Figure 5.2 Hill's Team Leadership model.

Source: Adapted from Leadership: Theory and Practice, 6th edn, by Peter Northouse, (2013).

CASE STUDY

HILL'S TEAM LEADERSHIP MODEL: THE SIR ALEX FERGUSON WAY

Never, ever cede control

Ferguson believed in quick, decisive and in many instances forceful action. If any of his players got out of control he quickly sidelined or removed them. In 2005, after captain Roy Keane publicly criticised his teammates, Ferguson terminated his contract. The next year, the team's top scorer, Ruud van Nistelrooy, showed his displeasure about being benched and Ferguson sold him to Real Madrid. As he comments:

> I told myself I wasn't going to allow anyone to be stronger than I was. Your personality has to be bigger than theirs. That's vital. . . . It's not about looking for adversity or for opportunities to prove power; it's about having control and being authoritative when issues do arise.

Q: How does this map itself onto Hill's model? What might be some of the potential issues that this sort of leadership brings?

Match the message to the moment

Ferguson's media image was as a hard taskmaster who regularly gave his players what was termed, 'the hair dryer treatment'. However, although Ferguson often gave tough talks to his players at half-time and at the end of games, he argues that he varied his approach depending on the situation:

> No one likes to be criticized. Few people get better with criticism; most respond to encouragement instead. . . . For a player – for any human being – there is nothing better than hearing 'Well done'. . . . At the same time, in the dressing room, you need to point out mistakes when players don't meet expectations. . . . I would do it right after the game. . . . I'd do it and it was finished.

Q: In terms of internal leadership functions where does this type of approach sit? Is instant feedback always effective in a sporting context?

Rely on the power of observation

At Manchester United, Ferguson delegated more of the training sessions to assistant coaches. But he always came to practice and watched his players:

> What you can pick up by watching is incredibly valuable. . . . Seeing a player's habits or a sudden dip in his enthusiasm allowed me to go further with him: Is it family problems? Is he struggling financially? Is he tired? What kind of mood is he in? Sometimes I could even tell if a player was injured when he thought he was fine. . . . The ability to see things is key – or, more specifically, the ability to see things you don't expect to see.

Q: How does this map itself onto Hill's model?

2   Are the actions necessary at an Internal or External level?
3   Is the intervention on the part of the leader task, relational or environmental? Depending on the type of intervention a specific functional is performed (see diagram for Function Interventions).
4   Correctly performing the above three steps creates high Performance through Development and Maintenance functions.

(Northouse, 2013, p. 290)

Hill's model is useful in providing a focus directly onto real-life team issues and leader interventions. However, it does assume knowledge rests at the top.

THE LEADERSHIP–TEAMWORK BLEND

Grint (2005) recognises the idea of institutionalised leadership when managers use historical symbolic references to define a problem as a *'critical problem'* that demands management authority to lead. He draws attention to a different kind of leadership that is required to solve what he calls a *'wicked problem'*, unique to the organisation with no preordained solution that management can relate to. Cultural change is an example of a wicked problem and only through leadership that engages in sense making with followers based on dialogical exchange can these problems be solved. This kind of leadership draws on power from below; it draws on the approval and authority of followers. In contrast, institutionalised leadership relies on hierarchical authority and formal position. For us, institutionalised leadership is not really leadership at all. It is best understood as a form of *pseudo leadership* that disguises traditional management as a process of authority and problem solving. The kind of leadership required to change organisational culture is of a strategic and authentic kind. Smircich and Morgan (1982, p. 260) explain that strategic leadership provides 'a conception and direction for organizational process that goes above and beyond what is embedded in the fabric of organization as a structure, i.e. a reified and somewhat static pattern of meaning'.

This means that leadership involves building new meaning systems. It involves reviewing existing meaning systems and changing or transforming these. It requires building meaning systems through dialogical processes as a platform for ongoing action to achieve cultural change. This process involves changing the patterns of meaning that inform established assumptions, values and cultural themes that contain or enable culture expression in an organisation. It is within the seeds of potential leadership that the promise of what the organisation may become lies.

Leadership is a creative and an imaginative process (Hatch, Kostera and Kozminski, 2005) but also one that cannot avoid issues of confrontation. Leaders do employ established interpretative frameworks to mobilise leadership processes (Goffman, 1959; 1967), but they also 'paint' new symbolic pictures for the attention of followers. In this way they artistically work with symbols to invoke images and meanings that followers interpret in ways congruent with the desires of their leaders. Smircich and Morgan (1982, p. 262) emphasise this point when they state that, 'the use of language, ritual, drama, stories, myths and symbolic construction of all kinds may play an important role'. The role they are referring to is the leadership role. The leadership skill is how they use these symbolic resources to dramatise

[handwritten margin note: Leadership : Creativity]

58

their ideas for consumption. Internal marketing can support the mobilisation of meaning in visually powerful ways.

The key issue for leaders is how to manage the conflicting views of key stakeholders and how to achieve harmonisation of meaning as a viable basis for action. This process in itself may be one of cultural transformation if the established culture is conflict adverse. If executive leaders cannot challenge cultural convention this is a leadership failure that will result in the collapse of any cultural change intervention. Changing organisational culture in a planned way is fundamentally concerned with motivation at the level of the group and of the individual. This involves the subjects participating in cultural change cooperating of their own free will through dialogical processes with organisational leaders to change the symbolic interpretations that they have either inherited or co-authored during their time in the organisation (Gramsci, 1971; Bohm, 1985; Johnson and Johnson, 1989; Argyris, 1990).

IT'S NOT THAT STRAIGHTFORWARD

dissenters

If we follow the line of thought outlined above we conclude that leaders will not only have followers they will have to deal with dissenters, subversives and change agnostics (Elsbach, 1999). Competing groups or individual actors may define situations through different inter-pretive lens, establishing abrasive cultural definitions and domains, which become a source of tension in the group dynamic (Brown, 1995; Dixon, 1998; Beech and MacIntosh, 2012; Alvesson and Sveningsson, 2008). In support of this view Smircich and Morgan (1982, p. 258) state: 'If a group situation embodies competing definitions of reality, strongly held, no clear patterns of leadership evolves.'

If the emerging leader cannot use competing definitions productively they may drive forward many of the negative and constructive politics within organisations (Buchanan and McCalman, 1989; Paton and McCalman, 2000). It is therefore important that leaders have to gauge the degree of support they will have for any situational definition they put forth.

LEADERS BUILD COMMITMENT

Argyris (1990) makes the significant point that unless the leadership within an organisation has the desire and the capacity for building internal commitment then any efforts to attempt cultural change are probably fundamentally flawed. He makes the significant point that unless the leadership within an organisation has the desire and the capacity for building internal commitment then any efforts to attempt cultural change are probably fundamentally flawed. Senior leaders need to be open to acknowledging the scale of cultural change – open to its challenges, its longitudinal nature – and most of all be prepared to sustain the stamina required for the cultural change process. They need to be willing to upset the cultural apple cart. Leaders must understand the dynamics of local culture in use and in an intelligent way work with cultural change theory to try to change the established cultural norms. Therefore, leaders need to be able to become competent at cultural analysis. This involves being open to the theories and practices of cultural change work. Thus a critical criterion for effective leadership is having an open and enquiring mind. Leadership and culture to a degree are two sides of the same coin. Established leadership styles are often local cultural productions and as such

59

future leaders are often appointed on their ability to reflect cultural norms. This is a problem for cultural change work. We call this phenomenon '*pseudo leaders*' – managers who are assumed to be local leaders and who may in fact be bureaucratic managers who are involved in smooth cultural reproduction, which simply maintains the status quo. It follows if we have pseudo leaders that there are '*pseudo followers*', who are people who pretend to be involved in a leader–follower relationship to maintain the cultural status quo and thus preserve or advance their own interests. Pseudo followers accept a senior manager in a leadership role who does not have the motivation and thus the ability in actual fact to lead anyone. In this situation there would be no real possibility of building commitment for cultural change unless it emerged from below and a senior manager was tasked or invited by others to shift form from that of a pseudo leader to that of a genuine leader with sincere followers.

BUILDING A NEW ORDER

The ownership of the function of planning, designing, implementing, reviewing and therefore leading is unquestionably a political process. It has the real potential to upset the historical dynamics of the management community that serves the needs of the business. To lead a cultural change programme requires access to the organisations top leadership and this can stimulate antagonisms rooted in jealousy. Tactics that managers may demonstrate to stem the increased influence of a cultural change leader would either be to attack the efficacy of the programme, its content, how it is being communicated or who it is involving. They may attack the language that is being advanced, the concepts being employed, the projects developed or whatever else they can use in their agenda to undermine the efficiency of the programme. If all of these tactics fail they can simply disengage and adopt a passive indifference towards the change programme and those who are central to its ongoing development. If the cultural change leader can outmanoeuvre all of these powerful tactics and start to define the change programme as a corporate success story then one may find that subversive tactics increase in their vigour. Smircich and Morgan (1982, p. 270) emphasise the political and power infused nature of leadership as a process: 'Leadership is not simply a process of acting or behaving, or a process of manipulating rewards. It is a process of power based reality construction and needs to be understood in these terms.' We can best illustrate this if we take the Ferguson case study example and cite one final part of his formula.

Prepare to win

United were known for coming from behind and winning. Ferguson had his players practice what to do if they needed to score a goal with minutes remaining. His strategy reflected a high risk/high reward approach about which he comments:

> I am a gambler – a risk taker – and you can see that in how we played in the late stages of matches. If we were still down say, 1–2 with 15 minutes to go, I was ready to take more risks. . . . We'd put in an extra attacking player and worry less about defence. We knew if we ended up winning 3–2, it would be a fantastic feeling. And

if we lost 1–3, we'd been losing anyway. . . . You can lose on the counterattack, but the joy of winning when you thought you were beaten is fantastic.

In support of the idea that leadership involves power contests over emerging meaning frameworks, Humphreys and Brown (2002) suggest that organisations may be defined as arenas where managers struggle for control over the discursive space. Leaders are central to this struggle, a struggle that is far more intense when the meanings being discussed are of a cultural nature and that may serve the interests of some and not of others. This is why building a dialogue with a critical mass is so important to the change leader, if they are to have any chance of success. This dialogical building process takes time but it is worth the effort as the dialogue creates the shared meanings that provide the foundations for the building of a new order.

SUMMARY

Analysis of team leadership revealed through the theories such as LMX and Hill's team leadership highlights the limitations of managerial authority to generate change. Senior management has the power to make decisions but they do not necessarily have the power to implement such decisions within a given cultural context. For example, we could contrast how team leaders in American Football and the global alternative could make tactical decisions in principle to introduce change but hypothesise that in the latter they would struggle to get them accepted by on-field stakeholders until half-time.

REFERENCES

Alvesson, M. (2002). *Understanding organizational culture*. Thousand Oaks, CA: Sage.

Alvesson, M. and Sveningsson, S. (2008). *Changing organizational culture: Cultural change work in progress*. Abingdon: Routledge.

Argyris, C. (1990). *Overcoming organizational defences*. Needham Heights, MA: Allen & Bacon.

Beech, N. and MacIntosh, R. (2012). *Managing change: Enquiry and action*. Cambridge: Cambridge University Press.

Bohm, D. C. (1985). *Unfolding meaning: A weekend of dialogue with David Bohm*. New York: Ark Paperbacks.

Brown, D. A. (1995). *Organizational culture*. London: Pitman.

Buchanan, D. A. and McCalman, J. (1989). *High performance work systems: The digital experience*. London: Routledge.

Burke, W. W. (2011). *Organization change: Theory and practice*. London: Sage.

Burns, J. M. (1978). *Leadership*. New York: Harper & Row.

Dansereau, F., Graen, G. G. and Haga, W. (1975). A vertical dyad linkage approach to leadership in formal organizations. *Organizational Behavior and Human Performance, 13*, 46–78.

Dixon, N. (1998). *Dialogue at work*. London: Lemos & Crane.

Elberse, A. and Ferguson, Sir Alex. (2013). Ferguson's Formula. *Harvard Business Review, 91*(10), 116–125.

Elsbach, D. (1999). An expanded model of organizational identification. *Research in Organizational Behavior, 21*, 13–200.

Gill, R. (2006). *Theory and practice of leadership.* London: Sage.

Goffman, E. (1959). *The presentation of self in everyday life.* London: Penguin Books.

Goffman, E. (1967). *Interaction ritual: Essays on face-to-face behaviour.* New York: Anchor Books.

Graen, G. B. and Uhl-Bien, M. (1995). Relationship-based approach to leadership: The Development of leader–member exchange (LMX) theory of leadership over 25 years: Applying a multi-level multi-domain perspective. *Leadership Quarterly, 6*(2), 219–247.

Gramsci, A. (1971). *Selections from the prison notebooks.* London: Lawrence & Wishart.

Greenleaf, R. (1977). *Servant-leadership: A journey into the nature of legitimate power and greatness,* Mahwah, NJ: Paulist Press.

Grint, K. (2005). Problems, problems, problems: The social construction of leadership. *Human Relations, 58*(11), 1467–1494.

Hatch, J. M., Kostera, M. and Kozminski, K. A. (2005). *The three faces of leadership: Manager, artist, priest.* London: Blackwell.

Humphreys, M. and Brown, A. D. (2002). Narratives of organizational identity and identification: A case study of hegemony and resistance. *Organization Studies, 23*(3), 421–447.

Johnson, D. W. and Johnson, R. T. (1989). *Co-operation and competition: Theory and research.* Edina, MN: Interaction Book Company.

Kotter, P. J. (1990). *A force for change.* New York: Free Press.

Opler, M. (1945). Themes as dynamic forces in culture. *American Journal of Sociology, 53,* 198–206.

Northouse, P. (2013). *Leadership: Theory and practice,* 6th edn. Thousand Oaks, CA: Sage.

Paton, R. and McCalman, J. (2000). *Change management: A guide to effective implementation.* London: Sage.

Schein, E. (2004). *Organizational culture and leadership.* San Francisco, CA: Jossey-Bass.

Smircich, L. and Morgan, G. (1982). Leadership: The management of meaning, *Journal of Applied Behavioral Science, 18,* 257–273.

Chapter 6

Destructive and toxic leadership

Laura Gail Lunsford and Art Padilla

CHAPTER OBJECTIVES

After reading this chapter you will be able to:

1   identify the three elements of the toxic leadership triangle present in sports organizations;
2   analyze the contribution of followers, leaders, and environments to destructive leadership outcomes in sports; and
3   describe checks and balances that sports administrators and boards might implement to reduce destructive leadership outcomes.

KEY TERMS

- destructive leadership
- colluders
- conformers
- checks and balances
- conducive environments

INTRODUCTION

There is an overemphasis on the role of the leader in all sorts of leadership episodes. This chapter defines the three elements of a toxic triangle in destructive leadership: leaders, followers, and environments. A flawed leader can cause much organisational damage and destruction, but such a leader needs help. Susceptible followers may enable destructive leaders' agendas through active or passive support. Conducive environments are marked by rapid changes, turbulent conditions, or lack of oversight, including, for example, new and hard to detect performance enhancing drugs, a lack of checks and balances in sporting associations and regulatory bodies, and cultural attitudes that promote and enable winning at any cost. Three case studies from American football, cycling, and track and field are presented to illustrate these elements and processes in sports environments. The chapter concludes with recommendations to mitigate destructive leadership.

REWRITING THE PAST

> We cannot look to NCAA history to determine how to handle circumstances so disturbing, shocking and disappointing. . . . These events should serve as a call to every single school and athletics department to take an honest look at its campus environment and eradicate the "sports are king" mindset that can so dramatically cloud the judgment of educators.[1]
>
> (NCAA President Mark Emmert, speaking about the Penn State scandal)

> Lance Armstrong is no longer the winner of the Tour de France from 1999–2005.[2]
>
> (Tour director Christian Prudhomme)

> [C]heating carries with it some very serious consequences, one of which is you forfeit the right to be called an Olympic champion.[3]
>
> (U.S. Olympic Committee spokesman Darryl Seibel speaking about Marion Jones)

Sports do not have a monopoly on destructive leadership but they certainly have the conducive environments that make it possible and even likely. Three prominent cases serve as illustration: Penn State University's football coach Joe Paterno, cyclist Lance Armstrong, and track runner Marion Jones.

■ Following a series of allegations and convictions associated with horrific child molestation episodes by a former assistant coach (Jerry Sandusky, now imprisoned), Penn State University's head football coach Joe Paterno was fired, along with the athletic director and the president of the university. The scandal tragically ruined the lives of several young men and the careers of various university administrators. The university was fined millions of dollars and Paterno's name was removed from the record books as the winningest American football coach when the Committee on Infractions of the governing body of intercollegiate athletics, the National Collegiate Athletics Association (NCAA), erased 111 of Paterno's games from the win column. This action left Paterno in second place with 298 wins behind Coach Bobbie Bowden, now the record holder with 377 wins. "[T]here is no rejoicing in the Bowden household," Bowden said, "Nobody would want to have a title given to him this way." (Zinzer 2012)

- The case of Lance Armstrong, arguably the best-known professional rider in the history of professional cycling, is a second example. An examination of the winners in the famed, three-week cycling race, the Tour de France, reveals that there are no first place winners from 1999 through 2005 and that the 2009 third place winner is also vacant. After Armstrong was compelled to confess his use of illegal performance-enhancing drugs in 2012, the Union Cycliste Internationale (UCI) removed all of Armstrong's first place wins. The various second- and third-place finishers during those years were ineligible to assume the titles because they too had violated the rules.
- Finally, the story of Marion Jones, an All American in basketball and track at the University of North Carolina and professional basketball player for the Tulsa Shock in the WNBA, and the first track and field Olympic athlete ever to win five gold medals, illustrates a sad toxic leadership episode. Jones won five medals in the 2000 Olympic games and for seven years the record books reflected her achievement. In 2007 the International Olympic Committee (IOC) withdrew the medals and vacated all seven of her medals. "Red flags should have been raised in my head when he [Coach Graham] told me not to tell anyone [about the supplement program]," she said.

A detailed examination of the circumstances surrounding these athletic scandals illuminates the processes of toxic leadership in sports. The chapter attempts to make three points. First, it presents an overview of destructive leadership and the elements and conditions that make it possible. Second, it examines these cases to illustrate the processes ultimately resulting in destructive outcomes. Third, the chapter concludes with suggestions to mitigate and reduce these destructive outcomes in sports.

DESTRUCTIVE LEADERSHIP

The tendency both in the academic and popular arenas is to wonder why the Joe Paternos, Lance Armstrongs and Marion Joneses of the world made the bad decisions leading to their downfall and to the downfall of others. We think of leadership, whether constructive or destructive, as the actions and behaviours of the individual leaders. Yet, individuals in positions of leadership always had followers who helped them to achieve the objectives that ultimately resulted in destructive outcomes. They also had or created environments that facilitated a toxic leader's agenda and consolidated power for them and their immediate circle of collaborators. In the case of Joe Paterno, the objectives included having a winning football team and the benefits that came with such success for a wide variety of individuals, organisations and commercial entities. Lance Armstrong's various cycling teams included eight other riders, in addition to multiple coaches, sponsors such as the U.S. Postal Service, Nike, Trek Bicycles and Anheuser-Busch, and assorted hangers on with deep stakes in Armstrong's successes. Marion Jones ran for herself, but also for the United States and for her coaches and commercial sponsors such as Nike, which aired an expensive series of 'Mysterious Mrs. Jones' television ads (in which Jones asked why women professional athletes earned less than men). As will be seen below, there were considerable, perhaps irresistible, environmental conditions and elements that undoubtedly contributed to the destructive outcomes associated with Paterno, Armstrong and Jones.

On definitions and leader-centrism

Leadership outcomes are rarely explained by the decisions, characteristics, or behaviours of a single person. Yet, we make statues of Coach Paterno, we take photos of Lance Armstrong on the platform with the race's yellow jersey, and we sing the national anthem when Marion Jones receives her medals on the Olympic platforms. We place these individuals on a pedestal and believe they are singularly responsible for their success and for their failures. While they are the most visible and recognizable, the leader is only one element in the toxic leadership triangle. Our main point is that the followers and the environments are also part of the process of leadership. Below we describe these three elements in greater detail.

The definition of "leadership" can be value-laden and polemical so it is useful to discuss the definitional issue at the outset. Many scholars in fact define "leadership" rather similarly (Yukl 2005). They write about a social process involving moving an organization, group, or team toward collective goals through an interactive and dynamic process between a leader and the followers. The process leads to certain group outcomes, some very good, some terrible, and most somewhere in between. Yet, most of the research does not focus on this dynamic process between leaders and followers or on the outcomes of the group. Instead, nearly three-fourths of studies concentrate on the traits and behaviors of leaders (Padilla *et al.* 2007). Even when outcomes are considered, they are explored from the perspective of the impact of the leader on followers. In addition, a number of non-neutral (or in the terminology of philosophy, normative) adjectives have been placed in front of the word "leader," such as authentic, responsible, transformational, servant, and toxic, making it even more challenging to arrive at a universal understanding of not only "leader" but also "leadership."

Regardless of the definitions—and although this is changing somewhat—the emphasis continues to be placed on leader traits and behaviors while followers and contextual environments are largely disregarded. It is our view that, particularly for toxic leadership situations and episodes, the importance of the role of followers and of the environments where leaders and followers interact cannot be overstated. Certainly, a flawed and destructive leader can have negative impacts on followers and on organizational results. But no matter how clever or devious the leader, he or she needs help to accomplish the destruction and this help comes from susceptible followers and from conducive environments that facilitate a leader's aims. Moreover, the process of leading and following is viewed cross-sectionally, with a snapshot in time. Most would agree that the leader during the first month is a different one from the leader in the fifth year, and that the relationships between leader and followers also move significantly over time.

Toxic leadership episodes may be seen as special cases of the more "normal" leadership episodes where group outcomes are largely positive and constructive. But toxic episodes have five characteristics that are useful to enumerate specifically. These are listed in Table 6.1.

Our perspective is that even "good" leaders are not always good, just as destructive leaders are not always "bad." For example, former Indiana University basketball coach Bobby Knight may be considered as a very flawed leader because he berated and slapped a few of his players, screamed obscenities at reporters, and frequently displayed an enraged temper on and off the basketball court. On the other hand, many of his players also respected and even loved him; his basketball teams had the highest graduation rate in the NCAA for many years; he was considered the best defensive tactician in the game; and he had the reputation for being highly

(handwritten margin note: dynamic process between leaders & followers)

66

Table 6.1 *Five elements of destructive leadership*

1 Destructive leadership is seldom absolutely or entirely destructive: there are both good and bad results in most leadership situations.

2 The process of destructive leadership involves dominance, coercion, and manipulation rather than influence, persuasion, and commitment.

3 The process of destructive leadership has a selfish orientation; it is focused more on the leaders' needs than the needs of the larger social group.

4 The effects of destructive leadership are outcomes that compromise the quality of life for constituents and detract from the organization's main purposes.

5 Destructive organizational outcomes are not exclusively the result of destructive leaders, but are also products of susceptible followers and conducive environments.

Source: adapted from Padilla *et al.* (2007).

esp. relevant in Sport.

ethical and was never investigated by the NCAA during his four decades of coaching. When he retired he was the winningest coach in Division I basketball. So do we focus on leader behaviors and traits or on results? Is there unanimity among observers about the success or failure of a leadership episode or do different "followers" evaluate such episodes differently?

Destructive leaders tend to possess a constellation of traits that lead to coercive behavior rather than persuasive behavior. Because the goals they pursue tend to be those that the leader values, and not necessarily those of the larger group, destructive leadership situations are associated with force, intimidation, manipulation, and coercion. Instead of motivating followers, instead of developing group goals consensually and in a way that empowers followers, the toxic leader dictates and rules with an iron fist. Walls are erected to keep people from fleeing, free communication is inhibited, and human rights are violated. The pervasive presence of police and military force in totalitarian regimes is not a coincidence. When persuasion doesn't work, force is the option of dictators.

While not all leaders who are considered by some as being charismatic are destructive, destructive leaders are often considered to be charismatic, have a personalized need for power, are narcissistic, often have dysfunctional or negative early life experiences, and an ideology that focuses on vanquishing competitors (Padilla *et al.* 2007). Armstrong's ambition was to beat everyone and not just once. There is also a selfish orientation that motivates destructive leaders. Their focus is a transparently self-interested one, how can they win or gain, rather than a focus on team or organizational goals. While all leaders, constructive as well as destructive ones, are self-interested and concerned with their personal advancement to some degree, the difference is that the destructive leader exhibits selfish behavior to an extreme. "Armstrong said, we had one goal and one ambition and that was to win the greatest bike race in the world and not just to win it once, but to keep winning it" (United States Anti-Doping Agency 2012, p. 11).

impact on culture

Less attention is given to outcomes of leadership, although outcomes are critically important, especially in sports where there are clear winners and losers. In sports, winning equates with increased fans, more ticket sales, and revenue from merchandizing and ads. Yet, even this seemingly clear evaluation is fraught with difficulty. Is a new coach responsible for a win if he or she did not select the players? In other words, who is responsible for a leadership episode? The tendency is to view the leader as the responsible party, yet this is too simplistic

67

an analysis. Destructive leadership outcomes tend to leave the organization in a worse state. In other words, leader derailment is when destructive leader outcomes are bad for the leader but destructive leadership occurs when organizations are affected. Lance Armstrong is an example of destructive leadership because he is not the only person who has experienced the negative effects. The drug charges against him also hurt his non-profit organization *LiveStrong* and interest in cycling in the United States.

Destructive leadership is also made possible by the interaction of leaders and followers in certain conducive contexts. We consider this interaction in the next section.

Susceptible followers

The importance of followers and environmental factors is beginning to garner attention. In most cases followers are afterthoughts, viewed as under the control of the leader. In fact, only 15 per cent of studies have examined the relationship between leaders and organizational outcomes that are accomplished by followers (Kaiser *et al.* 2008).

All followers do not react in the same way to destructive leaders. However, they may be categorized into two broad categories: *colluders* or *conformers*. *Colluders* actively support the destructive leader's agenda. Colluders are usually ambitious, share values with the destructive leader, and have unsocialized values that normalize greed and selfish behavior. *Conformers* passively support the destructive leader through their acquiescence. These susceptible followers are more likely to be present if they have unmet basic needs, low maturity, and lower core self-evaluations.

[handwritten margin note: Is there not something in between?]

Conducive environments

The environments, checks and balances, and industry conditions provide important and strong influences on destructive leadership episodes. Environments include the context, settings, circumstances, and conditions within which leaders and followers interact. There are three main elements of environments (Padilla and Lunsford 2013):

- institutional, including checks and balances;
- environmental, including economic, social, and technological conditions;
- cultural, including attitudes, experiences, and beliefs.

Regulatory bodies such as the United States Anti-Drug Association provide checks and balances for sporting organizations and events. New doping technology or acceptance of doping would be examples of environmental elements. Cultural elements are reflected in attitudes and experiences such the culture surrounding Penn State Football.

Section summary

Destructive leadership requires a focus on more than the leader. Susceptible followers who actively support the destructive leader (colluders) or who go along in fear (conformers) make destructive leadership possible. A lack of checks and balances, financial incentives, and rapidly changing technology in doping also contribute to environments that are conducive to destructive leadership in sports.

CASE STUDY
COVER-UP OF SEXUAL ABUSE IN HAPPY VALLEY

Penn State was a dominant team in American football during Paterno's tenure. The football organization has considerable support from the university, fans, alumni, and students. Many people have focused on Paterno as the leader who made many successful football seasons possible. Indeed, the Penn State Athletics website (www.gopsusports.com) opens a biography of Joe Paterno by noting: 'A career marked with distinction, glorious accomplishments and immeasurable contributions to The Pennsylvania State University.'

Paterno was a veteran of World War II and a star quarterback at Brown University. After graduation in 1950 from Brown, he joined the Penn State's Nittany Lions as an assistant coach and was named head coach in 1966. Within two years he had coached the Nittany Lions to a winning season. During his 46-year tenure he led his teams to win 409 football games, attend a record-breaking 37 bowl games, and win all four of the New Year's Day bowl games –the Rose, Sugar, Cotton, and Orange bowls. On average, he coached his teams to almost nine wins per season.[4] Penn State students and alumni, in whose eyes he could do no wrong, gave Paterno the affectionate nickname of "Joe Pa." Penn State football outcomes appeared to be a product of Paterno's effective leadership.

Three years after Paterno's appointment as head coach, Jerry Sandusky was hired as the defensive line coach. Paterno reportedly disliked Sandusky but also depended upon him. One biographer noted that Sandusky made many of Penn State's wins possible (Posnanski 2012). Like many college football coaches, who are considered celebrities in their communities, Sandusky wanted to "give back" to his community. In 1977 he founded a non-profit called "The Second Mile" to help troubled children. Paterno did not like the time Sandusky devoted to his non-profit or to children and did not miss Sandusky after he retired in 1999. Later, Paterno noted he had nothing to do with Sandusky's emeritus status or on-campus office (Posnanski 2012).

The scandal

> This was not a mistake by these men. This was not an oversight. It was not misjudgment on their part. . . . This was a conspiracy of silence by top officials to actively conceal the truth.[5]
>
> (Pennsylvania State Attorney General Linda Kelly)

It is hard to know when the sexual abuse began or even exactly when or what Paterno knew about it. The official record shows that Sandusky's sexual abuse of boys was witnessed by university staff and reported to administrators as early as 1994, even though it began years earlier. A janitor named James Calhoun observed Sandusky performing oral sex on a boy, known as Victim 8, in the showers of the Lasch Football Building. Calhoun, deeply disturbed, told his coworkers in tears what he saw. The employees feared they might lose their jobs if they reported the incident but persuaded Calhoun to tell Jay Witherite, Calhoun's immediate supervisor who then advised Calhoun to whom he should report the incident. Calhoun was a temporary employee and never made any further reports. He was afraid that "they'll get rid of all of us," the Freeh report later revealed (Freeh 2012).

In May, 1998, Gary Schultz, the university senior vice president for finance, was notified of a police investigation into Sandusky. Documented notes Schultz took show he knew about the alleged sexual abuse. Paterno denied knowing about the abuse, although notes from the Athletic Director, Tim Curley, show Paterno and Curley had several conversations about it. In February, 2000, Mike McQueary, a graduate assistant, witnessed Sandusky abusing a boy in the shower on campus. McQueary, who claims he omitted the details out of respect, told Paterno, who alerted Curley, but no further action was apparently taken beyond this point.

The Pennsylvania Attorney General started an investigation in 2009 after Victim #1's mother reported the abuse to the police. Sandusky was arrested two years later. Soon after Sandusky's arrest, Curley and Schultz resigned their posts and later surrendered to authorities on charges that they failed to alert the police about sexual abuse. Paterno said he would retire at the end of the football season but the following day the Penn State Board of Trustees fired both Paterno and university president Graham Spanier, one of the nation's longest serving university presidents. In addition, Jay Raykovitz, stepped down from his 28-year term as president of the non-profit Second Mile.

> I didn't know exactly how to handle it and I was afraid to do something that might jeopardize what the university procedure was,' he said. 'So I backed away and turned it over to some other people, people I thought would have a little more expertise than I did.
>
> Joe Paterno[6]

Outcomes

The ramifications of the Penn State Scandal are still unfolding, which underscores the importance of a time dimension in assessing leadership outcomes. Three of the university executives, the former president Graham Spanier, vice president Gary Schultz, and athletic director Tim Curley await trial, accused of covering up Sandusky's sexual abuse of minors. Before he died of cancer, Paterno's nomination for the Presidential Medal of Honor was withdrawn; his name was removed from numerous awards and trophies. A 900-pound brass statue of Paterno was relocated from outside the football stadium to a "secure location" in storage. Moody downgraded the university's credit rating, the university lost tens of millions in revenue, student enrolment declined, and the Board of Trustees struggled to find someone who would take on the Presidency. The Big Ten Conference also ruled that Penn State was ineligible for its conference title football game and that the Nittany Lions' share of bowl revenues for the next four seasons—about $13 million—will be donated to charities that "protect children."

Mark Emmert, President of the National Collegiate Athletic Association, commented that a $60 million fine against Penn State was, "100 times greater than any fine ever levied in the history of the NCAA." (The penalty has since been reduced after lobbying by the university trustees.) He also noted that, "The university has been very, very responsive in the openness of providing all of the information about this, and so we feel very comfortable where we are with these penalties."[7] Penn State Board Chairwoman Karen Peetz said, "we accept the consequences of failure and we are remedying any wrongs."[8] In fact, the board commissioned a former director of the Federal Bureau of Investigation Louis Freeh to conduct an independent investigation.

Susceptible followers and conducive environments

Few checks and balances, certain environmental and social conditions, as well as specific cultural attitudes mark conducive environments. Penn State football met all these criteria. There was relatively weak faculty governance of sports at Penn State (Thoroughgood and Padilla 2013) and an erosion of the usual internal checks and balances on student behavior. For example, student conduct violations fell under the Vice President for Student Affairs. Yet after the scandal broke, Vicky Triponey, who held that position in 2003–2007, released emails indicating that she was told not to discipline football players (Posnanski 2012). Paterno had been at Penn State for decades, which allowed him to amass power with little oversight from administrators (Thoroughgood and Padilla 2013). The media can provide an important check and balance but Paterno, Schultz, Curley, and Spanier reportedly made decisions on how to handle Sandusky's conduct to avoid bad publicity. Freeh (2012) noted that these leaders, "failed to protect children against a child predator and showed no empathy for his victims and concealed Sandusky's activities from the Board of Trustees and Penn State community" (p. 14).

Other environmental conditions included the enormous financial incentives in televised football games and bowl games. Boosters were proud of Penn State's reputation on player graduation rates and considered games to be important social occasions. Any hint of negative publicity or wrongdoing contrasted with Penn State's nickname as "Happy Valley".

The Freeh report strongly denounced Penn State for inadequate checks and balances. Freeh's recommendations covered strengthening safety and security policies; identifying and reporting misconduct; and governance. He made specific recommendations about policies and procedures for the Board of Trustees; administration and general counsel; campus police; athletic department; institutional reporting of misconduct and for the Penn State culture in general that focuses on transparency, ethics and increased reporting and accountability from leaders.

Some of the recommendations have been implemented, including a new policy to limit access to athletic facilities and a restructuring of the board to strengthen governance and independent oversight.

Summary

The Penn State scandal illustrates how the financial incentives from football combined with weak to non-existent checks and balances to create an environment conducive to toxic leadership. In this case the followers enabled the destructive episode because of their fear of saying anything negative about football at Penn State. Paterno was charismatic and Spanier and his executives showed traits of self-interest (versus group-interest). The case also illustrates the importance of timing when determining whether toxic leadership situations have occurred.

CASE STUDY
THE CYCLING CONSPIRACY

In grade school Lance Armstrong was an energetic kid who ran and swam. He soon added cycling and became a professional triathlete by the time he was in high school. The U.S. Olympic Development team invited him to train in Colorado and he went on to become a three time Olympic athlete.[9] Cycling was his best sport. He quickly became known as one of cycling's most promising riders. He rode in the Tour DuPont in 1991 and won the million-dollar "Thrift Drug Triple Crown" in 1993 by placing first in three competitive races. A diagnosis of testicular cancer in that same year seemingly ended Lance's cycling career when Team Cofidis cancelled his six figure contract.

The next chapters in Lance's story are well known. He went on to beat cancer, start the LiveStrong Foundation and its successful LiveStrong yellow wristband fundraising campaign. He also continued to win bicycling races, including cycling's premier event, the Tour de France. The tour is a 2,200-mile, 21-day, team cycling race up and down some of the steepest terrain in Europe. Armstrong came in first place seven consecutive years from 1999–2005, a feat previously not achieved. *USA Today* reported that, "Armstrong leaves the sport as the greatest Tour de France rider ever, and his record of seven consecutive wins probably will stand for a very long time."[10]

Outcomes

However, Armstrong's record stood a mere seven years, a period during which numerous allegations and charges and counter-charges were raised about the legitimacy of Armstrong's titles. In 2012 the United States Anti-Doping Agency (USADA) filed charges against Armstrong for drug doping, which continue as of this writing. The IOC vacated his wins and left no one in the winning spot because so many other cyclists had also been charged with doping. A search on the U.S. Olympic team web page finds a photograph of Lance Armstrong but no profile and no bronze medal.[11]

In 2010, Armstrong's former teammate and friend Floyd Landis sued Armstrong and others in a whistle blower lawsuit that has been joined in by the U.S. Federal Government, which is also seeking significant monetary damages. Landis may benefit from any legal verdict against Armstrong due to Landis' status as a whistle blower. The U.S. paid $40 million for the USPS team from 1998 to 2004, from which Armstrong's $17.9 million salary was paid.[12] The Federal Government filed a separate lawsuit for $120 million against Armstrong for defrauding the government when he rode for the United States Postal Service (USPS) team. The USADA issued a Reasoned Decision for their investigation to be transparent and to reduce the harm by Armstrong's frequent attacks on his accusers by clearing their names. SCA Promotions, a sports insurance company, has sued Lance for the return of the $7.5 million in bonus money they were forced to award him in a prior lawsuit filed by Armstrong. In sum, Armstrong and his associates and sponsors have endured, and will continue to endure, immense psychological and economic costs.

Susceptible followers and conducive environments

Colluders and conformers are present in this case. The USADA now calls the doping in which Lance engaged a conspiracy and has amassed sworn testimony from 26 people about the doping activities of the USPS Team.[13] Six of the 11 teammates who testified against Lance were themselves suspended for doping. Even Lance has said that he had to use performance-enhancing drugs if he wanted to be competitive in cycling because all the elite riders used performance-enhancing drugs (Holmes 2014). The evidence supports Lance's contention. The Reasoned Decision (USADA, 2012) noted that 20 of 21 cyclists on the podium from 1999–2005 were tainted by doping sanctions, questionable drug tests, or admissions of guilt. "[T]he judgment [is] that the era in professional cycling which he [Armstrong] dominated as the patron of the peloton was the dirtiest ever" (p. 12).

> More than a dozen of Armstrong's teammates, friends and former team employees confirm a fraudulent course of conduct that extended over a decade and leave no doubt that Mr. Armstrong's career on the USPS/Discovery Channel Pro Cycling Team was fuelled from start to finish by doping.
>
> (United States Anti-Doping Agency 2012, p. 10)

The people who stand to make money from these elite athletes also encourage their behaviour by actively supporting it (colluders). Over half of the USPS Team doped and so many cyclists doped that the Tour de France elected to leave Lance's vacated wins as empty slots in the record book. Dr. Ferrari was an Italian doctor who helped Lance enhance his cycling performance. Armstrong claimed to "not have a professional relationship with Dr. Ferrari" despite emails and financial records showing more than one million dollars in payments from Armstrong to Ferrari.[14]

The environmental conditions in cycling were conducive to destructive leadership. First, the *financial incentives* in cycling were difficult to resist. Enormous sums of money were paid to winners such as Lance to endorse Oakley's glasses, Nike shoes, Anhueser-Busch's beer, and Trek bicycles.[15] Lance lost an estimated $150 million in endorsement money and half of his $120 million fortune in lawsuits. Not only does Lance, and athletes like him, make a lot of money, so do the companies who pay these athletes to endorse their products.

Technological advances in performance-enhancing drugs make it difficult for agencies to administer tests to detect doping (Yesalis *et al.* 2001). The doping in cycling was so sophisticated that the agencies responsible for monitoring sports could not keep up. USADA results show that Lance never tested positive for drugs despite being tested 29 times in cycling and twice as a triathlete. There is a lack of resources to police drugs properly, which further contributes to a conducive environment for a destructive leadership episode.

A lack of *check and balances* also enabled Lance to enact such an extensive doping protocol over years. The Reasoned Decision from the USADA noted that, "On paper, Armstrong's team contract provided him with 'extensive input into rider and staff composition.' In practice, however, as a team owner and by virtue of the power his rapidly accumulating titles conferred, his effective control was even greater" (p. 11).

Section summary

The cycling conspiracy illustrates that leader traits such as self-interest and narcissism were present in Lance's leadership. However, the environment of professional cycling was conducive to destructive leadership episodes. The rapidly changing drug technology made it difficult for sporting agencies to monitor drug use. There were so many cyclists using drugs that it could be argued drugs were necessary to compete at elite levels. Followers, in terms of other cyclists, coaches, and support staff, both acquiesced and actively supported Lance and the team. The destructive outcomes included negative effects on Lance's charity LiveStrong and on the sport of cycling.

CASE STUDY
BALCO AND OLYMPIAN MARION JONES

Marion Jones was an extraordinary athlete. She was a stellar performer in California's high school basketball games and track and field meets. However, she put track on hold to play basketball at the University of North Carolina at Chapel Hill. She was a starting player on a team that won a national championship in her first year. By her second year on the team she was averaging an impressive 17.1 points a game as an All American.[16]

After college Jones returned to her best sport—track. She won Gold medals in the 1997 World Championships. In 1998 she won 34 individual events.[17] No track athlete, not even Carl Lewis, had ever won more than four medals in an Olympics. Jones won five medals in the 2000 Olympics in Sydney, Australia: three gold medals in the 100 and 200 meters and the 1,600 relay, and two bronze medals for the 400 relay and the long jump. Marion Jones had become "a one-woman, multinational corporation after her 2000 Olympic triumph: the feet of Nike, the face of Oakley Sunglasses, the wrist of TAG Heuer watches."[18]

By 2002, the regulatory agencies were beginning to catch up to the rapid technological improvements in the growing industry of illegal performance-enhancing drugs (PEDs). That year, U.S. Federal agents began to investigate the Bay Area Laboratory Cooperative (BALCO) for selling PEDs.[19] The investigation took a new turn after Jones' coach, Trevor Graham, anonymously sent a syringe with the banned and undetectable steroid called "the clear" to the USADA. Jones was accused of taking the clear. In an attempt to salvage her reputation, Jones promptly filed a $25 million lawsuit against the Victor Conte, BALCO's owner, for accusing her. She continued to deny drug use at a 2004 grand jury hearing. Conte finally pled guilty and many other athletes were caught up in the scandal, including several major league baseball players. In total, 550 athletes were tested and 20 were found guilty of taking PEDs. In a tear-filled news conference, Jones confessed to using illegal drugs and steroids as early as 1999 and during the Olympic games in 2000.

Outcomes

As a result of the scandal and its many revelations, BALCO's CEO and several implicated athletes, including Marion Jones, served time in jail. Jones was sentenced to six months in prison, the longest prison sentence in the BALCO scandal. The sign was taken down from BALCO's offices because it attracted too many curious on-lookers. The Marion Jones brand became bankrupt and sponsors withdrew their endorsements. The IOC vacated her five Olympic medals, reallocating two of the three individual medals to other competitors. Her relay team teammates contested this decision with the Court of Arbitration for Sport. The three-member appeal panel acknowledged the IOC ruling may have been unfair to Jones' teammates who did not use drugs, but nonetheless noted "the outcome of this case may [also] be unfair to the other relay teams that competed with no doped athletes."[20]

Susceptible followers and conducive environments

Marion Jones never tested positive in any drug tests. Yet rumors about her steroid use persisted, perhaps because of her marriage to two athletes, C. J. Hunter and Tim Montgomery, who had failed drug tests to detect PEDs. She maintained that her coach, Trevor Graham, started her on the illegal drugs, which she unknowingly took. "In 2000, I had no idea that I had been given something illegal," stated Jones, who now speaks to young people about the mistakes she made.[21] Her coach, among others, colluded with Jones to give her the illegal drugs. She claimed that her coach told her it was a nutritional supplement with flax seed oil. "Marion wasn't doing anything the others weren't doing. . . . Was she on performance enhancers? Yes, but she was the superior athlete. You don't just take performance enhancers and win gold medals," (Victor Conte, BALCO owner).

The anti-doping agencies and divisions, such as the USADA or the IOC, could not keep up with the changing technology—Jones never tested positive on any of the dozens of drug tests administered by the various agencies and organizations.[22] Because of limited funding and rapid innovations in technology, these regulatory agencies were challenged to serve the "check and balance" or oversight function they were meant to perform.

Whistle blowers also perform an important check and balance function. Some have called Jones' coach, Trevor Graham, the "World's Most Hated Coach."[23] It still is not clear why Graham anonymously sent a syringe to anti-doping authorities so they could identify the previously undetectable steroid called the clear. He was sentenced to one year of home confinement and five years of probation for lying in the BALCO case. He has also been banned from ever coaching in the Olympics again.

Section summary

This case illustrates the importance of colluders in making a destructive leadership episode possible. Coaches, doctors, and companies collude to "beat" the system and provide drugs. The regulatory environment is challenged to keep up with the technology to detect new drugs. Money and fame are seductive environmental conditions that also lead to destructive leadership.

SUMMARY AND RECOMMENDATIONS

Athletic enterprises are not immune from toxic leadership. Unfortunately, however, the popular and scholarly interest seems to focus on the leader. We have used three case studies from sports to highlight the contributions of negative leader traits, susceptible followers, and conducive environments to enabling destructive leadership episodes. Our main point is that all three elements are needed for destructive leadership to occur. In addition, a consideration of organizational outcomes is needed to determine whether toxic leadership has occurred.

What might coaches of athletic groups and leaders of organizations with oversight responsibilities conclude from our analysis? That is, how might an understanding of the toxic triangle help to reduce destructive leadership episodes in sports? We recommend a greater emphasis on shared governance, oversight, and controls. The Freeh report as well as the USADA's Reasoned Decision highlight a greater need for such controls to prevent destructive leadership. These checks and balances might include a method for anonymous reporting of illegal behaviors, independent advisory boards, and sanctioned monitoring of behaviors related to illegal activities.

Greater education of followers might be warranted to help them understand the dangers of "cheating" and the consequences of enabling or supporting cheating behaviors. Educational initiatives may contribute to reducing cultural attitudes that contribute to destructive leadership outcomes. "It goes back to that kind of shared culture in which all these guys are enmeshed, so it's hard for them to throw another guy under the bus, per se, even if they don't get along."[24] Coaches and leaders may influence these conducive attitudes in ways that help followers to speak out against wrong doing or illegal activity rather than colluding or conforming to it.

REVIEW QUESTIONS

1   Who are the colluders and conformers in each of the scandals?

2   What environmental influences made these destructive leadership episodes possible?

3   Who are the destructive leaders in each case study and how do they demonstrate destructive leader traits?

4   What was the role of checks and balances (or lack thereof) in these destructive leadership episodes?

5   What environmental factors might be changed to reduce the occurrence or effects of destructive leadership in sports?

NOTES

1 www.mlive.com/sports/index.ssf/2012/07/penn_state_draws_unprecedented.html
2 www.cbsnews.com/news/lance-armstrong-stripped-of-tour-de-france-medals
3 http://sports.espn.go.com/oly/trackandfield/news/story?id=3151367
4 http://espn.go.com/blog/statsinfo/post/_/id/37192/paternos-statistical-legacy
5 www.cbsnews.com/news/former-penn-st-graham-spanier-charged-in-sandusky-abuse-case
6 www.washingtonpost.com/sports/colleges/joe-paternos-first-interview-since-the-penn-state-sandusky-scandal/2012/01/13/gIQA08e4yP_story.html
7 www.cnn.com/2012/07/23/us/pennsylvania-penn-state-ncaa/index.html
8 www.cbsnews.com/news/psu-trustees-promise-close-look-at-freeh-changes
9 www.teamusa.org/News/2010/July/07/In-the-News-Lance-Armstrong
10 http://usatoday30.usatoday.com/sports/cycling/tourdefrance/2005–07–24-stage-21_x.htm
11 www.teamusa.org/Athletes
12 www.bloomberg.com/news/2014–06–20/lance-armstrong-must-face-u-s-fraud-suit-over-drug-use.html
13 http://cyclinginvestigation.usada.org
14 www.cyclingnews.com/news/usada-lance-armstrong-paid-ferrari-more-than-dollar-1-million
15 www.businessinsider.com/lance-armstrong-has-lost-his-last-sponsor-2012–10
16 www.npr.org/templates/story/story.php?storyId=15060426
17 www.sports-reference.com/olympics/athletes/jo/marion-jones-2.html
18 www.edgeofsports.com/2007–10–15–291/index.html
19 www.cnn.com/2013/10/31/us/balco-fast-facts
20 www.nytimes.com/2010/07/17/sports/17medals.html
21 www.washingtonpost.com/wpdyn/content/article/2007/10/04/AR2007100401666.html
22 www.usada.org/testing/results/athlete-test-history
23 www.nytimes.com/2009/10/25/sports/25graham.html?_r=0
24 www.nytimes.com/2014/09/26/sports/football/in-nfl-and-other-sports-players-have-a-muted-reaction-to-teammates-wrongdoing.html?mabReward=RI%3A5&action=click&pgtype=Homepage&region=CColumn&module=Recommendation&src=rechp&WT.nav=RecEngine

REFERENCES

Freeh, L. (2012, July 12). Report of the Special Investigative Counsel regarding the actions of the Pennsylvania State University related to the child sexual abuse committed by Gerald A. Sandusky. Freeh Sporkin & Sullivan, LLP. Available from http://progress.psu.edu/assets/content/REPORT_FINAL_071212.pdf (accessed August 18, 2014).

Holmes, A. (Writer) and Holmes, A. (Director) (2014). *The Lance Armstrong Story: Stop at nothing.* British Broadcasting Service.

Kaiser, R. B., Hogan, R. and Craig, S. B. (2008). Leadership and the fate of organizations. *American Psychologist, 63* (2), 96.

Padilla, A. and Lunsford, L. G. (2013). The leadership triangle: It's not only about the leader *European Business Review,* May–June, 64–67.

Padilla, A., Hogan, R., and Kaiser, R. (2007). The toxic triangle: Destructive leaders, susceptible followers, and conducive environments. *The Leadership Quarterly, 18,* 176–194.

Posnanski, J. (2012). *Paterno.* New York: Simon & Schuster.

Thoroughgood, C. N. and Padilla, A. (2013). Destructive leadership and the Penn state scandal: A toxic triangle perspective. *Industrial and Organizational Psychology*, 6 (2), 144–149.

United States Anti-Doping Agency (2012). "U.S. Postal Service Pro Cycling Team Investigation", Colorado Springs, CO: Author. Available from http://cyclinginvestigation.usada.org (accessed July 10, 2014).

Yesalis, C. E., Kopstein, A. N., and Bahrke, M. S. (2001). Difficulties in estimating the prevalence of drug use among athletes, in W. Wilson and E. Derse (eds.) *Doping in elite sport: The politics of drugs in the Olympic movement* (43–62). Champaign, IL: Human Kinetics.

Yukl, G. (2005). *Leadership in organizations* (6th ed.). Englewood Cliffs, NJ: Prentice Hall.

Zinzer, L. (2012, July 23). Punishing Paterno by erasing the past. *New York Times*. Available from www.nytimes.com (accessed September 3, 2014).

Part B
Leadership in sport management

Chapter 7

Facilitative leadership in sport management

Ian O'Boyle

CHAPTER OBJECTIVES

After completing this chapter you should be able to:

1   describe how a network of organisations can work together for common goals;
2   understand the role of the facilitative leader in coordinating the efforts of autonomous entities;
3   discuss how trust and distrust are powerful forces in determining the success of collaborative relationships;
4   demonstrate the link between face-to-face dialogue and trust building;
5   describe the keys to being a successful facilitative leader.

KEY TERMS

- network
- federated governance
- Chief Executive Officer (CEO)
- Netball Australia
- face-to-face dialogue

INTRODUCTION

Over the past decades, the contemporary sport industry has been transformed from a predominantly volunteer led system to a commercially driven professional environment that has required closer alignment with practices and processes from its traditional business counterparts to ensure sustainability and success. Although many sport organisations have without question become more business-like in their operations, there are still unique qualities and characteristics associated with these entities that make them different from solely profit driven organisations. One of the stark differences is the make-up of the sport industry and the federated structure that exists with many organisations relying on support (financial or otherwise), or at a very basic level, affiliation, with larger national and indeed international organisations. For instance, a local sporting club will generally be affiliated with a regional or state body, that regional/state body will usually be affiliated with a national sport organisation (NSO) and in turn that NSO will usually be affiliated with a global sport organisation (GSO). Given the interplay and often interdependence that exists within this type of structure, leadership in sport management is clearly an important component for facilitating a vibrant, sustainable and successful sport industry.

The board and the CEO within sport organisations are integral players in facilitating a cooperative and collaborative leadership approach to the whole of sport decision making and attempting to establish a shared understanding and vision for their sport. This chapter will focus on a number of issues that relate to how boards and CEOs at the NSO level can establish a facilitative leadership culture through a consensus orientated approach by engaging and involving numerous affiliated bodies with the whole of sport decision making. A case study of Netball Australia is adopted to illustrate facilitative leadership taking place within a NSO and the issues and challenges that are faced by the organisation and its leaders in relation to this leadership approach.

FACILITATIVE LEADERSHIP IN SPORT MANAGEMENT

There is a wide consensus that in order to bring various parties together to work towards a common goal and to create a shared understanding, whether sport related or not, leadership is a key component (Ansell and Gash, 2008; Gunton and Day, 2003; Hoye and Cuskelly, 2007). Sporting bodies within a network may have a history of strong collaboration and individuals may have built relationships with their counterparts in other organisations that has allowed for sharing of ideas or mutual benefits for each organisation. Likewise, organisations within a particular network may have a deep history of antagonism and conflict that may act as a barrier to a collaborative approach to leadership within their sport. 'Unassisted' negotiations are often possible within sport if there have indeed been positive interactions between entities previously but to ensure that all parties within a network are engaging in a collaborative spirit many authors have argued that facilitative leadership is crucial (Ansell and Gash, 2008; Reilly, 2001; Susskind and Cruikshank, 1987).

Leadership at the NSO level is clearly an important mechanism for setting policy and rules, building trust, facilitating face-to-face and other dialogue, and exploring mutually beneficial gains; even if these are small in nature they may contribute to momentum building and increase the level of trust within inter-organisational relationships. Effective leadership can empower affiliated organisations to create collaborations that lead to outcomes that are of a higher level than what could have been achieved if these entities continued to work without interaction with other organisations in their network (Vangen and Huxham, 2003). Lasker and Weiss (2003, p. 31) suggest that the facilitative leader should have the ability to: promote broad and active participation; ensure broad-based influence and control; facilitate productive group dynamics; and extend the scope of the process.

Facilitative leadership also relies on the willingness of other leaders within the network to engage in the process, both formally and informally, which may in fact lead to more successful collaborations (Bradford, 1998; Lasker and Weiss, 2003). One of the major benefits of implementing a facilitative leadership approach within sport is that 'weaker' stakeholders such as those at the bottom of the pyramid structure (clubs/grassroots sports) become more involved in the decision-making process. Empowering and representing these stakeholders is seen as an integral component of the facilitative leadership process (Ozawa, 1993). Ansell and Gash (2008) argue that within a facilitative leadership approach, the traditional balance of power that exists within a network becomes less critical and mediation procedures help to ensure all stakeholders enter the process on an equal footing. They add that 'this style of facilitative leadership also helps stakeholders to explore possibilities for mutual gain' (p. 555). This view is further supported by work undertaken by Lasker and Weiss (2003) who also suggest that facilitative leaders must give meaningful voice to all participants and encourage participants to listen to each other. The facilitative leader should stimulate creativity by taking on board the diverse views of all stakeholders within the sporting network and synthesising those views so new directions and ideas can be established and acted upon.

As noted above, a prior history of conflict that can often exist within sporting networks may severely limit the state of collaboration and interplay between entities within a network. Likewise, if parties feel there is little incentive to participate in a collaborative process or the balance of power is unjust, leadership then becomes an all-important mechanism for bringing these parties together and attempting to build trust and cooperation between affiliated entities. The qualities and characteristics required of boards and CEOs to enact facilitative leadership will often depend on the levels of conflict, distrust and antagonism that currently exist within the network. When incentives to participate are seen to be lacking, or lines of communication have completely broken down, the board or CEO will often be required to intervene in order 'to keep stakeholders at the table or empower weaker actors' (Ansell and Gash, 2008, p.555). Shilbury et al. (2013) argue that deft skill is required to co-ordinate wholly or partially autonomous organisations on behalf of interests to which they both contribute. They suggest that 'leadership, and the skill-sets of the personnel involved therefore, are also important factors' (p. 13). Henry and Lee (2004) also highlight the importance of the skill-sets of individuals in leadership positions within sport management. They argue that leaders should not simply have skills in planning and directing but should also have the ability to negotiate effectively and be willing to undergo mutual adjustment for the benefit of the sport as a whole and ideally for the benefit of all parties in the network.

These varying functions of the facilitative leader can unquestionably create tensions within the network, particularly if they are required to intervene to empower under-represented stakeholders, which others may view as favouritism. If there is a significant prehistory of conflict within the network, Ansell and Gash (2008) suggest that the only viable alternative may be

83

to obtain an external mediator to replace the board or CEO as the facilitative leader within the collaborative process. This of course is far from an ideal situation as external parties or individuals may struggle to gain acceptance and exert influence over the actions of affiliated bodies in the absence of any real leverage or preconceived levels of trust. In order for both external mediators or the current board or CEO to gain the trust of the network they must remain impartial to any parochial views of affiliated parties and be seen to act in a transparent manner, upholding the integrity of the collaborative process while clearly working towards the whole of sport outcomes.

TRUST AND DISTRUST

Within the networked model that many sport organisations find themselves operating in, trust within and between organisations can be a crucial factor in determining the level and ability for successful collaborations within that network. Although the issue of trust within inter-organisational networks in sport management has not specifically been examined by researchers, there is a plethora of scholarly works that focus on the issue within traditional business environments. The consensus in this body of work is that trust is an essential component of the collaborative process within any network of organisations (Child, 2001; Walsh et al., 1999). If trust therefore is an integral ingredient for success, the facilitative leader must ensure that strategies are in place to build trust within the network, particularly if there has been a prehistory of conflict where distrust may exist between parties limiting the capabilities for collaboration. This may prove extremely difficult for the board or CEO who are attempting to build trust within the network as parties may have had negative experiences with organisations in the past and may enter new collaborative arrangements with scepticism due to these past experiences. Ring (1997) suggests that even if trust is non-existent within a network, it may emerge from formal or informal processes of 'transacting'. However, the same can be said of distrust, and long histories of distrust within the network will present major challenges for the 'would-be' facilitative leader.

It is more than likely that in some networks distrust will be a major obstacle in attempting to undertake collaborative arrangements through a facilitative leadership approach (Weech-Maldonado and Merrill, 2000). The facilitative leader may have to undertake specific trust building initiatives within the network such as intentionally seeking intermediate outcomes (small wins) that help to build momentum and act as a platform for greater collaboration in the future. Ansell and Gash (2008) suggest 'the building of trust can be a time-consuming process that requires a long-term commitment to achieving collaborative outcomes' (p. 559). An additional feature that has been acknowledged as helping to build trust between parties is the extent of face-to-face dialogue that is undertaken within the network. Within some networks, face-to-face dialogue may take place on a regular basis whereas in contrast, in countries such as Australia with a large geographical size, face-to-face contact may only take place within the network at an Annual General Meeting. Developments in technology such as video conferencing have allowed organisations in such situations to have increased face-to-face dialogue and may be an adequate substitute for in person correspondences.

Face-to-face dialogue allows for the breaking down of stereotypes or preconceived notions about individuals or entities within a network (Bentrup, 2001). Warner (2006) argues that face-to-face dialogue is the core component for trust building, creating shared understanding and ensuring parties are committed to the collaborative process. The facilitative leader must exploit all opportunities for face-to-face dialogue within the network and encourage parties to correspond as often as possible through this medium. Of course, it is important to also note that face-to-face dialogue in some instances may in fact reinforce negative stereotypes and increase antagonism and distrust within the network. In this case, the facilitative leader will need to intervene to examine ways in which the relationship can be repaired. Regardless of this possible situation, effective collaboration based on high levels of trust is unlikely without significant face-to-face dialogue between parties within the network (Ansell and Gash, 2008).

TRUST

THE KEYS TO BEING A FACILITATIVE LEADER

Facilitative leadership, in particular within federated networks such as sporting environments, requires the leader to actively engage key stakeholders in the network so talents and contributions can be maximised. There are abundant instances of the need for individuals with facilitation skills within the sporting setting, most notably at the governance level where the majority of these relationships are played out. With increased pressure from funding bodies to ensure that affiliated sport organisations are working towards common goals, the need for board members and CEOs to possess the traits of a facilitative leader is becoming even more important. Furthermore, the increase in professionalism and the expertise of individuals working across all levels of sport should be brought to the fore of the decision-making process that the facilitative leader can help to achieve. Based on Cufaude's (2014) synopsis of facilitative leadership, there appears to be a number of key traits that are important for becoming an effective facilitative leader within the sporting environment:

1 Make connections with issues across the sport

The sport industry is a fast paced environment where information regarding financial, operational and strategic issues can change rapidly across various areas of the industry. The ability to make connections between all these pieces of information is crucial for the facilitative leader to attempt to join pieces of the puzzle together and ensure accurate up-to-date information is received by key stakeholders. It is the facilitative leader's responsibility to listen to the concerns of a group of stakeholders and make connections with the concerns of other stakeholders within the network. An effective facilitative leader must periodically ask the question: 'How do the concerns of these stakeholders fit in with the concerns of others within the network?'

2 Providing direction

It is important that the facilitative leader provides a direction for the sport or the issues at hand while still actively engaging stakeholders in the collaborative process. It often requires deft skill to balance the need for providing direction while simultaneously ensuring stakeholders 'own' the process, as in the absence of ownership true commitment to the process may not be sustainable. The facilitative leader must be concerned with guiding the collaborative process through asking the right questions at the appropriate times as opposed to a more traditional

85

directive style that may lead to adversarial encounters (O'Boyle and Shilbury, 2013; Shilbury *et al.*, 2013).

3 Balancing the agenda and the collaborative process

The facilitative leader is required to ensure that the content of matters being discussed by parties in the network is complemented by an appropriate collaborative process. Ensuring that the collaborative process is being undertaken correctly provides the greatest opportunity for additional collaborative processes to be undertaken in the future and helps to establish the all-important issue of trust within the network. Pre-empting the collaborative process by establishing agreements of how interaction will take place between parties in the network allows the facilitative leader to evaluate the process itself, irrespective of the outcomes that are achieved. Ignoring the group process and solely focusing on the outcomes or decisions that have been made runs the risk of alienating individuals or groups within the network who may feel that their contributions have not been appropriately acknowledged and considered.

4 Bringing the core issues to the fore (the elephant in the room)

The facilitative leader is required to tease out the underlying causation behind obstacles to effective collaboration within the network. There may be personality clashes, a prehistory of conflict or antagonism, or personal and professional issues that are preventing the network from collaborating effectively. Individuals may be reluctant to discuss these issues or attempt to avoid them. However, if these issues are truly preventing the network from achieving outcomes it is the role of the facilitative leader to use either subtle or forceful questioning to bring these issues to the fore so they can be addressed and the network can move forward. When the network can freely raise concerns and issues without fear of retaliation, openness, honesty and trust can be increased.

5 Facilitating sustainable collaboration

Facilitative leadership is not simply about achieving immediate outcomes or one-off collaborations within the network. The true value in employing a facilitative leadership approach lies in the establishment of the collaborative process itself where future collaborations may continue within the network based on the momentum, trust and good will that has been created through initial outcomes and collaboration. This long term focus ensures that the facilitative leader does not assume all responsibility for future collaborations. After the initial collaborative process, where strong facilitative leadership is clearly required, the ideal situation is that the facilitative leader simply oversees future processes as opposed to becoming directly engaged with additional collaboration in the network.

6 Commitment by the facilitative leader

Finally, the facilitative leader must ensure that they themselves are fully committed to enacting this style of leadership and must be authentic in their relations with others in the network. Enacting this style of leadership with some parties and not with others serves little benefit to the collaborative process and the leader may be judged to be insincere or even manipulative. Facilitative leadership requires thoughtful planning and execution to ensure its success. Leaders who spontaneously alter the way in which they interact and engage with stakeholders in the network must be sensitive to how parties may react and speculate on true intentions. Openness and honesty about the alteration of leadership style may relieve some of the concerns of the parties in the network. A staggered change from director to facilitator may prove to be more palatable for the network as parties get used to more involvement in the decision-making process and become comfortable with increased collaboration.

CASE STUDY
NETBALL AUSTRALIA

The following case study highlights quotes that illuminate issues related to collaboration and facilitative leadership within netball in Australia based on interviews with managers and directors of Netball Australia and its member organisations (MOs).

Introduction

Netball Australia is the NSO responsible for the governance of netball within Australia, including developing and implementing policy related to the sport and promoting the sport at both the grassroots and elite levels. Netball within Australia operates under a federal model of governance reflective of the political system within the country. This federated structure results in each of the six states (New South Wales, Victoria, South Australia, Western Australia, Queensland, Tasmania) and two territories (Australian Capital Territory, Northern Territory) having separate legally autonomous organisations responsible for governing netball within those locations that are affiliated with the national body. The federated structure of governance is in place within the majority of sports within Australia with few sports operating under alternative models.

The alternative models that do exist within Australian sport governance are the unitary model of governance and hybrid models – which see a mix of both the unitary and federal systems. The unitary model exists when a sport has a national body with 'offices' in each state and/or territory as opposed to separate autonomous bodies as seen within the federal model. The unitary model allows for direct reporting lines to the national body, pooling of resources, potentially achieving economies of scale, and crucially the leadership within the sport to exert power and influence over the offices within each state. In this situation it can be argued that having a CEO and board members who have skills in facilitative leadership is important but not essential. However, as the majority of sport organisations within Australia, other nations and indeed global sport organisations operate within a federated structure, facilitative leadership becomes a core requisite to ensure the successful collaboration between affiliated bodies within these networks.

Collaboration

In order to achieve successful collaboration and get 'buy-in' from each MO (state and territories), Netball Australia places a large emphasis on ensuring that the CEO and the board act as facilitative leaders within the sport. The CEO of the organisation reflects the importance of collaboration between all bodies in the network when stating:

> The reality is for a sport like ours, it operates in such a competitive environment, I think the major incentive is knowing that when we work together we add value to each other and we get more alignment around our priorities and planning and so get better outcomes. So it's as simple as that really.

In addition, to facilitate this process the CEO has developed a system to ensure that each MO is made aware of the discussions at Netball Australia board meetings.

> [A]fter every board meeting, which we've been doing for quite some time, we give out a board to board report, 'here are the key things that we discussed and here are our key decisions'. But then the next part is, I do a summary of the key discussion points for each of our directors and I allocate them a president of a [MO] and they are responsible for ringing them and discussing what came out of the board meeting . . . there's been a real breakthrough because of this and we swap them every month . . . and the whole idea is that all of our directors will get to know all of the presidents and then the presidents will feel more comfortable ringing them.

However, the President of Netball Australia outlines the history of collaboration in the sport and concedes that a collaborative culture was not always present with the member organisations:

> [P]robably ten years ago I would say that there were eight very separate organisations that had a loose affiliation and loose cooperative appetite. What's happened in probably over the last six years is that we have been able to put frameworks together where each and every one of those member organisations now agree to a national framework on a whole lot of different levels. And this has necessitated then obviously a lot more communication, a lot more planning, the willingness of the member organisations and the trust, I suppose, of the member organisations to allow Netball Australia to take the lead on a lot of these things. And of course the reason why they're giving us that trust and allowing us that leadership is because they think they're going to get something out of it. . . . the fact that we are able to offer a totally national footprint and sell that. It's also about not having competing commercial interests within Australia and within the sport, so that you're actually loyal to either a financial institution or a fast food chain or whatever . . . it's about that collective good . . . if everybody feels they're part of a team and you're headed in the right direction and it's exciting and there's energy and things are happening, then I think that those sorts of issues seem to be able to be resolved a little bit easier than when and if there's confrontation.

As mentioned previously within the chapter, a pre-history of conflict can have a significant impact on the success or failure of collaborative arrangements within the network. Inevitably as within most federated sporting networks, Netball Australia has experienced conflict with their MOs in the past. A board member from an MO states:

> There may be one or two states [MOs] that still view Netball Australia as a hindrance in terms of achieving. But as I said, I think it's a much stronger and much more aligned [sport] . . . and even those two larger states where the baggage from previous years may still be lingering, when you listen to their outlines of their strategic plans and objectives there is significant alignment. There's just a little lingering thing there maybe with some that they occasionally do hinder what they're trying to do.

Other board members from different MOs also comment on the pre-history of conflict within the sport and its impact on current collaboration:

> I think we would all benefit from relieving ourselves of the burden of unproductive history a bit more than we do in our relationships, and I say that respectfully from both sides, because I think it's easy to carry baggage, and that's both from the states and the national body, and it's not helpful.

and

> You know, you're always going to have some, perhaps a personality issue occasionally, but in saying that . . . everyone works for the betterment of netball, because . . . if people get caught up in their own little world as an individual, you've just got to remind them, 'What are we here for?'

Facilitative leadership

As discussed throughout the chapter, facilitative leadership is clearly required to allow for successful collaboration between various organisations that make up a federated sporting network. The following views taken from interviews with participants involved in the leadership and management of netball summarise how facilitative leadership from the CEO and the board within the national body has unified the sport within Australia and created a strong culture of collaboration, trust and shared understanding throughout the federated network. Commenting on facilitative leadership, the CEO of one of the MOs states:

> [I]t all gets back to communication and it gets back to leadership. What I see is a very strong leader . . . and that leadership style permeates across her senior team . . . and it comes back to what is the strategy of the board, and if the board want to drive a collaborative approach, then they take the lead with the individual boards of the MOs, but they also appoint a person with the skill-set to undertake that process. So, you know, you can have a CEO that doesn't have the skills, and I think the skills are engagement, that constant communication and ability to lead in that

sort of 'come with me approach and style', versus the autocratic 'this is what you'll do and you need to do it'. If you have strong appropriate leadership from [the CEO] and the president, then that filters down through to the boards of the MOs.

Facilitative leadership is not only practised by the President and CEO within Netball Australia but it is evident from the views of interview participants that the board itself as a collective body is seen as a facilitative leader within the sport:

> I think back to five or six years ago when we had a different president and a different chief executive, and the styles of the two that are there now in those roles are significantly more collaborative, and I think that's assisted in improving the relationship. I think provided you've got some key people on the board that show leadership and you can go to them if you have an issue or want to talk through anything, which we do have with our current president . . . I think it's doing a lot of the right things that we're expecting the board to do.

Another board member of a MO agrees with this view:

> In the end you've got to get people collectively getting a view of where the sport should go, and if it's just about one group telling another group, that's not a model for [collaboration] . . . having more authority does not therefore mean a more successful sport.

Netball Australia does not follow a delegate representation structure within its board composition. Candidates for board membership can be nominated or nominate themselves and the members of Netball Australia will then interview each candidate and vote on who they would like to join the national board. The elected board members (currently six) then have the option to co-opt an additional two directors onto the national board. Generally within sport governance, boards are moving towards this style of election/appointment process with candidates becoming successful based on a particular skill-set they may have. However, often overlooked within the election/appointment process are the personality traits and leadership styles and characteristics that may facilitate a collaborative environment within the sport. When asked about these traits and characteristics and whether or not they are viewed as important during the selection phase, various board members of the MOs stated the following:

> I certainly do, and I know for the last couple of years we've had that as a factor in when we vote people onto the board. We're looking at what types of people, what skills do they bring to the board, how are they going to work with the board, are they going to be engaged with us as members? As in board to board . . . are they going to just dismiss us and look at big picture stuff? You need a balance and you need some people that can work collaboratively with a number of different stakeholders. If you have a good facilitator we can be moved in the right direction.

> I think like a lot of relationships, it relates to personalities of individuals, because at the end of the day relationships are not between organisations, they're actually between people.

It's great for people to have, you know, all the financial skills and the corporate skills, and all those, and a lawyer or whatever else you want on your board. But I think a board is about building relationships as well, so I think you know that is a real key ingredient. Your board isn't there just to do the strategic stuff; they're actually there to make those partnerships.

I honestly believe, you've got to go out of your comfort zone and put that effort in, you've got to get a personal relationship at that higher level to make a difference.

Trust

The importance of trust in relation to effective facilitative leadership was outlined previously in the chapter. Within any form of collaboration in a network, trust is a necessary precondition to allow for collaboration to flourish. Prehistories of conflict or antagonism where trust has been damaged will inevitably make collaboration difficult. The facilitative leader may be required to engage in specific trust building initiatives such as intentionally seeking out intermediate outcomes that act as trust building exercises and help to establish momentum for further larger scale collaboration. The CEO of Netball Australia states:

The more national projects we have and being really clear that Netball Australia's role is this and your role is that . . . the more we have to work together; the more we work together the better we get to know each other; the more cooperative and collaborative we become.

The CEO of one of the MOs also concurs that intermediate outcomes are important for trust building within the network:

I think small wins are important, and especially in that trust area. If you can demonstrate something that there's been an issue in the past and we've worked collaboratively and you've achieved something, then I think that breaks down some of those barriers that may exist. I know how frustrating it would be from a NSO to try to get that buy in, but that's where you've got to have small wins, you've got to work hard at it.

Within a network of organisations such as those that make up the sport of netball in Australia, trust must be a reciprocal characteristic of the relationship to allow for facilitative leadership to take place. It was evident from interviews that there was a significant level of trust from the national body towards its MOs and vice versa. A board member of Netball Australia stated:

I think trust is extremely important and at the end of the day you will always find somebody that'll say, 'Oh, they don't like this and they don't like that'. The member organisations of netball have traditionally always supported their boards and [that] is evidenced by the fact that not always do we have lots of people standing for the [national] board.

Participants from the MOs also agreed that there were significant amounts of trust within the network to allow facilitative leadership to be adopted but also signalled that there have been instances where elements of distrust have been present within the relationship with the national body. A board member from one MO stated:

> I think that Netball Australia listening better to their member organisations has built their trust. The times when it's shaky are when they do something without consulting, and there's a difference between consulting and informing. When you discover that something's happened that you didn't actually know anything about and it could impact on a whole lot of things that you're thinking about . . . that's not a good flavour.

A strong theme that emerged from the interviews in relation to trust was the extent to which face-to-face dialogue takes place within the network. It is apparent that Netball Australia and the MOs understand the importance of face-to-face dialogue as a mechanism for building trust within the network. An example of an MO board member's view in relation to face-to-face dialogue is provided: 'I knew about them, but I hadn't met them, but when you actually sit down and have that networking you know offline, I think that's where you build the trust. And I think that's a key thing.'

SUMMARY

This chapter has discussed the importance of facilitative leadership as a necessary skill required for both CEOs and board members within sport organisations that operate within a federal or network style of governance. Trust and distrust have been presented as key issues that can have a significant impact on the success or failure of a facilitative leadership approach within a sport. In addition, the extent to which face-to-face dialogue takes place between key stakeholders within the sport can help to build trust between entities and individuals within the network, increasing the possibility of 'buy-in' from all organisations within the network to work towards common goals.

The keys to being a successful facilitative leader were outlined, including the requirement to be authentic in the leader's own actions among other issues. A case study of Netball Australia was presented to illuminate key issues related to facilitative leadership and trust within a national sport organisation. It becomes apparent through the quotes provided as part of the case study that leaders within Netball Australia have attempted to enact a facilitative leadership style to foster high levels of collaboration and trust within the federated governance system in which they operate. It is anticipated that this style of leadership will become increasingly popular within sporting networks as funding agencies place more pressure on sport organisations to work more closely together, allowing for greater collaboration through interdependence, a shared vision and common goals.

REVIEW QUESTIONS

1   What does the term 'federated structure' mean in relation to sport governance?

2   Discuss two barriers that may exist when attempting to enact a facilitative leadership approach.

3   Describe two ways a facilitative leader may attempt to build trust within a sporting network.

4   Why is it important that the facilitative leader is seen to be fully committed to the collaborative process?

5   What are the key benefits and challenges of facilitative leadership according to the data presented in the Netball Australia case study?

REFERENCES

Ansell, C. and Gash, A. 2008. Collaborative governance in theory and practice. *Journal of Public Administration Research and Theory*, 18(4), 543–571.

Bentrup, G. (2001). Evaluation of a collaborative model: A case study of analysis of watershed planning in the Intermountain West. *Environmental Management*, 27, 739–748.

Bradford, N. (1998). Prospects for associative governance: Lessons from Ontario, Canada. *Politics and Society*, 26, 539–573.

Child, J. (2001). Trust–the fundamental bond in global collaboration. *Organizational Dynamics*, 29, 274–288.

Cufaude, J. (2014). Facilitative leadership: Maximising the contributions of others. *The Systems Thinker*, 15(10), 2–5.

Gunton, T. I. and Day, J. C. (2003). The theory and practice of collaborative planning in resource and environmental management. *Environments*, 31(2), 5–19.

Henry, I. and Lee, P. C. (2004). Governance and ethics in sport. In J. Beech and S. Chadwick (eds), *The business of sport management* (pp. 25–41). Essex: Pearson Education.

Hoye, R., and Cuskelly, G. (2007). *Sport governance*. Oxford: Elsevier Butterworth-Heinemann.

Lasker, R. D. and Weiss, E. S. (2003). Broadening participation in community problem-solving: A multidisciplinary model to support collaborative practice and research. *Journal of Urban Health: Bulletin of the New York Academy of Medicine*, 80, 14–60.

O'Boyle, I. and Shilbury, D. (2013). Collaborative governance in non-profit sport. *Sport Management Association of Australia and New Zealand (SMAANZ). Book of Abstracts* (p. 22–23). Nov 20–22, Dunedin, New Zealand.

Ozawa, P. (1993). Improving citizen participation in environmental decisionmaking: The use of transformative mediator techniques. *Environment and Planning C: Government and Policy*, 11, 103–117.

Reilly, T. (2001). Collaboration in action: An uncertain process. *Administration in Social Work*, 25(1), 53–73.

Ring, P. S. (1997). Transacting in the state of union: A case study of exchange governed by convergent interests. *Journal of Management Studies*, 34(1), 1–25.

Shilbury, D., Ferkins, L. and Smythe, L. (2013). Sport governance encounters: Insights from lived experiences. *Sport Management Review*, 16, 349–363.

Susskind, L. and Cruikshank, J. (1987). *Breaking the impasse: Consensual approaches to resolving public disputes.* New York: Basic Books.

Vangen, S. and Huxham, C. (2003). Enacting leadership for collaborative advantage: Dilemmas of ideology and pragmatism in the activities of partnership managers. *British Journal of Management*, 14, 61–76.

Walsh, J. P., Wang, E. and Xin, K. R. (1999). Same bed, different dreams: Working relationships in Sino-American joint ventures. *Journal of World Business*, 34(1), 69–93.

Warner, J. F. (2006). More sustainable participation? Multi-stakeholder platforms for integrated catchment management. *Water Resources Development*, 22(1), 15–35.

Weech-Maldonado, R. and Merrill, S. (2000). Building partnerships in the community: Lessons from the Camden Healthcare Improvement Learning Cooperative. *Journal of Healthcare Management*, 45(3), 189–205.

Chapter 8

Communication in sport management

Andrea N. Geurin-Eagleman

CHAPTER OBJECTIVES

After completing this chapter you should be able to:

1 understand the role of communication within sport management;
2 explain the ways in which communication in the sport industry is constantly changing and evolving;
3 describe the various communication styles exhibited by sport management leaders;
4 discuss the impacts of new media on sport leaders' and organisations' communication strategies with various stakeholders.

KEY TERMS

- sport communication
- crisis communication plan
- sport leadership communication
- new media
- social media

At the core of nearly everything that takes place within the field of sport management is one commonality: communication. Whether it be a coach giving a pre-game inspirational speech to her team, a hockey team's marketing manager placing an advertisement in the local newspaper for an upcoming game, a public relations manager for a road race posting a message to followers on Facebook, or a basketball player signalling to a teammate that he is open for a pass, communication is a central component of each of these scenarios.

THE COMMUNICATION PROCESS

At its most basic level, the communication process involves a source, the message and a receiver. The source is the originator of the communication message that is delivered to the receiver or the recipient of the communication. For example, when a sport public relations professional for a professional soccer team sends a press release to a group of news reporters about an upcoming game that the team is hosting, the PR professional is the source, the press release is the message, and the news reporters are the recipients. Additional elements to this process can include feedback and noise. Feedback is a one-way or two-way form of communication between the receiver and source. If a news reporter reads the press release and is interested in covering the soccer game, he might contact the PR professional to ask for additional details. If the PR professional responds with answers, this is an example of two-way feedback. If a reporter simply responds to the press release to thank the PR professional for sending it and the PR professional does not respond, that is an example of one-way feedback. Noise occurs when something prevents the message from being delivered as it was intended to the recipient. Noise can be both literal and figurative. For example, while attending a live basketball game, you might have a conversation with the friend seated next to you. Suppose a player from the home team scores a crucial three-point shot and the arena erupts into claps and cheers. Suddenly you are unable to hear what your friend is saying. This is an example of noise literally getting in the way of your communication with your friend. Using the story about the press release above, here is another example. Imagine that the press release file was not saved properly and the entire first paragraph is missing from the release that the PR professional sent to reporters. In this instance, the noise is figurative – it is the lack of information given in the first paragraph. This noise will likely result in confusion and questions from the reporters.

SPORT COMMUNICATION

While the communication process generally applies to all communication in our lives, Pedersen et al. (2007) explained that additional aspects of communication and media apply to sport situations. Therefore, they defined the term sport communication as 'a process by which people in sport, in a sport setting, or through a sport endeavour share symbols as they create meaning through interaction' (p. 76). There are a wide variety of communication symbols, including non-oral cues, that are often thought of as body language symbols or facial expressions, such as nodding a head or shaking a hand; oral symbols, such as speaking directly to another person or group of people; or written symbols, such as a newspaper article or billboard along the road. When these symbols are shared with another person, this represents an interaction, and meaning is created from this interaction. For example, there are multiple symbols, interactions and potential meanings created in the following scenario: imagine an athlete rolls her eyes and attempts to walk away from her coach as the coach is speaking to her, and the coach subsequently grabs the athlete's jersey and angrily continues the speech. The symbols involved include the body language and facial expression of the athlete, the coach's tone of voice and the content of her speech, and the coach's attempt to grab the athlete. If the athlete remains upset as the coach continues to talk to her, the meaning created for the athlete is one in which she is upset or annoyed and does not appreciate the coach grabbing her by the jersey. From the coach's perspective, the meaning created might be that she needs to demand greater respect from the athlete or that she becomes increasingly upset with the athlete due to her behaviour. In addition to shared symbols creating meaning through interaction, Pedersen *et al.* (2007) noted, 'sport communication is intentional or unintentional, complex, circular, irreversible, transactional, unrepeatable, and dynamic' (p. 79).

THE STRATEGIC SPORT COMMUNICATION MODEL

The Strategic Sport Communication Model (SSCM), created by Pedersen *et al.* (2007), highlights the unique aspects of the sport industry related to communication. The model consists of three components: personal and organisational communication in sport, sport mass media, and sport communication services and support. Each component is made up of communication methods unique to that component. Within personal and organisational communication in sport are aspects of personal communication (e.g. intrapersonal, interpersonal and small group), and aspects of organisational communication (e.g. intraorganisational and interorganisational). The sport mass media component consists of publishing and print communication, electronic and visual communication, and new media applications. Finally, the sport communication services and support component is made up of advertising, public relations and crisis communication, and research.

Sport organisations and sport managers use all of these communication methods to communicate with both those within the organisation and outside stakeholders of the organisation. Depending on the internal or external stakeholder, different communication methods may be utilised. Internal stakeholders include the organisation's business employees, athletes, coaches, game day staff and volunteers. Broadly speaking, external stakeholders include groups such as the organisation's fans and customers, the community in which the organisation operates, business partners or sponsors, media organisations or journalists, and donors or investors. According to Stoldt *et al.* (2012), sport organisations should not assume that everyone within one of these broad stakeholder groups holds similar views and attitudes towards the organisation. Therefore, they suggest that sport organisations must target 'specific publics within broader stakeholder groups' (p. 3), or what is referred to as segmentation. This requires careful strategic thought about the best method for delivering messages to the various subgroups within each stakeholder group.

Message delivery, or the method by which a sender delivers the message to the receiver, is an important consideration for organisations and sport leaders. The SSCM outlines a wide variety of communication methods, and within each of these methods there is an ever-expanding number of options for communicating a message. For example, advertising is a communication method listed within the sport communication services and support component of the model. If a professional baseball team wants to advertise a promotion for a free t-shirt to the first 10,000 fans who enter the stadium at an upcoming game, they have an almost endless number of options for delivering this message. They could choose to place an ad in the newspaper, on television or radio, via a billboard, or even on the side of a bus or top of a taxi. Aside from these more traditional advertising methods, they might also consider buying ad space on websites that are popular with their target audiences or advertising on social media outlets such as Facebook. These are just a few of the many communication delivery choices available to the team. Along with advertising, they might consider public relations methods such as sending press releases to media outlets, posting a story about the t-shirt giveaway to their team's website, writing posts about it on the team's social media pages such as Facebook and Twitter, posting a photo of the free t-shirts on Instagram, or sending a text message blast to fans. In some instances, organisations might even turn to personal communication methods such as cold calling fans to tell them about the promotion or sending personalised emails to those fans who are most likely to be interested in the promotion.

As you can see from the previous example, sport organisations are faced with an ever-expanding number of options for communicating a message, even one as simple as a t-shirt promotion. Choosing to advertise a product or service is not quite as simple as paying the money to the advertising outlet (e.g. newspaper, television, website), and a great deal of strategic thought must go into this decision. Questions that must be asked when determining the delivery method include: Who is my target audience? How can I effectively reach my target audience, or where does my audience consume information? What is my budget for communicating this message? How can I effectively reach the most people in my target market while staying within this budget? The delivery method must be carefully thought out and matched to the target audience. For example, the Pew Research Center (2011) reported that 65 per cent of people under 30 consume the majority of their news via the Internet instead of traditional news sources such as the newspaper or television. Therefore, if the baseball team's target market includes a high proportion of people aged 30 and under, it would be wise to focus their advertising efforts on online media. From there, the team's marketing and communication employees can conduct research to further determine which online methods would be most effective for reaching their target market.

COMMUNICATION AMONG SPORT COMMUNICATION PROFESSIONALS AND SPORT LEADERS

Although this chapter has largely focused on sport communication from a public relations perspective thus far, it is important to remember the initial point made in the introduction – that communication permeates all activities within a sport setting, and therefore communication is important for all areas of sport. The following section will explain the importance of communication for two sport groups – first, among the sport communication and public relations professionals, and second, among all sport leaders (e.g. chief executive officers, presidents, board members, coaches, etc.).

Sport communication professionals

Depending on the size of an organisation, most sport organisations employ at least one staff member whose primary role is to communicate with both internal and external stakeholders. Some larger organisations employ entire departments of such professionals. These staff members typically have titles involving the words or phrases communication, sports information, public relations, media relations, community relations or external relations. Pedersen *et al.* (2007) noted that although the job duties of various positions within sport communication may vary, anyone in one of these careers must be able to communicate with key audiences. Furthermore, Stoldt *et al.* (2012) listed five key skills that sport communication professionals must possess.

First, writing skills are important because of the amount of writing that most of these roles require. Whether it be writing a press release, putting together information for the team's media guide, writing emails to media and other stakeholders, or writing content for the organisation's website, writing is a core competency for sport communication leaders. Next, public presentation competencies must be honed. While Stoldt *et al.* (2012) noted that not all communication professionals will be asked to give speeches, they are often required to complete tasks such as moderating press conferences, serving as an organisational spokesperson at events and giving statements to the media. The third skill necessary for sport communication professionals is desktop publishing capabilities. As noted earlier, those in sport communication roles are often called on to write press releases or put together the organisation's media guide. Because of this, it is imperative that these employees have a strong understanding of page layout and design principles, as well as the knowledge to create high-quality professional publications using software applications such as InDesign, PageMaker or PhotoShop. The fourth required skill is Internet-related competencies. This skill has become increasingly important in recent years as organisations move further into the digital online space with innovative use of websites, smartphone applications, blogs, podcasts and social media. It is important for communication professionals to not only understand how to use those various online-based communication outlets from a user's perspective, but also to understand how such outlets can be best utilised to reach and connect with the organisation's various audiences. Finally, the fifth important skill that sport communication professionals must possess is interpersonal skills. Although these roles require a great deal of writing and working with various computer and new media applications, communication professionals also must have the ability to effectively interact with a wide variety of people. For example, a public relations professional working for a professional motorsports team must be able to effectively communicate with the various journalists who wish to cover her driver. She also must be able to carry on meaningful conversations with the driver's fans at events, entertain and inform executives from the team's sponsoring organisations, and work well with the different personalities of the race team's other business staff, the driver and the crew members.

A crucial leadership role that sport communication professionals play in any sport organisation is that of the crisis communication leader. When crises occur, sport communication leaders must be prepared to proactively handle the situation from a communication perspective. A crisis is anything that occurs and has the opportunity to harm or damage the reputation of the sport organisation. Examples of crises in sport include athlete or organisational employee indiscretions in their professional or personal lives, such as the Tiger Woods scandal in which he was found to have cheated on his wife with several women or the Lance Armstrong performance-enhancing drug scandal; serious athlete injuries or deaths, such as when Minnesota Vikings football player Korey Stringer died during a practice session from heat stroke; scandals involving the business operations of an organisation, such as when the Salt Lake City Organizing Committee (SLOC) was found to have bribed members of the International Olympic Committee (IOC) in order to win the bid for the 2002 Winter Olympics. Stoldt *et al.* (2012) identified five crisis categories, including physical plant crises, on-field crises, family crises, corporate crises and player personnel crises.

Clavio *et al.* (2007) stated, 'Responding to a crisis means more than simply responding to media inquiries' (p. 15). They noted that crisis management kits can assist an organisation in its handling of crisis situations. Stoldt *et al.* (2012) described this crisis management kit as a crisis communication plan, which can 'offer guidance on how to proceed after a crisis has occurred' (p. 197). Such plans are necessary because organisations can find themselves under intense media and public scrutiny as soon as a crisis occurs, and organisations often do not have a great deal of time to develop a plan if one is not already in place. The development of a crisis communication plan involves forecasting all potential crises to determine which scenarios are most likely to occur. These scenarios should be included in the plan, and for each scenario, a response team should be outlined. These teams might vary based on the specific crisis. At least one member of the organisation's communication or public relations staff should be on each response team. Each team member will be assigned specific responsibilities, such as contacting any family members of the person or people involved in the crisis, serving as the primary organisational spokesperson with the media, and communicating with external governing body stakeholders. Along with a plan for communicating with external stakeholders such as the media, sponsors, fans and other publics, crisis communication plans should also include an internal communication plan. It is important that the organisation's employees are all made aware of the crisis event, although some employees might need to know more details about the situation than others. The media will often contact anyone who is available from an organisation for a statement, so it is important that all employees understand what to do if they are contacted by the media. Typically, there will be a specific person within the organisation to whom they should direct the journalist for a statement. Stoldt *et al.* (2012) noted that sport organisations that do not respond to crises in an appropriate manner face significant damaging implications. Crisis plans can 'empower sport organizations to limit the damage and, in some cases, make positive impressions' (p. 198). Sport communication professionals can take on meaningful leadership roles within the organisation through the introduction, development and implementation of crisis communication plans.

Sport leaders

All sport organisational leaders, whether they are a CEO, president, head coach or the vice president of sales, must have strong communication skills in order for the organisation to function smoothly and efficiently. Pedersen *et al.* (2007) stressed that the importance of communication skills for sport management leaders cannot be overstated. Further, Baldoni (2003) listed three components in a continuous cycle that leaders should practise daily. The first is to develop a leadership message, such as a mission or vision statement. The leader should determine exactly what it is that he or she wants to say or do, and should then select the appropriate communication channel. Second, this message needs to be delivered to an audience. It is important that the leader knows his or her audience in order to deliver the message effectively. Finally, the leader must sustain this message, keeping it alive and meaningful, which can be accomplished via feedback, repetition and coaching.

Pedersen *et al.* (2007) defined sport leadership communication style as 'the way a leader behaves toward and interacts and communicates with followers' (p. 139). It is important to understand the communication styles exhibited by leaders, as these have direct implications for the entire organisation and its culture. Leadership behaviours can vary based on contextual, situational and other influences. There are two dimensions of sport leadership communication styles, as identified by Pedersen *et al.* (2007): task-oriented communication, which focuses more on the task at hand than on the people completing said task, and relationship-oriented communication, which is more concerned with relationships and things such as listening, asking for opinions and making requests. Within these two dimensions lie four supervisory communication styles employed by sport communication leaders: autocratic style, consultative style, participative style and laissez-faire style. Each of these is described in greater detail below.

Autocratic style

Sport communication leaders with an autocratic style rank high on the task-oriented communication scale and low on the relationship-oriented communication scale. These leaders have been described as dictator-like for their strict control over others within the organisation. These leaders tend to regulate policies, procedures and behaviours quite firmly. Specifically relating to their communication style, autocratic leaders tend to have one-sided communication, meaning that they often offer detailed instructions and close supervision of their subordinates. Additionally, they seek little input from communication receivers. For example, the director of a professional tennis tournament writes a memo to all staff to notify them of a new policy restricting the social media use by employees during tournament play. This is an example of an autocratic leadership communication style.

Consultative style

Those leaders with a consultative communication style rank high on both task-oriented and relationship-oriented communication. They are concerned with whether or not the subordinate employee is interested in the message, but there is limited openness from the leader regarding whether or not the subordinate accepts the task. Therefore, the leader has the final say in most matters. For example, a leader who takes the time to explain to an employee exactly how a task should be completed and answers the employee's questions about it, but does not accept input from the employee regarding ways to make the task better or more efficient, exhibits the consultative style of communication.

Participative style

Leaders with a participative communication style exhibit low task-oriented communication and high relationship-oriented communication. This style has been described as democratic, as the leader and followers engage in supportive, two-way communication. These leaders tend to be good listeners and value input, discussion and feedback from employees. For example, a sport organisation leader with a participative communication style would likely seek input from subordinate employees when developing an updated organisational mission statement. The leader might host roundtable discussions in which employees could voice their opinions, or possibly solicit feedback and ideas on the updated mission via email submissions.

101

Laissez-faire style

The laissez-faire communication style is marked by low task-oriented communication and low relationship-oriented communication. Pedersen *et al.* (2007) describe this style as 'nonleadership or avoiding leadership' (p. 143) because the leader tends to accept subordinates' decisions and gives those employees a sense of being in charge. These leaders tend to have faith in their employees that they will complete tasks well, and therefore the leaders take a hands-off approach, rarely providing direction or feedback on tasks. Using the previous example of developing a revised mission statement, a leader with the laissez-faire style of communication might ask a group of subordinates to review the old mission statement and update it on their own. This leader would not have any involvement in the process and would likely trust the decision that the employees made regarding the updated mission statement.

Clearly, all four communication leadership styles outlined in the previous sections are quite different from each other. While most leaders tend to exhibit one dominant leadership communication style, it is possible that leaders might utilise more than one style depending on the situation at hand. The following four variables were identified by Pedersen *et al.* (2007) as being important in determining which leadership communication style a sport leader should use:

1   *Time* – the sport leader must determine whether there is enough time to engage in two-way communication before the task at hand must be completed.
2   *Information* – the sport leader must account for whether he or she has enough necessary information to communicate, make a decision or employ a course of action.
3   *Acceptance* – sport leaders must predict whether their follower or followers will accept a message fully, with some reluctance, or whether they will reject it.
4   *Capability* – the sport leader must determine the motivation – both ability and willingness – of the subordinate employees in completing the task at hand.

Once a sport leader determines the answers to the questions posed in each of these four criteria, he or she can better determine the appropriate communication leadership approach to take.

SPORT COMMUNICATION AND NEW MEDIA TECHNOLOGIES

Over the past decade, new media technologies have begun to drastically change the landscape of sport communication. Changes in the ways sports fans consume sport, interact with other fans and sport organisations, and a 24/7 news cycle all have impacts on sport organisations' communication efforts and strategies. The following section will outline the changes that have taken place in the communication landscape, the ways in which sport organisations are using new media, and the challenges sport leaders and organisations face due to these new technologies.

First, the term new media is often used interchangeably with the term social media, but it is important to note that the two are different, though related. New media refers to any forms of media beyond those classified as 'traditional' (newspaper, magazine, book, film, television or radio). New media platforms such as the Internet, websites, mobile phone and tablet applications, streaming videos and virtual reality environments all combine and integrate data, text, sound and images, which are stored in a digital format. Social media is just one category of new media, and Kaplan and Haenlein (2010) defined it as, 'a group of Internet-based applications that build on the ideological and technological foundations of Web 2.0, and that allow the creation and exchange of user-generated content' (p. 61). The creation and exchange of content relates to the interactivity involved in social media, which is an aspect that sets it apart from new media. Interaction is a key aspect to social media, as users can write comments and responses to each other, share content with others, and interact with content via symbols, such as the 'like' button on Facebook or the 'favourite' feature on Twitter.

Both new media and social media have become incredibly important to sport organisations and sport communicators in recent years, as they provide a plethora of new options for communicating with a variety of stakeholders. There are several characteristics of new media that are important to sport organisations, and sport communication leaders specifically. The first is geographic distance. New media allows sport organisations to transcend geographic boundaries. For example, a rugby team based in Australia still has the opportunity to communicate with fans all over the globe using means such as the organisation's website and any social media accounts such as Facebook, Twitter or Instagram. Additionally, because sport media outlets update content as soon as events occur, fans can follow game action via live blogs in almost real-time, and can find out about things happening tens of thousands of miles away simply by logging on to the Internet or using an app on their mobile phone.

The next important characteristics of new media for sport communication professionals are the volume and speed of communication. Because there are so many new media options for gathering information about a specific team or sport topic, fans and other stakeholders can easily find the information that they need. It is ideal if the sport organisation can be the source to provide this information, as they should be the primary source of important information relating to their team, athletes or sport. Because there are so many different new media platforms on which to communicate, the sport organisations can also connect with fans and stakeholders in multiple locations. In terms of the speed of communication, as mentioned in the previous paragraph, new media allows for real-time communication and real-time feedback, meaning that teams and organisations have the opportunity to collect feedback on events or issues immediately after they occur.

Finally, new media provides the opportunity for both interactivity and interconnection. From an interactive standpoint, sport organisations can communicate with stakeholders via a variety of mechanisms, whether it be through email, feedback on stories posted on the organisation's website or blog, or through online conversations on social media sites such as Facebook or Twitter. Interconnectivity refers to the ability to connect media from multiple platforms. For example, a sport organisation might post a new story about a new coach on its website. From there, they can post a link to that story on Facebook, which their fans can share on their own Facebook pages. If they tweet the link, it has the opportunity to be retweeted to thousands of other Twitter users, and if other media outlets pick up the story, there is the opportunity for the link to the website to be posted in those articles.

ORGANISATIONS' UTILISATION OF NEW MEDIA

As new media applications tend to change and evolve at a very quick pace, it can be difficult for organisations to understand exactly how to best use these platforms, as they are not static.

103

Best practices for new media use have begun to emerge, but these recommendations are still in their infancy stage and a great deal of scholarly research has not yet been devoted to these practices.

One thing that is certain is that it is no longer an option for sport organisations to have their own website; it is an absolute necessity. The organisational website is often the first place that stakeholders visit for information. Fans and customers might visit it to view the team's schedule or to purchase tickets or merchandise. Overseas fans or those who live far from the team might visit it to view past results or read previews about upcoming games. Sponsors and potential sponsors might visit it to get a better sense of the organisation's structure, fan base and potential sponsorship opportunities. Members of the media might visit it to access athlete biographies, statistics, historical facts and media relations staff contact information. Community groups might access it to learn about opportunities for athlete appearances or the team's charitable efforts within the community. It is important for organisations to have a website that is easy to navigate, informative and provides all of the necessary information that the various stakeholder groups might want to access.

Along with an organisational website, sport organisations must determine how they want to use social media outlets, which requires them to understand the opportunities and threats that each social media sites potentially pose to their organisation. Maintaining an organisational social media account can be quite a time-consuming endeavour, so it is important that the organisation understands its limits in terms of how many outlets it can be active on, and how much time its employees can devote to maintaining these accounts. Some sport organisations employ entire departments of professionals to maintain social media accounts. It is important for the organisation to ensure that whichever outlets they choose to use, they have very clear goals in place for what they hope to accomplish with that site. For example, a sports team that has a Facebook page might set goals relating to engaging current fans to strengthen their affiliation with the team, as well as targeting potential customers who might attend future games. The organisation might also decide to open an Instagram account, which might have completely different goals from the Facebook page. The goals should be clearly articulated to all employees to ensure that everyone within the organisation is on the same page regarding the social media usage.

NEW MEDIA CHALLENGES FOR SPORT LEADERS AND ORGANISATIONS

Although new media outlets provide a wide range of opportunities for sport organisations in terms of reaching and communicating with a variety of stakeholders, these new platforms also present some challenges to organisations. First, as previously mentioned, it can be difficult to maintain and update these outlets on a regular basis depending on the organisation's staffing capabilities relating to new media. In order to be successful with new media use, organisations must ensure that they are able to consistently update their website and social media accounts. Without staff who can do this on a regular basis, it can be difficult for organisations to maintain a strong new media presence. Additionally, social media users are not always kind, and some organisations find that they must carefully monitor the comments that users make on their posts, which requires more time from sport organisation employees. In other situations, fans or customers ask questions on the organisation's social media accounts, and it is important to have someone who can respond to these questions or concerns in a timely manner.

As alluded to in the previous section, it can also be difficult for organisations to determine exactly which social media or new media applications they should use. Some organisations attempt to set up accounts on every social media outlet possible, and find that this is extremely time-consuming and difficult to maintain. Therefore, organisations should define clear goals for social media use and only engage on those platforms that will assist in achieving these goals. Once again, they must also take into account how much time is available for staff to devote to these efforts.

Finally, a challenge sport organisations face revolves around the 24/7 news cycle. This relates somewhat to the section on crisis communication, as news media, fans and even the athletes or organisational employees themselves can report news about the organisation before the organisation itself has time to release a statement on an issue. When this occurs, facts sometimes tend to become twisted or rumours are started. Therefore, the organisations must be cognizant of the things that are written or said about it, and must be able to respond in a professional and timely manner. This makes the sport communication leader's job more difficult, as they might find that they spend a great deal of time attempting to correct misinformation that is written about the organisation.

While these challenges can at times be time-consuming and difficult, they are a reality for today's sport organisations and sport communication leaders. These challenges highlight the importance of leadership within a sport organisation, as strong leaders must be able to adequately address and control these challenges for the success of the organisation as a whole.

SUMMARY

Communication is inherent in every interaction within the sport industry. From coaches, athletes, sport organisation leaders and sport communication professionals, all involved in sport must understand how to communicate effectively in order for the organisation to operate at its optimal level. The strategic sport communication model outlines the wide variety of communication mechanisms utilised within the context of sport by both sport communication professionals and sport leaders. Sport communication professionals play a crucial leadership role within organisations with their crisis communication management skills and the ability to develop a crisis communication plan. In addition to sport communication professionals, sport leaders possess a wide variety of sport leadership communication styles. While most sport leaders have a dominant style, the variables of time, information, acceptance and capability have the opportunity to change the leader's style in certain situations. Finally, new media technologies have drastically changed the environment in which sport organisations operate, and specifically in how they communicate with various stakeholders. Both new media and social media technologies offer a wide range of opportunities for sport organisa-tions, although they present a number of challenges as well. As these technologies are ever changing, sport organisations must be able to adapt quickly in order to remain successful in these spaces.

REVIEW QUESTIONS

1 Assume that you are a sport communication leader for a professional Australian Football League (AFL) club and you've been given the task of developing a strategy for communicating an upcoming autograph session. You have been told that your primary target market for this autograph session is young fans under the age of 17. What would be the most appropriate communication methods to make your target market aware of the autograph session?

2 Think about a recent crisis that occurred in the sport industry. Look up news articles about the event and determine whether you would have handled the crisis differently if you were the communications director for the sport organisation involved. Develop a crisis communication plan that outlines how you would prepare for a similar crisis in the future.

3 Review the four communication styles employed by sport leaders (autocratic, consultative, participatory and laissez-faire) and think about the sport management leaders you are familiar with. These could be from personal experiences or from seeing these leaders in the media. Find one leader for each category and write down the leaders' attributes that led you to believe they fit that style of sport communication leadership.

4 Assume that you are the communication manager for a national sport organisation of your choice (e.g. Athletics Australia) and that you have two dedicated staff members who will maintain all of your organisation's new media endeavours, including the website. Which social media outlets would you choose to become active on as an organisation? Why these sites? What would your organisational goals be for using them?

REFERENCES

Baldoni, J. 2003, *Great communication secrets of great leaders*. McGraw-Hill, New York.
Clavio, G., Eagleman, A. N., Miloch, K. S., and Pedersen, P. M. 2007, 'Communicating in crisis: A case study of media management on public perception and brand image', in J. D. James (ed.), *Sport marketing across the spectrum: Research from emerging, developing, and established scholars*, Fitness Information Technology, Morgantown, WV, pp. 15–28.
Kaplan, A. M., and Haenlein, M. 2010, 'Users of the world, unite! The challenges and opportunities of social media', *Business Horizons*, 53(1), 59–68.
Pedersen, P. M., Miloch, K. S., and Laucella, P. C. 2007, *Strategic sport communication*. Human Kinetics, Champaign, IL.
Pew Research Center 2011, Internet now main source of news for young adults, Pew Research Center, retrieved 30 August 2014, www.pewresearch.org/daily-number/internet-now-main-source-of-news-for-young-adults/.
Stoldt, G. C., Dittmore, S. W., and Branvold, S. E. 2012, *Sport public relations: Managing stakeholder communication*, 2nd edn. Human Kinetics, Champaign, IL.

Chapter 9

Strategic leadership through strategic planning

David Shilbury

CHAPTER OBJECTIVES

After completing this chapter you should be able to:

1 describe the strategic planning process;
2 discuss the roles of leadership in shaping strategy;
3 understand the role of strategic leadership and strategic thinking;
4 demonstrate the link between strategic leadership and strategic visioning;
5 understand the role of collaborative leadership on key organisational functions including strategic planning.

KEY TERMS

- collaborative leadership
- national sport organisation (NSO)
- sport governance
- strategy
- strategic leadership
- strategic planning
- strategic thinking

INTRODUCTION

During 2012/13, Bowls Australia (BA), in conjunction with its nine state and territory member associations, crafted a vision statement to support its Bowls in Australia strategic plan 2013–17. In completing its strategic plan, BA adopted a challenging but powerful vision – 'To be the sport for life'. In so doing, senior leaders in the bowls community had mapped out the competitive space in which bowls competes, which in essence included sports offering lifelong participation (e.g. golf, table tennis, billiards and snooker) and, at the same time, articulated the goal of being recognised as the leading sport in this category. This vision was developed and adopted as part of a collaborative process to formulate a strategic plan for bowls in Australia.

Bowls Australia is the national governing body for the sport of lawn bowls in Australia and is composed of nine constituent member associations, all of which are separate legal entities. During the strategic planning process it was agreed that BA and its state and territory member associations would seek to form a common vision and mission for the sport, as well as an agreed set of strategic priorities, which ultimately would provide direction for member associations to develop complementary plans. Significantly, the resulting strategic plan was not a plan for BA, but rather a plan for the entire sport, inclusive of member associations.

The catalyst for the formulation of this strategic plan was initially driven by governance tensions typically found in a federated structure in which each member association is a separate legal entity. Often, member associations engage in actions and activities that do not always align with a national governing body's preferred strategic direction. In other words, to ensure alignment and consistency of strategic direction, a collaborative approach to governance was required to generate a common vision for bowls and, at the same time, build trust and rapport throughout the sport. What evolved from the BA case is relevant to this chapter as it focused on strategic planning and leadership.

The purpose of this chapter is to examine the role of leaders and leadership in the strategic planning process and strategy development generally. This chapter will introduce the process of strategic planning and its component parts, and consider the role of senior leaders in the strategy setting function. The chapter will elaborate further on the BA case providing a real-life application of the role of leadership in strategic planning, and, significantly, the role of the collaborative leadership process required when working within a federal sport structure, as is the case in Australia and many other countries. The BA case will be used to illustrate the component parts of the strategic planning process as well as examine how strategic leadership, both at an individual and organisational level was critical in developing a common vision for the sport.

Strategic leadership will form an important focus for this chapter, as it is the role of senior leaders to lead the strategy formulation process. Ireland and Hitt (1999: 43) defined strategic leadership as a 'person's ability to anticipate, envision, maintain flexibility, think strategically, and work with others to initiate changes that will create a viable future for the organization'. Initiating change is often an outcome of the strategic planning process, which is defined by Bryson (2011: xii) as a 'deliberative, disciplined approach to producing fundamental decisions and actions that shape and guide what an organization (or any other entity) is, what it does, and why it does it'.

Strategic planning of itself is not a replacement for leadership, it is merely a 'set of concepts, procedures and tools designed to help executives, managers, and others to think, act, and learn strategically on behalf of their organizations' (Bryson 2011: 385). In other words, leaders, through strategic leadership, bring to life the direction setting function through strategic planning. Leaders can empower others and invite them to contribute to the direction setting function, as well as invite them to share the vision generated through the strategic planning process. Fairholm (2009: 2) highlights the importance of strategic thinking by leaders, stating that:

> While strategic planning is upward focused, looking at ensuring how tactics link up to corporate goals and strategies, strategic thinking is downward focused, looking to ensure that meaning and purpose are diffused throughout the organization so that appropriate goals and tactics can be developed to meet the needs of the organization. Strategic planning in this sense is more linked to the work of classical management, while strategic thinking is linked more to the work of leadership.

An important feature of the BA case is the influence and interface of volunteer administrators at the executive (governance) level of the sport and paid staff (predominantly CEOs). Volunteer involvement in the governance and delivery of a sport such as bowls is a critical success factor that warrants special consideration in the ongoing professionalisation of sport organisations. Professionalisation continues to create tensions as paid staff seek to streamline decision making and implement traditional and new managerial tools and techniques, such as strategic planning, while volunteer administrators typically strive to maintain and 'live' their leisure time through their involvement in sport. For most, but not all, volunteers the demands of implementing strategic planning and other sophisticated managerial tools and techniques can be threatening, and inconsistent with their motivations and time available for involvement in the first place (Ferkins, Shilbury and McDonald 2009). This has implications for leadership in sport organisations. Notwithstanding these tensions, change has been evident in Australian sport during the last 20–30 years, albeit the pace of change is inconsistent from sport to sport.

To overcome the barriers to effective governance, leadership and strategy implementation, created in part due to a federal sport structure and a leisure orientation of volunteer board directors, a collaborative approach to governance and leadership was utilised by Ansell and Gash (2008) in their examination of collaborative governance which found that leadership was an important factor in explaining the success or otherwise of this approach to governance. This is consistent with the definition of leadership espoused by Crosby and Bryson (2005: xix) in which they state that leadership is, 'the inspiration and mobilization of others to undertake collective action in pursuit of a common goal'. This is especially the case in non-profit sport organisations where many people from varying backgrounds (i.e. the board of directors, service volunteers) are involved in the collective enterprise (e.g. national and state sporting organisations, community clubs) of delivering sport to the community.

This definition also supports Ansell and Gash's (2012: 1) view that, 'leadership is widely recognized as an important ingredient in successful collaboration', and therefore it follows that it is an essential feature of sport governance, strategic planning and the successful delivery of sport programmes to the community. The authors describe collaborative leadership as

109

facilitative, with collaboration voluntary in nature, even when it has been mandated (Ansell and Gash 2012). Three collaborative leadership styles are identified by Ansell and Gash (2012), including roles as an organisational steward, as a mediator and as a catalyst. The exact meaning of each of these terms will be explicated later in the chapter in the context of the BA story.

Before developing the BA story, it is worth defining strategy and its origins as determining that strategy is the purpose of the strategic planning process. Strategy can be thought of as a pattern of actions employed by firm leadership to position an organisation for competitive advantage. Competitive advantage is the 'edge' firms believe they have created as a result of the bundling of resources in a new and distinctive way, or by way of efficiencies gained through cost leadership. The iPhone, when first released, was an example of a unique bundling of resources to develop a product that created a competitive advantage for Apple, at least until competitors could imitate the iPhone. In other words, whatever the edge, it should not be easily replicated by competitors and can be reasonably expected to endure over time.

Strategic management, as distinct from strategic planning, refers to the managerial process of formulating the patterns of actions and implementing them. The difference between the two is that strategic planning is only concerned with identifying the best pattern of actions (strategies) to pursue over an identified time period, whereas, strategic management is also concerned with the implementation of these strategies, which, of course, among many other factors includes leadership to ensure adherence to the strategy. To that end, strategic management is considered a more contemporary and relevant term because it is focused on a broader perspective of organisational life and how patterns of actions are delivered through people, systems and processes.

Although strategy itself is an old concept and readily apparent in many aspects of life, such as on the battlefield during war and of course the playing field during sport, its centrality to corporate life is relatively recent, and even more recent in terms of its application to sport organisations. The birth of the field of strategic management, according to Rumelt *et al.* (1994), can be traced to three key texts including Alfred Chandler's *Strategy and Structure* (1962), Igor Ansoff's *Corporate Strategy* (1965), and Kenneth Andrews' *The Concept of Corporate Strategy* (1971), which was originally published in 1965 as a Harvard University textbook, *Business Policy: Texts and Cases*. All three texts are characterised by a prescriptive formula of 'strategy' relying on managerial action in response to environmental circumstances.

Other prominent writers in this field include Drucker (1946) and Mintzberg (1973), with the latter having written many articles and books solely dedicated to strategic planning and its role within organisational life. Notwithstanding the growing interest in, and importance of strategic planning and strategy generally in the 1960s, the field was somewhat impaired by a range of quick-fix approaches designed to provide management with formulistic methods by which to choose the best strategy (Marx 2013), which, in essence, minimised the need for leadership.

Montgomery (2012: 12), in her book entitled *The Strategist: Be the Leader Your Business Needs*, observed that, 'leadership and strategy are inseparable' but these 'two aspects of what leaders do, once tightly linked, have grown apart'. She argued that, 'strategy and leadership must be reunited at the highest level of an organization. All leaders . . . must accept and own strategy as the heart of their responsibilities'. This is also a theme picked up by Shilbury (2012) in his overview of strategy-related research in sport management. Consequently, senior managers require high level reasoning, analytical and conceptual skills to formulate strategy, while implementing strategy requires organisational and interpersonal skills in an environment in which progress towards strategy is not always clear, and does not automatically progress in a linear manner. Leadership is essential to ensure clarity of purpose in relation to strategy and its implementation. Clarity of purpose is often captured through the vision that typically says something about a company's competitive position and also communicates an aspirational goal, as was the case in the Bowls in Australia vision – *to be the sport for life!*

BACKGROUND TO BOWLS AUSTRALIA AND PROBLEM IDENTIFICATION

The BA study was undertaken as part of a larger focus on sport governance using action research as a method to work with boards of state and national sport organisations. The research question asked of BA was – how can BA enhance their governance capability? Using developmental action research, the research team worked with the BA Board of Directors to address this question, with the aim of identifying a specific problem and then implementing an intervention or series of actions that would enhance governance capability by addressing the problem. Before revealing the actual problem identified and the intervention designed to overcome the problem, a brief definition of governance is provided followed by some background about BA to provide necessary context to the case.

What then is governance? Essentially, to govern is to steer; it is undertaken by a board of directors with ultimate responsibility for establishing the overall direction and monitoring of the performance of an organisation. In this case, the BA Board consists of nine directors, six of whom are elected by the member associations, and another three appointed as independent directors to provide diversity of knowledge and skills on the Board. In the sport context, therefore, Ferkins and colleagues (2009: 245) defined sport governance as, 'the responsibility for the functioning and overall direction of the organization and is a necessary and institutionalized component of all sport codes from club level to national bodies, government agencies, sport service organizations and professional teams around the world'.

The national office of BA is located in Melbourne, Australia, and at the time the fieldwork commenced BA employed 15 staff to discharge its charter in the areas of participation, high performance sport, conduct of national events, and commercial operations. Staff numbers were boosted in 2012 by the appointment of 16 community development officers based in major cities and regions across Australia. The CEO had good experience as a CEO in other sport organisations, complemented by postgraduate qualifications in sport management. He had been with BA for five years at the commencement of the study. In summary, BA financial outcomes leading into the study show:

- $4.8 million 2011/12, an increase of $861,000 from the previous year (BA 2012);
- $1.3 million from the ASC split almost equally between high performance and participation (ASC 2012);
- $6,596 operating surplus in 2011/12, previous year result of $66,779 (BA 2012).

Participation in bowls had shown an 'increase in the numbers of participants . . . from 853,000 to 935,000 in 2011' (BA 2012: 20), up 9.6 per cent from the previous year. Although

111

impressive, these numbers are tempered by a trend towards declining membership in bowling clubs across Australia. The following club membership trends leading into the fieldwork showed:

- 234,725 members in 2,002 bowling clubs (BA 2010);
- declining to 221,052 in 1,974 clubs in 2010/11 (BA 2011);
- declining to 210,041 members in 1,961 clubs by commencement of the fieldwork (BA 2012).

The larger participation numbers reported in the annual census are attributed to the growing number of casual and recreational bowlers utilising club facilities but choosing not to avail themselves of a club membership.

After working with the BA Board (which consisted of nine directors) over a series of three workshops, it was identified that the sport was being hamstrung by an amateur culture and a lack of aspiration to grow and professionalise the sport. In what has been a fairly typical process in many national sport organisations (NSOs), the pace of change in relation to professionalisation had been slow and uneven across the sport. Frustrations expressed by directors included an inability to obtain agreement on a consistent strategy, and poor governance processes throughout the sport. The inability to consistently implement BA's preferred strategic direction by member associations was seen as a particularly frustrating impediment to good governance and the execution of a coherent strategy for bowls. At both an organisational (BA and member associations) and individual (individual directors, CEOs) level, leadership issues were apparent, with the BA Board of a view that, as the NSO, the member associations should fall into line with national strategy. This hierarchical, or position power, view of leadership has not traditionally been well received, as some of the member associations are quite strong in terms of their membership numbers, financial strength and power within the sport. Clearly, a wider base of leadership influence is required rather than relying solely on legitimate or position power to direct member association actions.

Ultimately, it was decided to use the formulation of the next strategic plan as the means to educate and influence the culture of the bowls community in relation to governance and, as it emerged, to focus on leadership styles. To commence the process, it was agreed to hold a two-day planning workshop in April 2012, in which all Presidents and CEOs of member associations would join the BA Board, senior staff and a number of other invited stakeholders representing groups including coaches, players, officials from local bowling clubs, sponsors and suppliers. As it had been agreed to formulate a plan for bowls in Australia, this workshop was an important first step in inviting member association representatives to collaborate to develop this whole-of-sport strategic plan. This was the first time such a planning workshop had been held in the sport of bowls.

STRATEGIC PLANNING WORKSHOP

Strategic planning is a process and, as was noted earlier in this chapter, its aim is to 'produce fundamental decisions and actions that shape and guide what an organization is, what it does, and why it does it' (Bryson 2011: xii). Typically, this process involves a review of market conditions, customer needs, competitive strengths and weaknesses, an environmental scan to discern prevailing economic, political, societal, technological and legal conditions impacting the sport organisation, and the availability of resources to take advantage of identified opportunities and mitigate threats. This scanning process leads to the formulation of vision and mission statements for the firm followed by organisational objectives and strategies, which ultimately cascade down to the various business units, or functional areas in a firm. Both strategic planning and management are driven by senior managers within organisations, and it is at this point that the interface between planning and leadership is noted. Strategic planning explicitly requires leaders to be the catalyst to formulate strategy, and strategic management extends the formulation process via implementation.

The bowls planning workshop essentially worked through the above key variables central to strategic planning. These variables are shown in Figure 9.1, which is also designed to highlight the importance of strategic leadership and thinking in the planning process. As you will note when studying Figure 9.1, the vertical box, with graduated shading from solid at the top to lighter shades at the bottom, captures an important concept for leaders. As was indicated earlier in this chapter, Fairholm (2009) described the importance of leaders at the strategic thinking stage of the strategic planning process. In the BA planning process, the strategic thinking stage and principal work of key organisational leaders is shown in the top half of Figure 9.1, and includes the environmental scanning (political, legal, social, technological, economic) and SWOT analysis, which stands for strengths, weaknesses, opportunities and threats. Both of these steps in the process are designed to capture external environmental influences, with the large outer oval shape denoting the environment in which bowls exists and interacts.

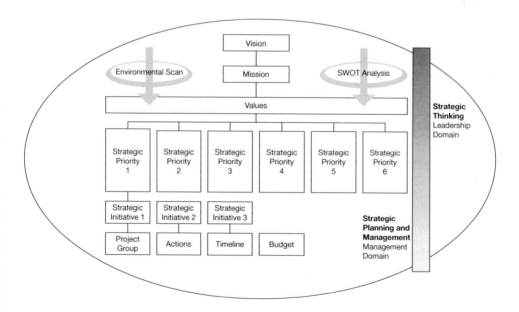

Figure 9.1 *The strategic planning process.*

Source: Adapted from Fairholm (2009).

It is at this stage that a range of information internal and external to BA was used to gain a common understanding of the forces affecting the sport of bowls. Following a review of the outcomes of the plan about to end (2008–12) and the infusion of relevant data, such as membership trends, various working groups were formed to undertake a SWOT analysis as the starting point for the workshop. The workgroups were important as they were composed of a mix of participants from different states, territories and organisations. It was also important to commence engaging BA directors and member association leaders (i.e. Presidents and CEOs) and other stakeholders with a style of collective leadership. Collectively, this group was required to connect with the higher order strategic thinking phase shown in Figure 9.1, in the hope that the collective voices would permeate back to member associations to seek engagement with the common issues identified and how they informed the vision, mission and core values.

The vision statement formulated has already been noted in the introduction to this chapter but, as yet, we have not considered what a mission and vision statement is and why they are needed. Traditional mission statements are aimed at addressing the reason for a company's existence. Typically, a firm addresses two questions: what business are we in; and what business should we be in? In the case of non-profit organisations such as BA, the mission is often referred to as a charter because the reason why the organisation exists in the first place is usually quite clear and less complex than for-profits businesses, which have more flexibility to change their product offerings, or the businesses they are in at any time. BA and its member associations exist *to grow the sport of bowls*, and that is exactly the mission statement that was eventually agreed to, although not until some months after the workshop and following considerable debate with member associations.

The use of a vision statement is particularly important in a federal sport structure where, in reality, the sport is delivered by a number of member associations and clubs across Australia. The vision, therefore, must have the potential to become a unifying feature of the plan, which is well understood across the country. The vision should be inspiring, aspirational and map out a competitive space for a sport organisation. A good vision statement should also be succinct, crisp and clear. The agreed vision for the Bowls in Australia plan, as previously noted, is: *To be the sport for life*. This vision meets the above criteria in the following ways:

- define competitive space – bowls is competing against low physical impact sports that encourage lifelong participation;
- aspirational – by using the word 'the', it is clear bowls strives to be the Number 1 sport in the sport for life category;
- inspirational – the aspiration to be Number 1 is motivating and galvanising, and the merits of the sport are easily identified by those involved;
- succinct – six words.

The final piece of the 'pure' strategic thinking stage is the formation of core values or behaviours that organisations seek to encourage. Workshop participants eventually agreed on eight core values: collaborative, professionalism, innovative, evidence-based decision making, respect and diversity, progressive, service excellence, and creating a sense of community, given the community focus of bowling clubs. The core values together with vision and mission

114

trigger leader behaviour that aims to operationalise core values for others to see and follow. Leaders continue to give ongoing meaning to vision and mission through their own voices and actions, and, significantly, by the actions or strategies a firm adopts and how they contribute to the vision and mission.

Once draft vision and mission statements were recorded, together with core values, the workshop moved to the next stage of the planning process: to identify the key strategic priority areas for bowls in Australia. As shown in Figure 9.1, identifying the strategic priorities remains grounded in strategic thinking by key organisational leaders, but, at the same time, a transition is occurring from pure leadership to managerial concern for how the priorities will align with specific strategic initiatives in each priority, and how to manage these initiatives, timelines and budget allocation. This alignment increasingly becomes the focus of strategic planning and management at the lower levels, as seen in Figure 9.1.

OUTCOMES AND IMPLICATIONS FOR LEADERSHIP

To progress the outcomes following the planning workshop, participants were challenged to identify the most meaningful way in which they could continue to contribute to the completion of the planning process, given their geographical dispersal. Completing the plan required determining the key initiatives, or objectives, in each of the six strategic priorities. To ensure the collaborative process continued, workshop participants were invited to consider the use of technology to support seven sub-groups to work on an allocated area of the plan. Six of the groups were allocated one strategic priority area each, with the seventh working through the list of draft mission and vision statements, seeking to refine them and present a sample for further discussion. Despite some initial resistance to meeting via technology such as GoToMeeting, it was agreed that it was a viable way to ensure ongoing representative input of organisational leaders, and also maintain the momentum on collaboration.

Strategic sub-groups were subsequently formed after the planning workshop, and a balance of relevant expertise and member association representation was sought, with five people allocated to each group. For the bowls community, meeting and collaborating in an environment mediated by technology was new and challenged traditional approaches that had tended to see member associations operating as isolated entities in between the one or two national meetings held each year. As Mandell and Keast (2007: 579) observed, the effectiveness of new arrangements depends on 'whether the members of a collaborative network are able to develop new processes that will lead to new ways of working, new structural arrangements and integration of the members into a new whole, which will lead to the accomplishment of innovative solutions'. Despite some early adjustment issues, directors and member associations were supportive of these new arrangements, largely based on sustaining collaborative practices to build trust through ongoing face-to-face dialogue, albeit mediated via technology. Two rounds of strategic sub-groups were conducted (between May and August, 2012), which led to the identification of strategic initiatives in each strategic priority area, actions, priority rankings, targets and deadlines.

With a full working draft of the plan, the collaborative process continued via the BA Board meeting with each of the member association boards, BA staff engagement with BA directors, and a further two meetings with the member association presidents and CEOs at the time of the annual general meeting in October 2012 and again in April 2013. The board-to-board meetings were a significant investment of time and resources by BA and it was only possible to convene four full board-to-board meetings, with the other meetings attended by the BA CEO and one or two directors. The purpose of the meetings was to allow each member association board to communicate their strategic issues, and then work through the draft Bowls in Australia plan as it stood at the time of the meeting. Typically, this involved a review of the vision, mission and six strategic priority areas and, later in the process, the evolving strategic initiatives attached to each priority area.

Although these meetings, as was the case with the planning workshop, were facilitated by a member of the research team, it provided an excellent insight into the call by Erakovic and Jackson (2012) for a stronger emphasis on ensuring leadership in, or through, governance and governance in leadership. They observed that leadership and governance scholars rarely engage with each other and contend that the reason for this lack of engagement is because 'leadership and corporate governance draw upon quite disparate roots for their guidance and inspiration – corporate governance is primarily rooted in accounting and commercial law, leadership in the disciplines of psychology and, to a lesser extent, sociology and political science' (Erakovic and Jackson 2012: 69). Moreover, the authors note the differing frames of reference each adopts when studying organisations, with governance motivated by a 'structural frame' emphasising policies and procedures (Erakovic and Jackson 2012) while leadership focuses on a 'human resources frame' emphasising people and interrelationships (Bolman and Deal 2003; Erakovic and Jackson 2012).

In our discussions of leadership, which tend to focus on individual leaders, this case analysis of BA reminds us to also think about the role of boards of directors in the leadership context. Although a form of collective leadership, in that all directors need to be working towards the same outcomes, logically, governance sets the stage for leadership at the top of an organisation. Essentially, 'good leadership can energize governance, while good governance can serve to sustain leadership' (Erakovic and Jackson 2012: 70). Governance and leadership tend to interface in three areas: 'team leadership, the chair's leadership of the board, and strategic leadership' (Erakovic and Jackson 2012: 70). Although the first two areas are important, the second – the role of the chair – highlights a quite specific leadership role. The BA case, however, demonstrated a specific example of strategic leadership, consistent with Ireland and Hitt's (1999) identification of the importance of strategic leadership.

Board directors in cooperation with the CEO must seek to exercise and apply strategic thinking on behalf of their organisation, and it explains why all the Presidents and CEOs of the member associations were invited to collaboratively contribute to formulating a whole-of-sport strategic plan. This form of collective strategic leadership is an under-researched area generally, and specifically more needs to be done in the sport organisation context to better understand the role boards fulfil in the leadership domain. One important outcome from the BA case is the extent to which a whole-of-sport approach can be maintained, once a neutral facilitator is not available to oversee the implementation. In essence, the sustainability of this approach is dependent on BA's ability to produce what Ansell and Gash (2012: 6) describe as organic leaders, 'or leaders that come from within the community of stakeholders'. This could be an individual but, in reality, it is about the BA Board and its role, and its ability to energize governance through collaborative leadership and to lead by example.

An interesting paradox to emerge from this study was the view expressed by the BA Board when identifying governance-related issues early in the study, suggesting that the member associations were largely at fault in terms of the inability to implement strategy determined by BA. The paradox in this case was noted in the hierarchical expectations of strategy implementation, but it only led to inconsistencies and resentment. Yet, when the BA Board agreed to implement a genuine collaborative approach to the strategic planning process with a view to improving governance across the sport, the member associations began to behave in a more cooperative manner. Interestingly, member associations began to afford BA the leadership they thought they should be exercising in the first place.

The style and nature of communication was also influenced, with differences expressed through open and robust discussion treated positively and seen as developing a greater understanding of the issues, and improving levels of trust and working relationships. The following responses from BA directors during evaluation interviews conducted as part of the study provide evidence of this change:

- Meetings are now much calmer and nicer. They are different meetings.
- There is more trust because people are working together. There is a perception now that BA is there to help the states.
- There's been a definite change in the relationship between BA and the states and I think a lot of that, or just about all of that, can be put down to the collaborative approach that we've taken with this project. There's a definite thawing, I suppose, of atmosphere at meetings compared to what there was, and I think a lot of that is because the states have been involved in working together.

Clearly, collaborative leadership was a key reason explaining the changing attitudes. Ansell and Gash (2012: 6) define collaborative or facilitative leadership as, 'helping others to make things happen'. When thinking of contingency theory, which recognises that there is no best way to lead, but rather leadership styles adjust to the situation, Ansell and Gash identified three leadership roles to help people make things happen. Collaborative leadership could, therefore, oscillate between the board's roles as an organisational steward, mediator and catalyst (Ansell and Gash 2012).

All three roles are important and are applicable when seeking to perform different aspects of the charter of a NSO. NSOs are, at different times, required to build social capital across the sport and facilitate outcomes, as was the case in the BA case study. Social capital outcomes as a consequence of fulfilling the role of *organisational steward* can be assessed in terms of improved levels of trust through an enhanced and common understanding of both BA and member association issues, improved working relationships and enhanced cooperation to improve governance of the sport. Improved working relationships and enhanced cooperation were a direct outcome of framing a shared vision for bowls in Australia. All these changes are consistent with cultural change sought when the BA Board agreed to implement a collaborative approach to governance. Perhaps the most important outcome, given the collaborative and facilitative approach adopted by the BA Board and member associations, was the influence on individual leadership styles which also began to move from adversarial to facilitative. This is a good example of how governance leadership can influence leader behaviour across the organisation. Although the findings from the BA case are couched in terms of collective strategic board leadership, the reality is that individual leadership styles and behaviours of board members and CEOs were also influenced.

BA, as an NSO, is also required to act as a *mediator* to arbitrate and nurture relationships between member associations, either on or off the field, and as a *catalyst* to identify value-creating opportunities, as well as to activate member associations to ensure the progressive and innovative development of bowls in Australia. Contingency theory would indicate that these three leadership roles should oscillate, depending on the situation with which BA is confronted. What remains clear from this case is that the BA Board cannot revert to an authoritarian style of leadership, which would likely see a return to previous levels of distrust and a lack of harmony. It was these issues, and the adversarial behaviours associated with these feelings, that led the BA Board to experiment with a collaborative style of leadership.

In April 2013, when the BA Board met with member association presidents and CEOs at the first of their two meetings during that year, the main focus was on the approval and adoption of the Bowls in Australia plan. Following final presentations summarising the plan and its contents, it was the purpose of this meeting to resolve whether to proceed and implement the plan scheduled to commence from 1 July 2013. When the question was put, there was unanimous agreement to adopt and implement the strategic plan for Bowls in Australia. The only subsequent discussion related to operationalising the plan, including cost-sharing arrangements for the major projects shared between BA and member associations. It was recognised that member associations required considerable lead time to factor in budget allocations for the major projects in which they would be involved. With this acknowledged and a timeline outlined in relation to operationalising the plan, all that was left was to assess how the member associations aligned their own state-based plans to the whole-of-sport plan. All agreed to this, but with changing personnel and other political and individual factors to consider, only time will answer how well-aligned each member association plan becomes, as each moves to renew their existing plans in the forthcoming 12 months.

This study of collaborative leadership and governance has demonstrated a positive response through changes described in levels of trust, respect, culture and recognition of the need for a unified vision for bowls. To maintain the momentum on this collaborative approach will require the BA Board to continue to rigorously foster collaborative leadership, and remind its member associations of what has been agreed to and how their leadership is critical in ensuring bowls becomes the sport for life. What commenced as a governance problem was ultimately grounded in leadership, with collaborative leadership demonstrating its potential to enhance governance capabilities.

SUMMARY

This chapter has introduced the strategic planning and management process, including its key component parts. It was noted that strategic planning was simply a management tool for use by senior leaders to assist with setting strategic direction. Strategic leadership and thinking were two important concepts introduced to demonstrate the importance of leaders guiding the process. High level strategic thinking, largely the domain of senior leaders, was shown to be necessary in assessing the external and internal environments, as well as aligning this information with sharply focused vision and mission statements supported by core values and key strategic priorities. This is often referred to as the visioning process, and captures higher order thinking, aiming to assess how a firm can position itself for prolonged success in its markets.

A chapter-long case study of Bowls Australia explicated how collaborative styles of leadership had the potential to re-shape governance behaviours and, indeed, individual leader behaviour. The BA case illustrated how to involve a large group of people in a strategic planning process, not just to determine key strategic directions, but also as a process to unify a sport to ensure all of its parts are implementing a consistent and coherent strategy. The power of a good vision statement was also noted, as it, through organisational leaders and their collective voice, had the power to sustain consistent implementation of strategic direction. The BA case exemplifies the importance of a collaborative culture, driven by leadership and governance in a federal sport structure in which all member associations are separate legal entities, with a history of thinking that their sole responsibility is to their geographical region. Strategic visioning, driven by strategic leaders, demonstrating strategic thinking, encapsulates the higher order leadership skills required to lead the strategic planning and management process.

REVIEW QUESTIONS

1   What is strategic planning and how is it different from strategic management?

2   What is strategic leadership and what is its role in the strategic planning process?

3   Describe the role of strategic thinking in the strategic planning process and management of sport organisations generally.

4   What is collaborative leadership and how does it relate to collaborative governance?

5   Describe the role of collaborative leadership in the Bowls Australia case, and at what level it was important.

6   In the Bowls Australia case, in what ways did collaborative leadership change governance and individual leader behaviour?

REFERENCES

Andrews, K. 1971. *The concept of corporate strategy.* Homewood, IL: Dow-Jones Irwin.
Ansell, C. and Gash, A. 2008. Collaborative governance in theory and practice. *Journal of Public Administration Research and Theory*, 18(4): 543–571.
Ansell, C. and Gash, A. 2012. Stewards, mediators and catalysts: towards a model of collaborative leadership. *The Innovation Journal: The Public Sector Innovation Journal*, 17(1): 1–21.
Ansoff, H. I. 1965. *Corporate strategy: an analytical approach to business policy for growth and expansion.* Homewood, IL: Richard D. Irwin.

119

Australian Sports Commission (ASC), 2012, *Annual report 2011/12*, Australian Government Printing Press, Canberra.

Bolman, L. G. and Deal, T. E. 2003. *Reframing organizations: artistry, choice, and leadership.* San Francisco, CA: John Wiley & Sons.

Bowls Australia (BA). 2010, Annual reports 2009/10, Bowls Australia, Melbourne.

Bowls Australia (BA). 2011, Annual reports 2010/11, Bowls Australia, Melbourne.

Bowls Australia (BA). 2012, Annual report 2011/12, Bowls Australia, Melbourne.

Bryson, J. M. 2011. *Strategic planning for public and non-profit organizations.* 4th edn. San Francisco, CA: Jossey-Bass.

Chandler, A. S. 1962. *Strategy and structure.* Garden City, NY: Doubleday.

Crosby, B. C. and Bryson, J. M. 2005. *Leadership for the common good: tackling public problems in a shared-power world.* San Francisco, CA: Jossey-Bass.

Drucker, P. F. 1946. *Concept of the corporation.* New York: John Day & Co.

Erakovic, L. and Jackson, B. 2012. Promoting leadership in governance and governance in leadership: towards a supportive research agenda, in A. Davila, M. Elvira, J. Ramirez, L. Zapata-Cantu (eds) *Understanding organizations in complex, emergent and uncertain environments.* Basingstoke: Palgrave Macmillan: 68–83.

Fairholm, M. R. 2009. Leadership and organizational strategy. *The Innovation Journal: The Public Sector Innovation Journal,* 14(1): 1–16.

Ferkins, L., Shilbury, D. and McDonald, G. 2009. Board involvement in strategy: advancing the governance of sport organizations. *Journal of Sport Management,* 23(3): 245–277.

Ireland, D. R. and Hitt, M. A. 1999. Achieving and maintaining strategic competitiveness in the 21st century: the role of strategic leadership. *Academy of Management Executive,* 13(1): 43–57.

Mandell, M. and Keast, R. 2007. Evaluating network arrangements: towards revised performance measures. *Public Performance and Management Review,* 30(4): 574–597.

Marx, T. G. 2013. Teaching leadership and strategy. *Business Education Journal,* 5(2): 12–19.

Mintzberg, H. 1973. *The nature of managerial work.* New York: Harper & Row.

Montgomery, C. A. 2012. *The strategist: be the leader your business needs.* New York: HarperCollins.

Rumelt, R. P., Schendel, D. E. and Teece, D. J. 1994. Fundamental issues in strategy, in A. Davila, M. Elvira, J. Ramirez, L. Zapata-Cantu (eds) *Fundamental issues in strategy: a research agenda.* Boston, MA: Harvard Business School Press: 9–54.

Shilbury, D. 2012. Competition: the heart and soul of sport management. *Journal of Sport Management,* 26(1): 1–10.

Chapter 10

Leading organisational change

Lesley Ferkins, Ljiljana Erakovic and
Judith McMorland

CHAPTER OBJECTIVES

After completing this chapter you should be able to:

1   explain the drives of change that have impacted the way sport organisations are led;
2   discuss the relationship between processes of professionalisation and commercialisation
    and sport organisation leadership;
3   describe and apply the stages of the Common Good Organisation (CGO) Development
    Model in relation to a sport organisation;
4   analyse how the CGO Development Model highlights the transition challenges for sport
    organisation leaders.

KEY TERMS

- professionalisation
- commercialisation
- CGO Development Model
- affiliates

INTRODUCTION

Sport sector organisations are not alone in their challenge to embrace a rapidly changing environment. Change is everywhere and in all sectors of contemporary organisational life with many commentators pointing to the pervasive nature of technology contributing as a primary driver (Kotter 2012; Scharmer and Kaufer 2013). Change is also not a new phenomenon. Sport organisations have been evolving since their inception. Many national and international governing bodies as we know them today were created in the late 1800s, and we have seen much innovation in the way sport is organised, led and delivered since this time. Perhaps the most well-known example is the International Olympic Committee (IOC), founded in 1894, which staged its first major event in 1896 (summer Olympics in Athens). In tracking its evolution since inception, the IOC can be considered an example of an organisation that has predicted, embraced and adapted to environmental change (Toohey and Veal 2007). At once an historical, perhaps conservative organisation, proud of its traditions and history, the IOC leadership has appeared to steer the modern Olympic Games and the Olympic Movement through many political, technological, socio-cultural and economic challenges (see Toohey and Veal 2007 for a comprehensive account of this evolution). It is this ability to adapt that has enabled the IOC and its showpiece Olympic Games to continue to survive and thrive amidst turbulent societal change.

Cohen (2009) attributed the quote, 'The best way to predict the future is to create it' to Peter Drucker, in his text *Drucker on Leadership*. Although the origin of the quote is contested, the Drucker attributed statement points toward the role of those who champion change. In many instances this has been the assigned leaders of the organisations (i.e. the board, CEO and senior management). Where sport organisations have radically reformed, it has been the board and CEO who have been the face of this change (Ferkins and Shilbury 2010). It is a well-accepted notion that organisational change is inextricably linked to leadership. Scharmer and Kaufer (2013: 3), in their book *Leading from the Emerging Future*, consider that the 'ability to shift from reacting against the past to leaning into and presencing an emerging future is probably the single most important leadership capacity today'. They go on to say that leadership capacity is 'critical in situations of disruptive change, not only for institutions and systems, but also for teams and individuals' (2013: 3).

Thus, we can conclude that leadership is indeed a 'bed-fellow' of change, but what kind of leadership is needed for what kind of change? Kotter (2012), a seminal author on leading change, argued that the twenty-first century businesses must overcome a culture of being 'over-managed' and 'under-led'. He also argued that, 'as the act of management deals largely with the status quo and the act of leading mostly deals with change, in the next century we are going to have to try to become much more skilled at creating leaders' (Kotter, 2012: 45). How well has the sport sector embraced notions of leadership? What do we know about leadership in sport?

The complementary chapters to this in the present text explore this question, and in so doing offer a much needed contribution to the conversation on the leadership of sport. This particular chapter focuses on the link between leadership and change within sport organisations. We begin with summarising what we consider to be the key drivers of sport sector change, drawing a relationship between these key drives and sport organisation leadership. We then offer a framework of thinking (the CGO Development Model) for sport organisation leaders and 'students' of sport leadership, grounded in the notion that leadership is about facilitating and developing capacity in organisations and capability of people. Developed outside of the sport sector, this framework offers a new lens through which to view the transitions challenges sport organisation leaders have faced and are currently facing. We also draw relevance between this framework and the nuances of the sport sector, demonstrating the highly applicable and instructive nature of the framework.

EVOLVING LANDSCAPE: DRIVERS OF SPORT SECTOR CHANGE

In specifically considering the sport sector, many authors agree that a pivotal contemporary issue in driving organisational change has been the professionalisation and commercialisation of the sector. By this, we mean the recent transition from amateurism and a largely volunteer 'workforce' running sport organisations to the payment of players and the funding of organisations to enable paid staff (as also variously described in previous chapters). Shilbury and Ferkins (2011: 110) captured this sentiment in their article on professionalisation and sport governance in stating:

> Although sport remains a 'pastime' for the bulk of the population, its management is no longer grounded in this pastime. Paradoxically, a key success factor for the management of sport is the ability to retain its play like features, yet deliver it in an increasingly professional manner. Therefore, governance, as the direction-setting mechanism in organisations, is the pivotal process around which leisure and business cultures must be created and co-exist.

In employing a governance lens through which to explore the transition process toward professionalisation, Shilbury and Ferkins highlighted the tensions evident for the organisations' strategic leaders, the board and CEO, and their central role in leading change. Their work also reinforces the socio-cultural context within which sport organisations operate. In other words, the so-called evolution toward commercial, business-like entities that present an entertainment product is tempered with the values and traditions of sport as a social good (Hassan and Hamil 2010). Indeed, many sport organisations around the globe remain not-for-profit entities charged with commercial imperatives to 'grow the game' as well as offer a 'social good' to the communities from which they have grown and to whom they serve.

In reinforcing this notion, Hassan and Hamil (2010: 344) argued that there is an important 'current debate surrounding to which realm – social, economic/commercial or political – sport truly belongs'. In their work on the changing nature of football governance the authors analysed a commentary by Michel Platini, then President of UEFA (the governing body of European football) who they considered, threw 'into sharp relief an age-old argument in the history of organized sporting activity, the encroachment of commercial forces into sport' (2010: 344). Of Platini's comments, Hassan and Hamil (2010: 345) considered that 'he was also concerned with how to manage these forces without losing something potentially very valuable – sport's wider contribution to the social and cultural "balance sheet" of society'. Arguably, it is the challenge of commercial and professional forces that is the central driver of change for sport organisations, and the central challenge for those enacting leadership within many sport organisations around the globe (Dowling, Edwards and Washington, 2014).

In searching for new thinking, to assist leaders of sport organisations navigate change processes in light of these drivers of change, we followed the approach by McMorland and Erakovic (2013) who have addressed the issues of management, leadership and governance in not-for-profit organisations by creating the CGO Development Model. The model weaves together organisational stages of development; different levels of work that organisations build on; and key factors of their development pathway. More importantly, the model addresses the *transitional* challenges (internal and external) that sport organisations are likely to encounter as they progress through development stages. In this, the model highlights the establishment of formal management systems (a transition from voluntary associations to agencies) and strategic governance (positioning of the agency within the sector).

In the use of the model, we also take the position that leadership occurs in many places across the organisation and indeed the sport sector which includes but is not limited to the assigned leaders (i.e. CEO, board). This approach is supported by Northouse (2007) who views leadership as a process that involves influence within a group context. In the sport setting, Kihl *et al.* (2010) also argue for the need to explore leadership as a phenomenon experienced by people within a group as distinct from the more common 'leader-centric' approach to understanding leadership. In the following sections, we present the development stages typical of many sport organisations (mostly in reference to sport codes and national sport organisations) where leadership is entwined in these major stages of change.

MODEL OF ORGANISATIONAL DEVELOPMENT: BUILDING BLOCKS

The CGO Development Model (McMorland and Erakovic 2013) comprises three conceptual building blocks:

1   the five stages of development, which present movement across time;
2   the five levels of work, which delineate organisational complexity; and
3   the five key factors that organisations need to pay attention to at each of the stages.

The five stages of development help us understand the importance of the sport organisation's history and memory, and point to how the purpose for which the sport organisation was established, gets reinterpreted and re-enacted in different times and in response to changing external factors. Consider, for example, the case of rugby union, which underwent a momentous change in 1995 when its world governing body (the then IRB) announced that the game would become 'professional'. The resulting impacts of this decision have been felt by national and state/regional rugby organisations around the world since. It has been argued, unsurprisingly, that professionalisation forces were at work well before this date, and in fact led to this insurmountable pressure for such a decision to be made (Ferkins *et al.* 2013). In this way, movement into a new stage is often well under way before we really notice that significant change is already occurring.

The Levels of Work model developed by Jaques and Clement (1991) shows what new work is required as complexity for the sport organisation increases. In the case of national

124

rugby union organisations this complexity included increased staffing, player payments, new competition design, commodification and commercialisation of it products and services, and global reach, for example, as new income from broadcast rights flowed into the game. This concept of work refers to the range of responsibilities carried by people charged with delivering results over different time frames. The longer the time span, the greater are the cognitive abilities required to handle the increased levels of complexity and intention. The first three levels of work are operational, while the work at higher levels is strategic in its focus. Management and governance tasks at different stages of organisational development are distinguished by the challenges these stages pose and the sorts of work that are required if these challenges are to be met successfully (Jaques and Clement 1991). As complexity increases at each stage and qualitatively new work is required to meet the demands of that stage, so changes are needed in both capacity (form, policy, practices) and the capability of individuals who contribute to the organisation processes (McMorland 2005; Stamp 1990).

Organisational arrangements develop through the dynamic interplay of *capabilities of individuals* involved in management, leadership and governance processes, *organisational capacity* – structures and processes that support various organisational arrangements, appropriate *composition* of skills and resources, *complexity* of organisational work, and the political, social and economic *context* in which an organisation acts. Capability, capacity, composition, complexity and context (5Cs) are five key concepts that organisations need to pay attention to as they transition through the stages of development (McMorland and Erakovic, 2013).

Taken together, the three building blocks provide a powerful and practical tool for considering how sport organisations might change and, therefore, how leadership and acts of leadership (assigned leaders and anyone influencing group processes) within sport organisation might steer this change process. Stages of development give an idea about organisational evolution, levels of work point out the work required as organisations become more complex, and the 5Cs provide the content of transitions from one stage to another (see Figure 10.1).

The next sections explain the application of the model to three transitional stages in which organisations change from voluntary associations to agencies with strategic goals, showing the impact of each new level of work, and how the 5Cs apply at each stage. In so doing, it offers for sport organisation leadership a sense of a distinct evolutionary path (i.e. an understanding of where the organisation has come from, and therefore greater perception of its future).

FROM ASSOCIATION TO AGENCY: CHALLENGES AND COMPLEXITIES

Employment of staff, and the development of tiers of managerial responsibility, signals a fundamental shift in a traditionally not-for-profit, voluntary based sport organisation. Billis (2010) explains this as the transition from *association* to *agency*. For Billis, the term *association* refers to organisations that are predominantly volunteer-determined. In contrast, the term *agency* identifies not-for-profit organisations where responsibility for the operation is devolved to a manager by the voluntary responsible body (Managing Committee or Board) and service provision is predominantly by paid staff. While many national sport organisations are often referred to as associations because they represent a collection of separate but affiliated organisations (e.g. among its affiliates, Tennis New Zealand has six regional entities), the

CGO Development Model					Level of Work	5Cs Major emphasis
				Charting New Waters/ Elaborating	5 New directions, purposeful intent	Capacity Capability Composition Context Complexity
			Leading/ Governing		4 Innovation, change and continuity	Capacity Capability Composition Context Complexity
		Becoming More Productive/ Managing			3 Effective work practice, system and productivity	Capacity Collective capability Composition Context Complexity
	Getting Established/ Organising				2 Effective coordination, collective improvement and efficiency	Capacity Individual capability Composition Context Complexity
Founding/Forming					1 Purposeful activity and service contribution	Capacity Capability Composition Context Complexity

Figure 10.1 Linking stages of development, levels of work and 5Cs.

Source: authors' own.

distinction made by Billis (2010) is useful in the context of an evolutionary view of organisation change. For many sport organisations that have undergone this very change (i.e. introduction of paid employees) over the last 40–50 years, this process has brought about both benefits and challenges. Many sport organisations have retained elements of their earlier voluntarism in frontline roles such as events support, coaching or competition management work, and/or at a strategic level on boards and committees. Kikulis *et al.* (1995: 136) capture this evolution in the context of Canadian national sport organisations:

> Historically, NSOs in Canada were small and independent associations that organized national championships and enforced rules governing the membership and competitions of their particular sport. Under the direction of volunteer executive members, this period of autonomous and fundamentally unstructured sport delivery, which for most NSOs began in the late 19th and early 20th centuries, continued

uninterrupted until the 1970s. It was at this time that the Canadian amateur sport delivery system entered a new period of evolutionary growth. In large part, the trigger for this shift was the *Report of the Task Force on Sports for Canadians* that identified the sorry state of the administrative and technical programs for sport in Canada and called for NSOs to improve their operations (Department of National Health and Welfare). As Macintosh *et al.* (1987) have documented, the recommendations made in the task force report gave the federal government the impetus for more direct involvement in the Canadian amateur sport delivery system and in particular the development of NSOs.

Employing a manager and assigned leader is a major step in the life of any organisation. It signals a new set of relationships and also new responsibilities for enacting mission. When staff members are employed, 'membership' and 'ownership' of the organisation changes. Responsibility for the expression of mission shifts from volunteers to 'stewards' paid to provide service. There are numerous examples of this within each sport code, where this has occurred at international, national, state/regional and then local level. The work of Kikulis *et al.* (1995), Kikulis (2000) and Amis *et al.* (2004) present the story of these transition processes within Canadian national sport organisations. In investigating change processes of six Canadian national sport organisations over a 12-year period, Amis *et al.* (2004: 158) conclude:

> Results showed that NSOs that completed the transformation possessed leadership with the technical and behavioural capacity for change, had an organizational structure in which volunteers were willing to share power with professional staff, and engaged in an all-encompassing transformation process that embraced the entire organization. By contrast, those NSOs that failed to complete the changed lacked effective transformation leadership, had a structure in which power was retained centrally by volunteer board members, and were characterized by ongoing struggles among subunits to protect their own interests.

Furthermore, when agencies become more dependent on external contracts they have to demonstrate their compliance with standards of service, health and safety, and employment regulations, as well as their financial transparency. As a result, they lose the freedoms of a purely voluntary association and take on aspects of fully fledged, productive organisations that are accountable for their actions. This is evident in many of the Commonwealth countries around the globe where there is strong government involvement and funding of the sport system (e.g. Canada, Australia, UK, New Zealand). In New Zealand, for example, Sport New Zealand is the peak body (Crown Agency) through which government 'investment' flows to national sport organisations. This funding relationship brings with it increased expectations of organisational performance (including 'on-field' results and participant involvement), accountability and transparency.

Managers as leaders. The range of work a newly appointed manager and leader undertakes depends on the size and complexity of the organisation and on the contribution that the responsible governance body continues to make. In the transition phase from the association to agency, some roles can become 'over-developed', such as the GM/CEO taking too much responsibility and, at the same time, long-serving board members can get stuck in the historical legacy rather than the future of their organisation. Over-developed roles can lead to rigidity in thought and action. The past, rather than the future is entrenched, and this can lead ultimately to organisational decline (McMorland and Erakovic 2013). In recounting the story of New Zealand Football's quest to develop board strategic capability, Ferkins, Shilbury and McDonald (2009) capture the issue of over-developed roles. In this, the board and the CEO worked to develop a model shared leadership to reduce an over dominance by the CEO and create greater board involvement in strategy development for the organisation.

The CGO Development Model is useful for identifying the capacity and capability required at this level of work. However, if the organisation lacks the resources to support this development, a manager may not necessarily be able to work at the level required. Trying to do everything with insufficient resources becomes frustrating, stressful and counter-productive. This is the plight of many not-for-profit sport organisations as they struggle to achieve sufficient scale to be efficient as well as effective. The paradox is that organisations are unlikely to achieve this scale without Level 3 leadership (General Manager level), leaving early managers in a vulnerable position. Consequently, frequent turnover for those in paid management and leadership positions within national and state/regional sport organisations has been acknowledged as a concern by various commentators (Leberman et al. 2012).

To make a successful transition from a voluntary association to agency, managers working at Level 3 need to be appropriately supported by staff working at operational levels (Levels 1 and 2). A general manager in a small sport organisation, with minimal staff, is frequently required to do everything to the detriment of their main work: from setting the budget, negotiating with sponsors, appointing coaching staff and overseeing competitions to relating to the board and talking with media. This might be the current reality for state/regional sport organisations, whereas this description represents the reality of many national sport organisations some 40 years ago (see Slack and Hinings, 1987).

Volunteers. Volunteers who, prior to changes in ways of working, have been used to a high level of autonomy may resent the intrusion of managerial control. Volunteers may have unreasonable expectations of what the manager will do for them. With a focus on their own (Level 1) work, they may not understand wider organisational constraints. Conversely, they may not accept the legitimacy of the manager's right to control their work. They may feel that their voluntary contribution is no longer valued and resent pressures to align voluntary efforts with the organisation's main values. It is therefore important for managers to make explicit their expectations of volunteers' roles, to affirm that voluntary work contributes to the overall mission, and to demonstrate how that meshes in with the work of paid staff. The embedded nature of volunteer control was reported on in the previously mentioned work of Kikulis et al. (1995: 150) on reforms in Canadian national sport organisations. They found that in the time period of their study, 'the pressures from the Canadian government for a professional bureaucratic form of organization were not strong enough to destabilize the structural inertia that had built up around the traditions of volunteer control of NSOs'.

Board. As also found by Kikulis et al. (1995), the developmental step between the association and agency is a big one for the board. When board members decide to divest themselves of operational work by taking on paid management staff, they are still guardians of the organisation's mission. While they may think they are devolving tasks, this major step, in fact, creates new responsibilities for board members. The informality of earlier stages is replaced by a formal obligation on the part of the board to be a good employer, and to work within the terms of a legally enforceable employment contract.

There are a number of reasons why the impact of this transition may be problematic. First, when the authority for operational affairs is handed over to the manager, it is not easy for a group of people (a board or committee) that used to be in charge to let go of responsibility in favour of an employee (usually an outsider) and afford them sufficient scope to make the job their own. Second, the board needs to take a big step up in the level of its work. In order to provide effective leadership, once a manager has taken over operations the board has to work at a level above the capability of the manager – in effect, leapfrogging from effective coordination to innovation, change and continuity. Third, the board needs a new set of capabilities. The skills, knowledge and general capabilities required of the responsible body going forward are not the same skills, knowledge and activities that brought the organisation to this point. This point of transition needs to be recognised and may require appointment of new people to the board. Fourth, the role of the board itself is also subject to a major change, shifting its identity from an organising or managing committee to a responsible governing body.

If the board does not develop adequate criteria to choose people appropriate for the new governance work required of them, old patterns of recruitment (friends, 'old boys network' or available volunteers) often prevail and the appropriate transition falters. There are numerous examples of this situation in the work of sport governance researchers who have studied national sport organisations in Canada, Australia, New Zealand and the UK since the 1990s to the present day (e.g. Auld and Godbey 1998; Ferkins et al. 2009; Hoye 2006; Hoye and Cuskelly 2003; Inglis 1994, 1997; Shilbury 2001; Shilbury and Ferkins 2011; Shilbury et al. 2013; Taylor and O'Sullivan 2009). After a two-year study with three national sport organisations boards in New Zealand, Shilbury and Ferkins (2011: 108) 'highlight the challenges associated with volunteer board engagement, given the increasing demands for strategic thinking and action, while also balancing this task with the conformance, policy and operation roles'. Of these challenges, the researchers also argue these tensions are evidence of sport's transition from a volunteer-driven and amateur pastime to a more professional and business-like sector.

In summary, according to the McMorland and Erakovic (2013) model, it is the manager as leader's responsibility to build up organisational capacity so that staff and volunteers of the sport organisation work at an appropriate level. Clear role descriptions are a crucial part of capacity building, providing structure and certainty for the organisation as new ways of working are adopted. It is important to develop good systems and practices and high standards of work, and to comply with statutory obligations. Planning for a two- to three-year time frame is more difficult if the context is uncertain. Maintaining strong links with stakeholders is essential for support and community recognition. Sustainability depends on the ongoing engagement of the board and management, and increasing capacity and capability at all levels.

FROM GOVERNING BY DOING TO STRATEGIC GOVERNANCE

The leadership of the organisation shifts as management takes responsibility for operational matters. The role of the governing body has to change and a new partnership has to evolve with management. In following the McMorland and Erakovic (2013) model, the work of the board at Stage 4 is to: champion a vision of the organisation, envision the desired future for the next three to five years, define the most effective direction and bring the organisation safely through any hazards met on the way. In this, the model recognises that good governance relies on good management: the partnership between management and board requires an equal level of capacity and capability on both sides. Capacity provides the appropriate structures and processes to ensure that separation of responsibilities can occur; capability determines the quality of the governance that will result.

As an organisation becomes more complex, so its capacity needs to grow. Ideally, the sport organisation's capacity needs to match the increasingly complex set of require-ments demanded by its stakeholder, such as members/affiliates, spectators/fans, players/athletes, casual participants, funders/sponsors, media and government. Developing the governance function is one of the most effective ways to do this, significantly adding to an organisation's capacity. The mark of a board's strategic capability is the questions it asks – of the CEO, of itself and of its organisation's environment. According to the work of McMorland and Erakovic (2013), many not-for-profit boards think that strategic planning addresses these questions, but they may work without a deep enough understanding of the issues to be addressed.

In studying national sport organisations in New Zealand, Ferkins and Shilbury (2012) explored what meaning board members attached to the concept of 'strategic capability'. They found four elements that 'served as reference points in mapping out the meaning of a strategically able board' (2012: 67). These were categorised as the need to have capable people on the board, a frame of reference (i.e. organisation strategy/strategic direction), facilitative board processes that allowed for board involvement in strategic design, and facilitative regional relationships with its members/affiliates. This study and others that investigated how boards of national sport organisations develop their strategic capability (Ferkins and Shilbury 2010; Shilbury and Ferkins 2011) exemplify a strong relevance of the model presented by McMorland and Erakovic (2013) for national sport organisations in the current era.

McMorland and Erakovic (2013) emphasise the ability to read the signals of change and the courage to take responsive strategic action as the key challenges for boards as their organisations move into the future. Strategic actions should be based on the critical analysis and evaluation of options for action, not on planning, which is more about implementation. In this, boards risk moving too quickly into implementation before they have established the rationale for their choice of action.

'Knowing the organisation's capabilities well enough to think deeply enough about its strategic direction' promotes 'governance as leadership' (Chait et al. 2005). This concept of 'governance as leadership' is a key idea for boards to grasp as they formulate strategy at this stage. To develop effective strategy, board members need to step up as organisational leaders. Stakeholders expect boards to actively represent and respond on behalf of their agencies, and to engage in strategic thinking and create the future for their organisations. These expectations demonstrate a radical shift in focus from the orthodox components of governance (control and monitoring) to its more powerful facets (partnership and involvement). In this respect, good leadership can energise governance, while good governance can serve to sustain leadership (Erakovic and Jackson, 2012).

Chait and colleagues (2005) created a framework to address and explain what governance as leadership involved. They identify three modes of governing, 'all created equal', that make up the work of a board when it is involved in governance as leadership.

Fiduciary stewardship. Many boards interpret fiduciary stewardship as financial monitoring and compliance, taking oversight of financial affairs and performance as their central governance responsibility. It is more than this. It is not just about money but the mission as well as the resource to promote it. Chait *et al.* (2005) use the concept in this wider sense, suggesting that a fiduciary responsibility is to ensure the effective and efficient use of assets and resources, to set policy (across a range of factors) and to assess the effectiveness of programmes/outputs that the agency produces.

Many boards get stuck at a low level of understanding of financial accountability. One temptation for business people on boards is to do more of what they ordinarily do – that is default to behaviours that are familiar in other contexts, including busying themselves over management decisions, questioning the integrity of reports presented or the prudence of financial decisions, rather than inquiring into the deeper issues of appropriate resource allocation. The role of 'strategic thinker' is under-developed if it relates solely to financial matters. If the first step in financial management is to get accuracy of records, then the board's role is to identify the implications of financial trends for the longer term, against criteria of mission integrity and organisational sustainability. Management often plays a crucial role in guiding boards to this wider role.

The notion of *fiduciary stewardship* moves a board beyond transactional accounting into the broader questions of strategic intent. What is the mission of the sport organisation? Why was it established? Is the desire to become commercially successful the only fulfilment of its mission or is there a broader social good aspiration?

Strategic partnership with management. The second leadership challenge for boards – the strategic mode – necessitates a partnership with management, as though responsibility for strategic direction ultimately rests with the board; at a practical level, boards do not know enough of the detail of organisational life to integrate present work with future direction. This is why Chait *et al.* (2005) state that a board needs intelligent questions, not excellent answers. Such questions must be related to strategic priorities. The answers will arise from two-way communications with different stakeholders. Mutual confidence in the partnership between management and the board takes time to develop. As noted above in the Ferkins *et al.* (2009) study, the Football New Zealand board identified shared leadership between the CEO as a critical element in developing the board's strategic capability. Outcomes from that study demonstrated that, in order to create shared leadership, the board needed to become more involved in designing the strategic direction of the organisation; they needed a 'frame of reference' that they had been involved in developing in order to step up and truly play a role in questioning and guiding the CEO.

Generative work. The driving forces behind strategic choice are the vision, mission and values of the organisation. Such choices are much deeper than the setting of policies for others to enact. This is the place of leadership. Collectively, a board provides, on the basis of their attachment to deep values and meanings, and in order to protect the integrity of the mission of the organisation, the template for future development. This leadership provides the mindful, explicit, statement of intentionality. Malcolm Speed, former CEO of the International

131

Cricket Council (ICC) recounted his governance experience, which spanned a 30-year period within Australian basketball, cricket, and with the ICC in Shilbury *et al.* (2013). In this he signals the place of leadership within multiple board room situations – many of which were highly adversarial – in order to protect the integrity of the mission of the organisation (also see Speed, 2011).

In the McMorland and Erakovic (2013) model, prerequisites to the generative governance mode are a healthy partnership between management and board, with well-matched organisational and individual capabilities, and enough people capable of addressing the complexity of greater uncertainty. Governance and leadership at this level are challenged to look beyond medium-term concerns of two–three years toward a bigger picture, a more distant horizon, a bigger goal.

If the previous stage (which focused on strategic development) was about making choices among alternative scenarios, the generative work (where the theme of work is strategic intent) challenges an organisation to seek new expressions of its bedrock mission. Board members may not have the deep knowledge that staff members have of how to translate deep vision into action, but they need to have an understanding of the value premises that underpin *organisational purpose*. Boards need to determine where the organisation stands on certain values and how far they would go in change efforts to bring about the objectives they have.

The generative mode has the power to invigorate the foundational mission and transform it appropriately for the context of the present and the anticipated future. At what point do the organisational actions require board members to revisit their analysis of the organisational purpose, and challenge their strategic intentions? What does it take for a national sport organisation to transform itself from appealing to those who like to play the sport to seeing the potential of sport to become a promoter of the community development? When do the ethical boundaries of action become evident (such as a refusal to seek funding from gambling derived sources)?

To conclude this section, the first transition from governance-by-doing to strategic governance involves the differentiation of governance from management and the setting of clear strategic direction by the responsible governance body. This meant letting go of operational matters now entrusted to management staff, and looking forwards and outwards to the long-term welfare and sustainability of the organisation. The board is challenged to give strategic direction, developed within the collective capability of its own structures and changes in the environment and within the organisation itself. The crafting of strategy was seen to require a healthy partnership between board and management.

BUILDING STRATEGIC IDENTITY AND MAKING STRATEGIC CHOICES

To adapt to more radical changes an organisation must undertake research and environmental scanning, exercise due diligence in the search for new opportunities, make prudent assessment of risk, and use considerable strategic imagination, leadership and courage to go beyond the readily known. Such change requires exploring what their 'strategic identity' might be in these wider places. Making these judgements is Level 5 work. Level 5 work is about providing strategic imagination for the future – a future that embraces five to ten years, and beyond, and shifts the organisation's perspective about its contribution and influence from the local to the societal level. It is about building generative capacity and capability, and working creatively with the complexity that inevitably, and necessarily, emerges. There is much evidence to suggest that national sport organisations, in particular, operate at this level of complexity (Ferkins and Shilbury 2010; Hoye and Doherty 2011; Shilbury and Ferkins 2011; Taylor and O'Sullivan 2009).

Sport organisations may adapt to increasing complexity by becoming more centralised, or may choose to diversify in order to respond to the specific needs and aspirations of their members and wider community. Responses may also involve developing a wider range of services, appealing to different audiences or forming relationships with other organisations, in the sector, at a national or international level. McMorland and Erakovic (2013) have identified three major strategic approaches that represent options for sport organisations to implement in response to more radical change: structural, relational and entrepreneurial.

In this instance, structural change encompasses both change to a single sport organisation entity (e.g. structural change to UK Sport, the government agency) or structural change to a sport code within a particular country, which involves a network or system of affiliated organisations. Examples of structural change of this nature include Tennis New Zealand, which reduced its regional affiliates from 25 to six, and Touch Australia, which attempted to collapse its state affiliates into one national body (see Ferkins and Shilbury 2010; Shilbury and Kellett 2006). The transitional challenges demonstrated by Tennis New Zealand and Touch Australia are to find and sustain governance capability at a national strategic level (Level 5 work), and to create the strong united voice needed to address changes at national and international levels.

On the ground this means that the governing body's composition must be able to provide the skills needed for Level 5 work. The branches and affiliates need to feel they have continued importance in creating momentum for change throughout the whole organisation. And the branch and affiliate boards need to be willing to embrace a new way of working, where the benefits of collective action (and the part that each branch and affiliate plays in that) are seen.

National sport organisations face an additional dilemma related to their high performance athletes (some of which are professional athletes). Increased complexity arises when the demands of recreational participants (club members and amateurs) and high performance athletes (amateurs and professionals) within the same national body require different organisational arrangements. The challenge is how to hold these components together; how to retain a single organisational identity, and the value of community reputation and outreach, while at the same time having the flexibility needed to meet the needs of high performance and professional sport at the national and international level. What structural arrangements can such organisations adopt to enable this? An example of this is the recent changes taking place within rugby union. In response to the announcement by the International Rugby Board that the game would become professional in 1995, the New Zealand Rugby Union (NZRU) continued to control licences to its 'Super Rugby' franchises. This meant that its affiliates as not-for-profit bodies held those licences. However, in 2013, the NZRU offered the opportunity for its Super Rugby franchises to involve private shareholdings that has resulted in some franchises structurally separating from the regional affiliate (e.g. in 2013, the Auckland Blues became a separate commercial entity from the Auckland Rugby Union and comprises 40 per cent private shareholding and 60 per cent affiliate).

Disruptive change of this nature is generative. In the deliberate process of radical change, purpose and intention drive the search for the appropriate capacity and composition (structural components) for action. For the generative work to develop, board members should have the ability to understand complexity in relationships among different parts of the system and the ability to juggle information three-dimensionally and consequentially: across different time frames and levels of input. In other words, they should be able to make strategic choices in congruence with the organisation's values and mission (Bradshaw, 2009). These choices call for more proactive change agendas and evaluation of the congruence between what an organisation advocates to be and what it actually is.

Relational strategies in this instance include management and governance efforts to step outside the organisational boundaries and develop mutual interests with commercial enterprises, governmental agencies and other sport organisations. This strategic approach accommodates individual and organisational needs for cooperation, collaboration and partnership, as a means of responding to challenges in complex situations and of building a more effective organisation.

One way in which synergies can work across organisations is in shared infrastructure (capacity elements), for example, multi-use facilities or the 'Sports House' concept adopted in many Commonwealth countries to house national sport organisations who share resources. Although there might be some closeness between the agencies involved, competition for funding might undermine their ability to work cooperatively. Some sport organisations forge deliberate relationships with commercial and other organisations from their communities. When this happens, organisation leadership invests time in building *strong community partnerships* in order to bring longer term benefits, or provide support to new endeavours (e.g. new events, facility development).

The intention behind relationship building of this kind needs to be explicit and valued by all the organisations concerned. The return on such 'investments' may be difficult to determine in the short term, but it is undoubtedly an important component of the social capital of organisations. In New Zealand, a major relational strategy has occurred in the collaboration of university, government, philanthropic and commercial entities, together with the government sport agency, and national sport organisations to design and develop a multi-million dollar community and high performance sport facility. This major initiative that has become the hub of high performance sport in New Zealand may not have been possible had the organisations not come together in a relation strategy for collective action (see www.AUTMillennium.co.nz).

ENTREPRENEURIAL ACTIVITIES

For many national sport organisations it is a major strategic imperative to become more financially independent from government funding (and influences). Organisations may engage in a variety of activities to achieve this. When organisations embrace the idea that they have to be more commercially or entrepreneurially focused, two issues arise: the first concerns alignment of business and mission values and the second alignment with stakeholder aspirations.

Entrepreneurial activities have the potential to transform not-for-profit sport organisations from agencies to quasi-businesses. Strategically, this requires developing new capacity (through generation of financial and social capital) and becoming more economically savvy. This, in turn, requires more elaborate infrastructure and new types of capability (economic analysis, risk-management and business acumen) in the board and senior management alike. It is the responsibility of leadership to ensure that these business activities stay aligned to core organisational purpose. Mission-drift can too easily occur: if organisational resources get unduly absorbed into making money, means become ends in themselves.

Furthermore, the organisation leaders need to address several other important issues. First, the board needs to seriously consider appropriate organisational arrangements for commercial activities. Typically, new commercial endeavours are unfamiliar territory for most board members, creating a real danger that the board will be swept along by an enthusiastic CEO. To fulfil its duties, a board has to assess carefully the additional or redeployed capacity and capability needed for these activities, and the associated risks. Second, the board and management should find the best way to 'sell' the need for changes in ways of working and funding to diverse stakeholders. It is very important to hold credibility with current organisational members and supporters while at the same time satisfy the needs of commercial partners.

The success of entrepreneurial strategies depends on the strength of the alignment between the values and mission of the shareholder and those of the business-development component of the organisation. Robust governance and management is a prerequisite for financial elaboration. Many revenue-generating activities are established quite pragmatically, without taking into account their sustainability or long-term implications for the organisations' capacity and capability. While new initiatives are potentially lucrative, they are never cost or effort neutral. Appropriate structures and processes have to be in place to ensure initiatives provide real added value. Cricket Australia, for example, has joined many other cricket organisations around the globe (e.g. Indian Premier League) in redesigning its core product to appeal to broadcasters, fans (gate and merchandise sales) and participants with a recent product being the 'T20 Big Bash' (see www.bigbash.com.au). Such strategies, in essence, represent many of the commercial activities that sport organisations have pursued in seeking new sources of income, and in the redesign of their products and services for income generation.

SUMMARY

This chapter has highlighted the evolutionary nature of sport organisation change and the role of leadership within these change processes. In this, we have demonstrated how the sport sector, as a traditionally volunteer led industry, has undergone substantial change over the past 40 to 50 years, driven in large part by the processes of commercialisation and professionalisation. We have also argued that, as a sector in transition, the positive influence of CEOs and board members has been pivotal to organisation and sector achievement, and how an understanding of the evolutionary nature of change within the sector is a vital component of leading sport organisations. To strengthen an evolutionary understanding we have offered a framework of thinking for sport organisation leaders and 'students' of sport leadership (the Common Good Organisation Development Model) grounded in the notion that leadership is about facilitating and developing capacity in organisations and capability in people.

In presenting the CGO Development Model (McMorland and Erakovic 2013), we weaved together organisational stages of development; different levels of work that organisations build on; and key factors of their development pathway. Most importantly, we showed the *transitional* challenges (internal and external) that sport organisations are likely to encounter as they progress through development stages. In this, the model highlighted the establishment of formal management systems (a transition from voluntary associations to agencies) and strategic governance (positioning of the agency within the sector). Developed outside of the sport sector, this framework has offered a new lens through which to view the transition challenges sport organisation leaders have faced and are currently facing as they seek to grow organisation capacity and impact within a turbulent environment.

REVIEW QUESTIONS

1 Identify the evolutionary changes that national sport organisations in Commonwealth countries have undergone since the 1970s.

2 Discuss each stage of the CGO Development Model in relation to sport organisation change.

3 Discuss the transitional challenges (internal and external) that sport organisations are likely to encounter as they progress through the development stages noted above.

4 Discuss the relationship between sport organisation change and leadership.

REFERENCES

Amis, J., Slack, T. and Hinings, C. R. (2004). Strategic change and the role of interests, power, and organizational capacity. *Journal of Sport Management, 18,* 158–198.

Auld, C. and Godbey, G. (1998). Influence in Canadian national sport organizations: Perceptions of professionals and volunteers. *Journal of Sport Management, 12,* 20–38.

Billis, D. (2010) (ed.). *Hybrid organisations and the third sector: Challenges for practice, theory and policy.* London: Palgrave Macmillan.

Bradshaw, P. (2009). A contingency approach to nonprofit governance. *Nonprofit Management and Leadership, 20*(1), 61–81.

Chait, R. P., Ryan, W. P. and Taylor, B. E. (2005). *Governance as leadership: Reframing the work of nonprofit board.* Hoboken, NJ: John Wiley & Sons.

Cohen, W. (2009). *Drucker on leadership: New lessons from the father of modern management.* New York: John Wiley & Sons.

Dowling, M., Edwards, J. and Washington, M. (2014). Understanding the concept of professionalization in sport management research. *Sport Management Review, 20,* 529–570.

Drucker, P. (2001). *The essential Drucker.* New York: Harper Business.

Erakovic, L. and Jackson, B. (2012). Promoting leadership in governance and governance in leadership: Towards a supportive research agenda. In A. Davila, M. Elvira, J. Ramirez and

L. Zapata-Cantu (eds), *Understanding organizations in complex, emergent and uncertain environments* (pp. 68–83). Basingstoke: Palgrave Macmillan.

Ferkins, L. and Shilbury, D. (2010). Developing board strategic capability in sport organisations: The national–regional governing relationship. *Sport Management Review, 13,* 235–254.

Ferkins, L. and Shilbury, D. (2012). Good boards are strategic: What does that mean for sport governance? *Journal of Sport Management, 26,* 67–80.

Ferkins, L., Shilbury, D. and McDonald, G. (2009). Board involvement in strategy: Advancing the governance of sport organizations. *Journal of Sport Management, 23*(3), 245–277.

Ferkins, L., Jogulu, U. and Meiklejohn, T. (2013). Sport governance in New Zealand. In I. O'Boyle and T. Bradbury (eds), *Sport governance: International case studies* (pp. 243–259). New York: Routledge.

Hassan, D. and Hamil, S. (2010). Models of football governance and management in international sport. *Soccer and Society, 11,* 343–353.

Hoye, R. (2006). Leadership within Australian voluntary sport organisation boards. *Nonprofit Management and Leadership, 16,* 297–313.

Hoye, R. and Cuskelly, G. (2003). Board-executive relationships within voluntary sport organisations. *Sport Management Review, 6,* 53–73.

Hoye, R. and Doherty, A. (2011). Nonprofit sport board performance: A review and directions for future research. *Journal of Sport Management, 25,* 272–285.

Inglis, S. (1994). Exploring volunteer board member and executive director needs: Importance and fulfillment. *Journal of Applied Recreation Research, 19*(3), 171–189.

Inglis, S. (1997). Shared leadership in the governance of amateur sport. *AVANTE Journal, 3*(1), 14–33.

Jaques, E. and Clement, S. D. (1991). *Executive leadership: A practical guide to managing complexity* (reprinted 2002). Falls Church, VA: Cason Hall & Co Publishers.

Kihl, L., Leberman, S. and Schull, V. (2010). Stakeholder constructions of leadership in intercollegiate athletics. *European Sport Management Quarterly, 10,* 241–275.

Kikulis, L. (2000). Continuity and change in governance and decision making in national sport organizations: Institutional explanations. *Journal of Sport Management, 14,* 293–320.

Kikulis, L. M., Slack, T. and Hinings C. R. (1995). Towards an understanding of the role of agency and choice in the changing structure of Canada's National Sport Organizations. *Journal of Sport Management, 9,* 135–152.

Kotter, J. P. (2012). *Leading change.* Boston, MA: Harvard Business Review Press.

Leberman, S., Collins, C. and Trenberth, L. (eds) (2012). *Sport business management in New Zealand and Australia,* 3rd edn. Melbourne: Cengage Learning Australia.

McMorland, J. C. I. (2005). Are you big enough for your job? Is your job big enough for you? Exploring 'Levels of Work' in organisations. *University of Auckland Business Review, 7*(2), 75–83.

McMorland, J. and Erakovic, L. (2013). *Stepping through transitions: Management, leadership and governance in not-for-profit organisations.* Auckland: CGO Transitions.

Northouse, P. G. (2007). *Leadership: Theory and practice* (4th edn). Thousand Oaks, CA: Sage.

Scharmer, O. and Kaufer, K. (2013). *Leading from the emerging future: From ego-system to eco-system economies.* San Francisco, CA: Berrett-Koehler.

Shilbury, D. (2001). Examining board member roles, functions and influence: A study of Victorian sporting organisations. *International Journal of Sport Management, 2,* 253–281.

Shilbury, D. and Kellett, P. (2006). Reviewing organisational structure and governance: The Australian Touch Association. *Sport Management Review, 9,* 271–317.

Shilbury, D. and Ferkins, L. (2011). Professionalisation, sport governance and strategic capability. *Managing Leisure, 16,* 108–127.

Shilbury, D., Ferkins, L. and Smythe, L. (2013). Sport governance encounters: Insights from lived experiences. *Sport Management Review, 16,* 349–363.

137

Slack, T. and Hinings, C. R. (eds) (1987). *The organization and administration of sport*. London, ON: Sports Dynamics.

Speed, M. (2011). *Sticky wicket: Inside ten turbulent years at the top of world cricket*. Sydney: HarperSports.

Stamp, G. (1990). *A matrix of working relationships*. BIOSS working paper.

Taylor, M. and O'Sullivan, N. (2009). How should National Governing Bodies of sport be governed in the UK? An exploratory study of board structure. *Corporate Governance: An International Review, 17*, 681–693.

Toohey, K. and Veal, A. (2007). *The Olympic Games: A social sciences perspective*, 2nd edn. Cambridge, MA: CABI International.

Chapter 11

Diversity in sport leadership

Laura Burton and Sarah Leberman

CHAPTER OBJECTIVES

By the end of this chapter you should be able to:

1 describe the advantages to diversity within sport organizations;
2 explain why women and other racial/ethnic minority groups are not well represented in leadership positions in sport organizations;
3 discuss your identity and lived experiences and how those have shaped your understanding of leadership in sport organizations;
4 provide recommendations for how to improve diversity in leadership positions in sport organizations.

KEY TERMS

■ diversity
■ multilevel perspective of leadership
■ leaderful practice
■ prejudice

INTRODUCTION

This chapter makes the business case for diversity and why it is important for the sector as we move through the twenty-first century. This is followed by an overview of the sport leadership landscape and the reasons why the situation is as it is. We then consider how more critical perspectives of leadership research can assist in improving diversity in sport leadership. This chapter will draw on examples from North America and New Zealand.

Writing a chapter on diversity is always challenging as it carries with it assumptions regarding how we conceptualize identity. Identities intersect and, depending on context, we often privilege one identity over another. As authors of this chapter, we acknowledge our position as white and able-bodied, yet also share the experience of being women within the male dominated field of sport. Given the lack of leadership diversity in some areas of sport, there is often a corresponding under-representation in the leadership of other groups in the sphere of sport (e.g. coaching). This chapter will focus on gender, race, and ethnicity. It is, however, important to recognize the wide range of diversity that exists in society, including sexual identity, physical and mental ability, age, religious belief system, social class, and appearance [weight, height, attractiveness] (Cunningham, 2011a).

ADVANTAGES TO LEADERSHIP DIVERSITY IN SPORT

So why is there any value in having more diverse leadership in any organization? The research internationally demonstrates the benefits to business of gender diversity. It improves financial performance, widens the talent pool, supports enhanced innovation and group performance, encourages adaptability, and improves employee retention. Encouraging more women into the workplace also enables a greater understanding of the buying preferences of women (Catalyst, 2013; Equal Employment Opportunities Trust, 2010; Pellegrino et al., 2011). As countries move through the twenty-first century, policy makers and organizations alike need to identify strategies to capitalize on the many and diverse strengths women and other under-represented groups bring to the workforce and to the development of successful businesses. According to New Zealand's Equal Employment Opportunities (EEO) Trust (2011), to bring out the best in diverse individuals and teams, a workplace culture that makes the most of everyone's talents, that values the transfer of valuable knowledge and experience from one generation to another, from one culture to another, and from one team to another needs to be cultivated. A restrictive, one-dimensional view of what people can provide to workplaces and leisure places is not going to bring out the best in individuals or teams in the years to come.

Within the U.S., benefits associated with increased gender diversity include improved financial performance for non-sport companies (Badal and Harter, 2014). Within sport, intercollegiate athletic departments in the U.S. that adopt an inclusive culture and were racially diverse had better performance outcomes (Cunningham, 2009). Further, athletic departments supporting an inclusive culture that had a higher number of LGBT employees performed better (more team success) than other less inclusive athletic departments (Cunningham, 2011b). As highlighted above, the research suggests that diversity befits organizations for a wide variety of reasons. Despite the evidence, the practice evident in sport worldwide is quite different.

LANDSCAPE OF SPORT LEADERSHIP

Though sport participation is universal and many groups are overrepresented in regard to participation, they are not equally represented in management, leadership, or governance in sport. People of different races, ethnicities, religious affiliations, ability levels, genders, sexual identities, and ages participate in sport. However, those who lead sport organizations

140

do not reflect this diversity. As noted by Cunningham (2010) "people who differ from the typical majority—that is, people who are not White, able-bodied, heterosexual, Protestant males—are likely to face prejudice and discrimination based on their personal demographic characteristics" (p. 395) when attempting to gain access to leadership positions in sport.

When considering sport leadership at the international level (e.g., International Olympic Committee, FIFA) the majority of those holding positions of power are White, able-bodied men. As we look to national organizations (e.g. National Football League, New Zealand Rugby Union), again we see White, able-bodied men as leaders (Lapchick, 2013; Sydney Scoreboard, 2014). Within the intercollegiate system in the U.S., again, those leading are predominantly White men (Fink et al., 2001). Even when considering youth sport governance, again, men dominate leadership positions (Messner and Bozada-Deas, 2009). Why, if sport is universal, do White, able-bodied, heterosexual men dominate leadership positions in sport organizations? This section of the chapter will explore this issue in detail, and describe the myriad of reasons why there is so little diversity in sport leadership.

Before we begin a discussion on the challenges facing minority groups seeking sport leadership positions, it is important to establish why one particular group, White, able-bodied men (Fink et al., 2001), is the dominant leadership group in sport organizations. Anderson (2009) has argued that sport "actively construct[s] boys and men to exhibit, value and reproduce traditional notions of masculinity" (p. 4), and that competitive sport serves as a social institution that defines certain forms of masculinity as acceptable, while denigrating others. Further, organized sport is used to define and reproduce hegemonic masculinity, in which one form of masculinity (i.e., exclusively heterosexual and physically dominant) maintains dominance by suppressing all other forms of masculinity and subordinating women (Connell, 2009). This dominant form of masculinity is maintained in and through sport because the presence of other groups is viewed as outsiders within sport. As noted by Kane (1995), women are often situated as "other" in the social institution of sport, and therefore when they are participants, coaches, managers, or leaders they are under constant scrutiny.

Women are not the only group perceived as "other" within sport, and more notably in sport leadership. Racism must also be recognized as negatively impacting the opportunities for racial and ethnic minorities in sport organizations. Racism is an institutionalized practice in sport (Singer, 2005). Coakley (2009) noted that sport in the U.S. has perpetuated the idea that Whites are smarter, more ethical, and better leaders than their Black counterparts. The situation is similar in many other countries, for example, in New Zealand, where the work of Hokowhitu (2003) and Laidlaw (2010) has challenged the notion that Māori and Pascifika people are only capable of participating in sport, not leading sport, as they do not possess the characteristics necessary for leadership positions in sport.

REASONS FOR THE LACK OF DIVERSITY IN SPORT LEADERSHIP

Multilevel perspective

The issues facing under-represented groups in sport are "situated in multi-level, sometimes subtle, and usually taken-for-granted structures, policies, and behaviors embedded in sport organizations" (Fink, 2008, p. 147). A multilevel perspective allows us to examine how society influences under-represented groups in sport (macro-level), stereotyping of leaders, issues of discrimination, prejudice, and organizational cultures (meso-level), and how perceptions of leadership inform our understanding of leadership in sport (micro-level).

Macro-level

As we consider leadership as "a collective process" (Ladkin, 2010, p. 11), including both leaders and followers within "particular social and historical contexts" (p. 11), we must explore how institutional practices favor leadership that represents one particular group of individuals over others. When examining institutionalized practices, we consider policies and practices that reinforce discrimination because agreed upon ways of operating within an organization can become institutionalized and accepted (Cunningham, 2010) (i.e., "the way things are done around here"). Sport organizations have institutionalized masculinity as the operating principle within sport, identifying male activity as privileged, and reinforcing masculinity and masculine behavior as the appropriate leadership qualities required in sport (Shaw and Frisby, 2006). For those who do not embody this type of masculine behavior, perceptions of their skills as leaders and the individual's recognition of leadership ability is called into question. As an example, when examining practices of leadership selection in Dutch national sport organizations, researchers noted there was a perception of gender neutrality in board member selection, however selection practices actually favored men over women (Claringbould and Knoppers, 2007).

Institutionalized discrimination also keeps minority groups from obtaining leadership positions in sport organizations (Bradbury, 2013; Walker and Sartore-Baldwin, 2013). The inability to recognize that women, racial/ethnic minorities, LGBT individuals, and individuals with disabilities have the capability to lead sport suppresses opportunities to obtain these positions. Considering the case of football, institutional racism and discrimination has significantly impacted, in a negative way, the experiences of minorities and limited their involvement in the organization and leadership of the sport internationally (Bradbury, 2013).

Further, perceptions of stakeholder groups within a sport organization (e.g. fans, alumni, donors, sponsors) can also influence who is perceived to be an acceptable leader. In the U.S., stakeholder perceptions of acceptable leaders in intercollegiate sport organizations are those perceived to "look like" them, meaning White men (Cunningham, 2010).

Meso-level

When we consider meso-level influences on how we understand leadership in sport organizations, we need to explore stereotyping of leaders, issues of discrimination, prejudice, and organizational cultures.

Organizational cultures (i.e., values, norms, beliefs) that embrace diversity are: characterized as having respect for differences, exhibit tolerance for risk and ambiguity, have a strong people-orientation, are proactive in utilizing the talents of their diverse members, and are organizational cultures that will attract and best utilize diversity (Fink et al., 2001). This type of culture will be proactive in their recruitment and hiring of persons from under-represented groups (Cunningham and Singer, 2009). However, many sport organizations operate with an organizational culture of similarity, where the leadership teams are not diverse and represent only the dominant group (White males), do not have structured hiring and promotion standards to improve diversity in leadership positions, and see diversity as a liability rather than an asset (Fink *et al.*, 2001).

Further, people tend to be drawn to people similar to themselves and will therefore select those like them. This is known as homologous reproduction and has been noted in sport leadership research (Kanter, 1977). Women have been excluded from the hiring process in sport as a result of homologous reproduction (Hoffman, 2011).

Leadership stereotypes or perceptions of what is required to be a successful leader have significant impact on the ability of minority groups to be provided opportunities for leadership positions in sport organizations (Burton, 2014; Burton *et al.*, 2011). Leadership categorization theory is a useful means to understand why minority groups face challenges in obtaining leadership positions; it explains that individuals develop a set of characteristics that form categories of a standard or typical leader (Lord and Maher, 1991). People will then compare an actual leader to the prototypical leader that is imagined and "those persons who possess characteristics that are consistent with the stereotypes are likely to be viewed as more effective than are their counterparts" (Cunningham, 2010, p. 401). As the prototypical leader for a sport organization is White, able-bodied, Christian and male, those who do not fit this stereotype are likely to be perceived as less effective and therefore less likely to be a successful leader.

Both access and treatment discrimination occur at the organizational level and negatively impact minorities seeking positions of leadership in sport organizations (Cunningham, 2011b). Access discrimination operates by excluding members of certain groups from entering the organization, while treatment discrimination occurs when individuals from certain groups receive fewer organizational resources than they would legitimately deserve (Greenhaus *et al.*, 1990). Within the U.S. sport system, minority groups have had fewer opportunities for leadership positions, yet make up a majority of participants at several of the higher levels of sport (i.e., intercollegiate and professional sport) (Lapchick, 2013), demonstrating a lack of access to such positions. When considering treatment discrimination, minority groups receive fewer returns for social and human capital investments to improve their managerial or leadership position (Sagas and Cunningham, 2005). Women in intercollegiate sport have been denied opportunities to engage in important oversight roles such as budgeting and leading men's sports programs, which negatively impacts their abilities to build skill-sets toward positions of athletic director (Grappendorf *et al.*, 2008). There are exceptions, for example, the hiring of Becky Hammon as an assistant coach for the 2014 San Antonio Spurs (NBA team). This is the second time a woman has been hired to coach for a major men's U.S. professional sports team, with Nancy Lieberman Kline being the first, though she coached for the development league of the NBA.

Prejudice has a significant impact on who is considered an acceptable leader within a sport organization. As noted by Cunningham (2010), prejudice is "a psychological term focusing on people's attitudes and beliefs" (p. 399) and has had a significant impact on the opportunities afforded to racial minorities in the U.S. (Lapchick, 2013).

143

Micro-level

Evaluation at the micro-level focuses on individuals and how they make meaning of their experiences, their expectations and understandings of power. The micro-level can also explore the assumptions made by individuals in how they interact within an organization, and also the self-limiting behaviors individuals engage in within their work. A case study at the micro-level explored the status of Pasifika and Māori within New Zealand sport governance roles in National Sports Organizations (NSOs) and the insights into the lived experiences of those board members (Holland, 2012). Pasifika and Māori have high player-participation rates in a number of national sports, but are under-represented in leadership positions within sport. The findings highlighted that Pasifika and Māori representation on New Zealand NSO boards is low, and many sports organizations are without Pasifika and/or Māori directors. Pasifika and Māori people experienced numerous challenges including ethno-cultural expectations concerning age, status, and respect; a lack of integration into the board environment; stereotyping and expectations; tokenistic appointments and a lack of Pasifika and Māori role models in sport governance roles.

An additional consideration with a micro-level framework is examination of how women's careers develop differently from those of men. While men generally have a linear, planned approach to their careers, women's careers often unfold without any planned strategy, and are shaped by many different influences (see for example, Hertneky, 2012; Mainiero and Sullivan, 2005; O'Neil et al., 2008). It is becoming increasingly apparent that the careers of women do not develop in a planned, linear fashion and younger generations in particular are less interested in traditional, planned careers (Mainiero and Sullivan, 2005).

Research has been undertaken on a variety of aspects relating to women in sport leadership. This includes the experiences of women as mothers and sports leaders (Dixon and Bruening, 2005; Leberman and Palmer, 2009), working mothers who volunteer as coaches in youth sport (Leberman and LaVoi, 2011), female sports graduates and the experiences of successful female chief executive officers of sports organizations (Leberman and Shaw, 2012). This body of research emphasizes the male dominated nature of the industry and that it is still very much an "old boys network."

Human and social capital is a micro-level factor that can help explain the lack of minorities in sport leadership. An individual gains human capital through education, job training, on the job experiences, and the like, and accrues social capital resources through a network of relationships with peers, supervisors, and subordinates. When considering how human and social capital impact men and women's career advancement, social capital was more influential for men advancing in sport organizations than it was for women (Sagas and Cunningham, 2005). With regard to race, Black men in U.S. intercollegiate coaching have indicated they are less able to utilize human and social capital to advance to the head coach position when compared to White men in coaching (Cunningham et al., 2006).

Given the landscape of sport leadership and the multiple challenges facing under-represented groups as identified from a multilevel perspective, we also want to call attention to how leadership research has been framed in the majority of studies on the topic. As a result of a focus on leadership that is devoid of cultural context, and is often focused on a heroic leader, our understanding of leadership and leadership effectiveness is narrowed. We must expand

144

our understanding of leadership and examine leadership in multiple contexts so that we may consider alternative ways of understanding the issues of diversity in sport leadership.

LEADERSHIP AS A WAY OF BEING

Individual leaders, in sport or any industry, cannot be "successful" on their own. Leaders need the support of followers and the systems that underpin their organization. If we think of a successful sports team, it is about group success, rather than only attributable to just the captain or coach—without the team there would be no success. Some of the current more critical thinking around leadership and in particular the work of Amanda Sinclair (2007, 2010) and Donna Ladkin (2010) challenge the existing theories of leadership. In her book *Leadership for the Disillusioned* (2007, p. XV), Sinclair argues that we need to think

> about leadership as a way of being that is reflective and thoughtful about self; that values relationships and the present; that is connected to others and embodied; that is not narrowly striving or ego-driven; and that is liberating in its effects.

She encourages readers to reflect upon their own experiences of leadership and how these experiences inform the way they are both leaders and followers. Similarly, she highlights how the leaders we should aspire to be are often business leaders, and questions how the voices and knowledge of certain groups of society are privileged, while others (i.e., those not leading businesses or sport organizations) are marginalized. These observations are at the core of what is required to challenge the dominant structures supporting leadership within the sport industry. Leadership is more than a position or a title, it is about being a person of influence, which can be exercised in many different ways.

Sinclair (2010) focuses on the importance of knowing your sense of place when learning and reflecting on leadership. Her key argument is that identities (e.g., gender, ethnicity, sexuality, belief system) and places (e.g., country, socio-economic context) have been largely absent from the leadership literature and yet form such an important part of thinking about both leadership and what it means to be a leader. She argues that we have multiple identities and often these are contradictory, requiring constant negotiation depending on the situation we are in.

Sinclair argues for the importance of 'placing ourselves' by thinking about the places we have come from and are in and the multiple identities that we have when we are thinking, studying, and writing about leadership. Where do I come from? How do I situate myself within this? In a sense what is my story and experience of leadership in response to the established theories and are there new or more appropriate ways of studying and explaining leadership? These are important questions as they frame the way we interpret and view leadership theories—do they resonate with us? Do they help explain our experiences? Can we engage with them? Much leadership is about knowing yourself and Sinclair focuses strongly on identity work with her students—where they come from in family and history as this provides the lens through which we see everything we do.

Similar to Sinclair, Ladkin (2010) also questions the traditional approaches used for studying leadership, adopting a phenomenological approach to exploring the notions of

145

leadership and leaders. Most existing leadership theories have been based on the positivist paradigm, where leadership is predominantly focused on one person, the "leader," and individual variables are separated out and evaluated. What these theories omit is any reference to time and context.

These different approaches are particularly important for people outside of North America and Europe, as much of the leadership literature is informed by those contexts, which may be quite different from those of people in Oceania or Southeast Asia, for example. Similarly, leadership research from a gender and/or indigenous perspective is still limited. With people from different backgrounds increasingly assuming leadership roles it is important to identify their experiences of leadership and develop models of leadership representative of their experiences.

For example, Palmer and Masters (2010) provide a greater understanding of the socio-cultural and structural issues that arise from the intersection between indigeneity and gender, illustrating the realities of indigenous issues in sport and emphasizing the importance of "hearing" indigenous voices when attempting to manage diversity in sport management.

Their research highlights how Māori women are one of the most marginalized groups in New Zealand society, and explores the experiences of Māori women within organized sport—"one of the most privileged, Eurocentric and masculine institutions in New Zealand" (p. 332). The research is based on in-depth interviews with four Māori women working within sport organizations, using a *kaupapa* Māori and Māori feminist approach, coupled with inter-sectionality theory. The findings highlight how these women took on sport leadership positions, as well as the barriers they experienced, the strategies they used to negotiate these, and the impact of identities on their sport leadership experiences.

LEADERSHIP CUBE

Ladkin (2010) uses the analogy of a cube to explain how phenomenology can assist in rethinking the way we conceptualize leadership. A cube has six "sides," but at any one time it is impossible to see all of them. Similarly, depending on which way you move the cube will vary the "aspect" with which you see the cube. Transferring these notions to leadership —a side could be "leader," "follower," "the organization," "the community," or "historical situation." In terms of aspect—imagine how a parent will view what is happing in a sports organization differently to the CEO, the coaches, or the children—perspective is therefore crucial when considering questions of leadership. For example, Messner and Bozada-Deas (2009) investigated leadership roles in youth soccer from the perspective of coaches. They draw on a combination of statistical background figures for U.S. Youth Soccer and Little League Baseball/Softball in Southern California. The findings suggest that, while the notion of choice to become a leader was raised by many participants, this choice is constrained by the social environment within which it operates. Men automatically volunteered to be coaches, whereas women chose the "team mom" roles—suggesting that the terms "coach" and "team mom" are inherently gendered and reflect the gender divisions inherent in the family and work lives of most of the participants. Similarly, as in family and work situations, men are in the visible leadership roles, while women are in the invisible support roles. The term "soft essentialism" is used by the authors to describe this notion that men in a sense have a destiny to be leaders and therefore coaches, whereas women exercise a choice to do so. This research has implications for sport managers on many fronts. If we are to change the culture of youth sport where women are just as likely as men to be seen in leadership roles as coaches, sport managers need to consider the way in which opportunities to take on these roles are presented and supported. It is moving beyond the formal to consider the "way things are done" and raise awareness about the informal ways in which gender segregation within leadership in youth sport is perpetuated.

Equally important to the side and angle is the notion of "identity." Following this line of thought, Ladkin argues that leadership is a "moment" of social relation, as it cannot exist independently—it requires people, a context, a purpose, and a point in time, and therefore moves beyond the focus on one aspect, namely, that of the leader. The way we interpret this leadership moment is very much dependent on our own perspective, experience, and how we are positioned in relation to that moment. Are we the parent, coach, umpire, or CEO? Leadership is inherently about people and great leaders get the best team together to achieve set objectives.

Reinforcing this perspective, recent work by Raelin (2011) shifts the focus from leadership as an individual act to leadership as the process of people working together to accomplish a particular outcome. The emphasis is therefore on understanding "where, how and why leadership work is organised and accomplished" (p. 196), rather than on who the individual is. Process and context are therefore vitally important, instead of the outcome per se. Raelin argues that leaderful practice, as distinct from leadership-as-practice, requires collectiveness, concurrency, collaboration, and compassion. Leaderful practice focuses on the democratic approach involving all stakeholders in working toward outcomes. What this means for sport management researchers is that it may be time to move away from the more individualistic approaches to leadership, which have provided the majority of leadership research in sport management, toward research that takes more account of context and the multiple realities of leadership.

RECOMMENDATIONS TO INCREASE DIVERSITY IN SPORT LEADERSHIP

Leveling the playing field

Many western countries have embraced the concept of meritocracy in the workplace. This assumes a level playing field for every individual. However, research has shown that perceptions of effective leaders are influenced by stereotypes, and these stereotypes often negatively impact under-represented groups (Eagly and Chin, 2010). Further, stereotypes can be self-limiting as women have a tendency to hold themselves back, can be risk averse, and less likely to put themselves forward for promotion, often needing encouragement to apply for more senior roles.

In order to level the playing field for diversity, senior executives must actively encourage and develop their talented employees—this needs to be an express strategic management priority, consistently applied over a long period of time. Equal Employment Opportunity policies are not enough. Neither is a focus on developing the skills and networks of individuals

147

from under-represented groups. A commitment to organizational change, led by senior executives, over a sustained period of time is required to bring about lasting results. However, leadership development programs often fail because there is little recognition of the context in which they are situated and the reflection associated with the program is often removed from the work environment. Similarly, the time taken for a change to take place is often underestimated and in many cases programs are seeking immediate outcomes for their organizations, and do not establish longitudinal research and therefore the results of such programs are seldom measured (Gurdjian et al., 2014).

The value and importance of women or minority-only leadership programs is supported, recognizing that the challenges under-represented groups face in the leadership environment not only vary by gender, but also depend on their individual backgrounds and cultures that they live and work within. It is therefore crucial to ensure that the curriculum for leadership development programs is tailor made to the specific context within which it is operating (Ely et al., 2011). Ely et al. (2011) strongly support the need for women only leadership development programs and argue that framing leadership development as identity work and developing a sense of agency assists women in moving into senior leadership roles. The value of leadership development programs for other under-represented groups is also advocated.

Mentoring, networking, and role models

Developing good networks, as well as the importance of mentors, particularly an informal mentor relationship, is a consistent theme arising from this body of research. Women leaders value the advice and encouragement from role models, mentors, peers, and friends (Leberman and Palmer, 2009). Mentors and sponsors are key to developing leadership skills and can be of critical importance in providing leadership opportunities for groups that are under-represented in leadership positions (Hewlett, 2013).

Self-confidence and self-awareness

Women and other minority groups face internal barriers that, if left unaddressed, can restrict their career progression. The development of self-confidence and assertiveness have been identified as essential areas for self-development. In order to survive in a leadership position in the male-dominated sports sector, women need to build resilience and develop confidence.

> You have to be incredibly resilient. It's not a place for soft people, because there is a lot of personal attack. It is not a popularity contest—so if you want to be popular, sports is not the place for you. But it is a place where you can earn a lot of respect for being upfront and honest and consistent.
>
> (Leberman and Shaw, 2012, pp. 27–28)

Self-confidence and assurance in one's decision-making is important to improve performance, as well as the ability to cope with difficult situations, such as interpersonal conflict motivation and emotional stability (Harris and Leberman, 2012). In order to develop these personal skills, self-awareness is required, a theme consistently raised by research participants.

148

Overall there is a need for sport organizations to better understand the benefits of diversity and for it to be embraced as a strategic management objective for the senior executive team, which includes greater diversity in leadership positions throughout the organization. It is important to emphasize that embracing diversity in leadership is not about "fixing under-represented groups," but about providing them with the best possible skill-set to enter the working environment. Once in the workforce, it is imperative that organizations consider how best to develop their top talent across the board, including women and other minority groups, so as to be successful sport organizations in the twenty-first century.

The reality is that women and other minority groups still contend with bias from society as leaders and also the internal biases, which might prevent them from considering senior level leadership opportunities. It is therefore important to have champions at the executive level as this strengthens leadership development for both the individual, the organization, and, where appropriate, the sector.

SUMMARY

Sport organizations must consider the benefits of diversity in order to be successful in the competitive landscape of twenty-first-century sport. Leadership across all levels of sport must include women and other minority groups if organizations are to truly gain the competitive advantages derived from diversity. More importantly, sport organizations must embrace a culture that values diversity and fosters a climate that supports and promotes under-represented groups in positions of leadership.

As we have described, we must all reflect on how our identities have formed our understanding of leadership and shaped how we view who should and should not be leaders in sport organization. Further, we must question our assumptions regarding those we perceive to be "appropriate" leaders in sport. We have called attention to the limitations of the study of leadership and have supported examining leadership in multiple contexts so that we may consider alternative ways of understanding the issues of diversity in sport leadership.

REVIEW QUESTIONS

1   Why should sport organizations seek leaders who represent different groups of people (e.g., women, minority men and women)?

2   What challenges have certain groups of people (e.g., women, minority men and women) faced as leaders of sport organizations? Describe micro- and macro-level forces.

3   Describe your understanding of the importance of including an understanding of self when considering how you would lead a sport organization.

4   Describe the leadership cube and how it can be applied to leadership in a sport organization.

5   Describe two different ways that sport organizations can improve the representation of women and minority men and women in leadership positions.

REFERENCES

Anderson, E. D. (2009). The maintenance of masculinity among the stakeholders of sport. *Sport Management Review, 12*(1), 3–14.

Badal, S., and Harter, J. K. (2014). Gender diversity, business unit engagement, and performance. *Journal of Leadership and Organizational Studies, 21,* 354–365.

Bradbury, S. (2013). Institutional racism, whiteness and the under-representation of minorities in leadership positions in football in Europe. *Soccer and Society, 14*(3), 296–314.

Burton, L. J. (2014). Underrepresentation of women in sport leadership: A review of research. *Sport Management Review.* Advance online publication. DOI: doi:10.1016/j.smr.2014.02.004.

Burton, L. J., Grappendorf, H., and Henderson, A. (2011). Perceptions of gender in athletic administration: Utilizing role congruity to examine (potential) prejudice against women. *Journal of Sport Management, 25,* 36–45.

Catalyst. (2013). Why diversity matters. New York: Catalyst. Retrieved July 17, 2014 from www.catalyst.org/knowledge/why-diversity-matters.

Coakley, J. (2009). *Sport in Society: Issues and Controversies* (10th ed.). Boston, MA: McGraw-Hill.

Connell, R. (2009). *Gender.* Cambridge: Polity.

Claringbould, I., and Knoppers, A. (2007). Finding a "normal" woman: Selection processes for board membership. *Sex Roles, 56,* 495–507.

Cunningham, G. B. (2009). The moderating effect of diversity strategy on the relationship between racial diversity and organizational performance. *Journal of Applied Social Psychology, 39,* 1445–1460.

Cunningham, G. B. (2010). Understanding the under-representation of African American coaches: A multilevel perspective. *Sport Management Review, 13*(4), 395–406.

Cunningham, G. B. (2011a). *Diversity in sport organizations.* Scottsdale, AZ: Holcomb Hathaway.

Cunningham, G. B. (2011b). The LGBT advantage: Examining the relationship among sexual orientation diversity, diversity strategy, and performance. *Sport Management Review, 14*(4), 453–461.

Cunningham, G. B., and Singer, J. N. (2009). *Diversity in athletics: An assessment of exemplars and institutional best practices.* Indianapolis, IN: National Collegiate Athletic Association.

Cunningham, G. B., Bruening, J. E., and Straub, T. (2006). The underrepresentation of African Americans in NCAA Division IA head coaching positions. *Journal of Sport Management, 20*(3), 387–413.

Dixon, M. A., and Bruening, J. E. (2005). Perspectives on work-family conflict in sport: An integrated approach. *Sport Management Review, 8*(3), 227–253.

Eagly, A. H., and Chin, J. L. (2010). Diversity and leadership in a changing world. *American Psychologist, 65*(3), 216–224.

Ely, R. J., Ibarra, H. and Kolb, D. M. (2011). Taking gender into account: Theory and design for women's leadership development programs. *Academy of Management Learning and Education, 10*(3), 474–493.

Equal Employment Opportunities (EEO) Trust. (2010). The business case for diversity. Auckland, New Zealand: Author. Retrieved June 20, 2014 from www.eeotrust.org.nz/toolkits/index.cfm.

Equal Employment Opportunities (EEO) Trust (2011). *Specifically Pacific: Engaging Young Pacific Workers.* Auckland: EEO Trust.

Fink, J. S. (2008). Gender and sex diversity in sport organizations: Concluding comments. *Sex Roles, 58*, 146–147.

Fink, J. S., Pastore, D. L., and Riemer, H. (2001). Do differences make a difference? Managing diversity in division IA intercollegiate athletics. *Journal of Sport Management, 15*(1), 10–50.

Grappendorf, H., Pent, A., Burton, L., and Henderson, A. (2008). Gender role stereotyping: A qualitative analysis of senior woman administrators' perceptions regarding financial decision making. *Journal of Issues in Intercollegiate Athletics, 1*, 26–45.

Greenhaus, J. H., Parasuraman, S., and Wormley, W. M. (1990). Effects of race on organizational experiences, job performance evaluations, and career outcomes. *Academy of Management Journal, 33*, 64–86.

Gurdjian, P., Halbeisen, T., and Lane, K. (2014). Why leadership development programmes fail. *McKinsey Quarterly*, January, 1–6.

Harris, C., and Leberman, S. (2012). Leadership development for women in New Zealand universities: Learning from the New Zealand Women in Leadership Program. *Advances in Developing Human Resources, 14*(1), 28–44.

Hertneky, R. P. (2012). Composing our lives—as women and as leaders. *Advances in Developing Human Resources, 14*(2), 140–155.

Hewlett, S. A. (2013). *Forget a Mentor, Find a Sponsor: The New Way to Fast-Track Your Career.* Boston, MA: Harvard Business Review Press.

Hoffman, J. L. (2011). The old boys' network. *Journal for the Study of Sports and Athletes in Education, 5*(1), 9–28.

Hokowhitu, B. (2003). "Physical beings": Stereotypes, sport and the "physical education" of New Zealand Māori. *Culture, Sport, Society, 6*(2/3), 192–218.

Holland, R. (2012). Governance of New Zealand national sport organisations: Pasifika and Māori voices. Unpublished PhD thesis. School of Management, Massey University, New Zealand.

Kane, M. J. (1995). Resistance/transformation of the oppositional binary: Exposing sport as a continuum. *Journal of Sport and Social Issues, 19*(2), 191–218.

Kanter, R. M. (1977). *Men and Women of the Corporation* (Vol. 5049). New York: Basic Books.

Ladkin, D. (2010). *Rethinking Leadership: A New Look at Old Leadership Questions.* Cheltenham: Edward Elgar.

Laidlaw, C. (2010). *Somebody Stole My Game.* Auckland: Hodder Moa.

Lapchick, R. (2013). The racial and gender report card. Retrieved June 20, 2014 from www.tidesport.org/racialgenderreportcard.html.

Leberman, S., and LaVoi, N. (2011). Juggling balls and roles, working mother-coaches in youth sport: Beyond the dualistic worker-mother identity. *Journal of Sport Management, 25*(5), 474–488.

Leberman, S., and Palmer, F. (2009). Motherhood, sport leadership, and domain theory: Experiences from New Zealand. *Journal of Sport Management, 23*(3), 305–334.

Leberman, S., and Shaw, S. (2012). Preparing female sport management students for leadership roles in sport. Wellington, New Zealand. Retrieved July 20, 2014 from https://ako-web.ako-kvm.catalyst.net.nz/download/ng/file/group-6/preparing-female-sport-management-students-for-leadership-roles-in-sport.pdf.

Lord, R. G., and Maher, K. J. (1991). Cognitive theory in industrial and organizational psychology. *Handbook of Industrial and Organizational Psychology, 2*, 1–62.

Mainiero, L. A., and Sullivan, S. E. (2005). Kaleidoscope careers: An alternate explanation for the opt-out revolution. *The Academy of Management, 19*(1), 106–123.

Messner, M. A., and Bozada-Deas, S. (2009). Separating the men from the moms: The making of adult gender segregation in youth sports. *Gender and Society, 23*(1), 49–71.

O'Neil, D., Hopkins, M., and Bilimoria, D. (2008). Women's careers at the start of the 21st century: Patterns and paradoxes. *Journal of Business Ethics, 80*(4), 727–743.

Palmer, F. R., and Masters, T. M. (2010). Māori feminism and sport leadership: Exploring Māori women's experiences. *Sport Management Review, 13*, 331–344.

151

Pellegrino, G., D'Amato, S., and Weisberg, A. (2011). The gender dividend: Making the business case for investing in women. Retrieved June 23, 2014 from www2.deloitte.com/content/dam/Deloitte/global/Documents/Public-Sector/dttl-ps-thegenderdividend-08082013.pdf.

Raelin, J. (2011). From leadership-as-practice to leaderful practice. *Leadership, 7*(2), 195–211.

Sagas, M., and Cunningham, G. B. (2005). Does having "the right stuff" matter? Gender differences in the determinants of career success among intercollegiate athletic administrators. *Sex Roles, 50*(5), 411–421.

Shaw, S., and Frisby, W. (2006). Can gender equity be more equitable?: Promoting an alternative frame for sport management research, education, and practice. *Journal of Sport Management, 20*, 483–509.

Sinclair, A. (2007). *Leadership for the Disillusioned: Moving Beyond Myths and Heroes to Leading that Liberates.* Crows Nest, NSW: Allen & Unwin.

Sinclair, A. (2010). Placing self: How might we place ourselves in leadership studies differently? *Leadership, 6*(4), 447–460.

Singer, J. N. (2005). Understanding racism through the eyes of African American male student-athletes. *Race Ethnicity and Education, 8*(4), 365–386.

Sydney Scoreboard. (2014). Global scoreboard: New Zealand. Retrieved July 6, 2014, from www.sydneyscoreboard.com/scoreboard/country/new-zealand/.

Walker, N. A., and Sartore-Baldwin, M. L. (2013). Hegemonic masculinity and the institutionalized bias toward women in men's collegiate basketball: What do men think?. *Journal of Sport Management, 27*(4), 303–315.

Part C

Leadership in sport coaching

Chapter 12

The sport coach

Andrew Cruickshank and Dave Collins

CHAPTER OBJECTIVES

After completing this chapter you should be able to:

1   understand some of the core differences between coaching requirements in participation and performance domains;
2   discuss diverse models of sports coaching and how these differ in terms of their emphasis, strengths and limitations;
3   describe a range of key factors that impact on the coaching process and how these can be integrated through a focus on professional judgement and decision making;
4   describe some crucial skills that can help coaches to understand and manage the complex and dynamic environments in which they work and best lead performers.

KEY TERMS

■   coaching process
■   professional judgement and decision making
■   adaptive expertise
■   nested thinking

INTRODUCTION

With the previous sections of this book having provided an overview of leadership theories and their application in sport management, we now open this section on leadership as applied in the context of sports coaching. To lay the foundations for later chapters, as well as provide a point of comparison and contrast with the previous section (note that organisational and sport participation/performance settings are similar but not identical!), this chapter will first introduce the sports coach and outline the requirements of this role across participation and performance environments. We then provide an overview of models that have attempted to conceptualise the coaching process, culminating in a focus on coach decision making. In the third and final section, we identify and discuss some core skills that help coaches to make consistently effective decisions when leading sports performers and teams.

INTRODUCING THE SPORTS COACH

While undertaking a host of supporting activities, the primary role of the sports coach is to develop and optimise the performance of individuals and teams. This mainly involves the coach organising practice sessions and training schedules, supporting the development and refinement of physical, technical and tactical skills for competition, and leading the performers or team throughout a season and beyond. In addition, however, a great deal of communication and support work should also go on outside the direct training environment. It is the subtle but optimum blend of these two types of coaching, direct and indirect, that characterises the best coach–leaders.

In terms of the specific requirements of coaches (i.e. their work in the 'direct' training environment), these will clearly vary in relation to the nature of the goal for the performer/ team (i.e. performance or participation), the aim of the governing body/organisation/club, the nature of the sport and the level of competition. For participation coaches, the focus will usually be tipped in favour of promoting positive sporting experience to a greater extent than performance outcomes. As such, participation coaches are required to *generally* focus less on results and more on the interpretation, development and well-being of the performers/team. Indeed, rather than winning and/or outperforming others (although these will still be factors!), coaches in this setting may also often work to foster individual and interpersonal skills that benefit individuals in their sporting and wider social contexts; for example, developing resilience and teamwork that can be applied at school/in their job. Coaching effectiveness will therefore be gauged against the delivery of these types of outcomes as well as how individuals generally feel about their participation (e.g. 'Did I have a good time?' 'Have I learned something new?' 'Am I getting better?').

For coaches operating under a performance remit, the focus will instead be tipped in favour of promoting performance outcomes to a greater extent than positive sporting experience. As such, performance coaches are therefore required to *generally* focus more on systems and processes that enable peak performance and competitive success rather than individual well-being. Indeed, although coaches in this environment will still look to foster positive broader individual and interpersonal skills, these are seen as the means to achieving the main goal of objective success (i.e. not the main goal itself). Coaching effectiveness will therefore be gauged more closely against performer/team evolution, their execution of performance, the consistency of this execution, and their hard results. This should not be taken to mean that participation coaching involves a greater percentage of indirect work (i.e. that done away from the immediate training environment) than performance coaching. Rather, as we will explore later, the judgement of what to do, how much, when and how is the crucial variable.

CONCEPTUALISING THE COACHING PROCESS

As outlined by Lyle (2002), the coaching process can be considered a purposeful series of goals, activities and interventions that are designed to improve the performance of teams and athletes. Although the prior section outlined some broad criteria that can define effectiveness in performance and participation domains, we must emphasise that identifying markers of successful coaching is an inherently difficult task due to the subjectivity of the coaching process, the variability of sporting outcomes (e.g. performer development and results) and, of course, the length of time that may be involved before the efficacy of the coaching process can be truly evaluated. For example, the 'making' of an Olympian may take 12–16 years, with several coaches contributing to the performance ladder. As a result, it is usually much better to look at the quality of the process (what is being done against logically derived criteria) than the outcome of how well the performer is doing. Indeed, the best coaches do not necessarily work with the best performers/teams, or performers/teams who seem to be having the best time. Unfortunately, before this was commonly acknowledged, coaching literature was dominated by a behaviourist approach that aimed to develop definitive coach profiles (through assessing coaches of successful performers/teams) which could then be prescribed to those learning their trade. In this way, expert coaching behaviours were perceived to be distinct, observable, measurable, predictable, controllable and generalisable. However, as asserted by many coaching researchers (Cushion et al., 2006; Nash and Collins, 2006; Nash et al., 2012), this behaviourist approach was based on a flawed assumption that coaching expertise can be simply copied and reproduced. With a focus on *what* (apparently) good coaches look like, it also overlooked the actual *process* of coaching (i.e. *how* coaches work) and, even more crucially, *why* (and *why not*) particular methods were used.

In a move away from the traits of (apparently) effective coaches towards the coaching process itself, a number of models have been developed to define and operationalise coaching effectiveness. Following the classifications of Lyle (2002) and Cushion et al. (2006), these models can be considered as either 'of' or 'for' the coaching process. Models 'for' coaching have typically been developed through the critical review and integration of prior theory and research (Franks et al., 1986; Fairs, 1987; Sherman et al., 1997; Lyle, 2002). In their review of coaching literature, however, Cushion et al. (2006) argued that these models are overly simplistic and often fail to account for core features of effective practice. More specifically, with their primary focus on the sequential structure and function of the coaching process (i.e. 'do this, then this, then this'), important social dimensions such as the quality of coach–performer interactions have been overlooked or downplayed (Borrie, 1996; Jones et al., 2004). Finally, as shown by various authors in coaching (e.g. Abraham and Collins, 2011) and sport science (e.g. Martindale and Collins, 2010), the complexity of the coaching environment suggests greater benefit from a focus on 'the why' of the coaching process.

157

In terms of models *of* coaching, and in contrast to those 'for' the process, these have been developed via the assessment of expert/successful coaches but not carefully evaluated against established theoretical ideas. More specifically, Cushion *et al.* (2006) argued that work in this area – despite adopting a more holistic approach – has positioned coaching as a largely implicit and uncontested process (e.g. Côté *et al.*, 1995a, 1995b; McClean and Chelladurai, 1995; d'Arrippe-Longueville *et al.*, 1998). Indeed, although complexity and context receive greater recognition, these models still present coaching as a one-way activity in which performers are passive recipients of coach knowledge and direction.

To address these shortcomings in models for and of coaching, Abraham *et al.* (2006) took the middle ground to develop a model 'for' coaching that was then assessed by expert coaches (who could comment on its depiction 'of' coaching). Rather than attempting to prescribe 'ideal procedures' or represent all interacting factors, the resultant model instead centred upon the *knowledge* that underpins effectiveness. More specifically, Abraham *et al.* identified that coaching excellence requires extensive knowledge of:

1   the performer(s) (i.e. through an understanding of scientific disciplines such as sport psychology, biomechanics, nutrition, motor control, etc.);
2   the techniques and tactics of the specific sport;
3   pedagogical principles (i.e. the systems and processes of performer learning and development).

By encouraging coaches to explicitly and simultaneously consider the performer/team, sport and learning environment in practice situations, this model promoted a more holistic approach to coaching that moved beyond the design and delivery of drills. Indeed, by considering these three areas in tandem, this model promotes a 'breadth-first' approach to problem solving and the generation of 'best-fit' solutions. Within this conceptualisation, the coaching process is therefore depicted as a continual series of goal-based decisions.

Although useful for promoting a focus on coach knowledge and decision making rather than 'prototypical' personality characteristics and behaviours, evidence has gathered to suggest that Abraham *et al.*'s (2006) model does still not fully reflect the multidimensional nature of coaching (Abraham and Collins, 2011). In addition, Cushion *et al.* (2006, p. 90) described the challenges of coaching models that focused on pedagogy alone:

> The coaching context is more than an individually dominated setting and a place for learners to simply 'acquire' sport skills. It also often doubles as an interactive workplace, is consequently racked with competing egos, hierarchies, constraints and opportunities and is, in its own right, an intricate, multifaceted and wide ranging social system.

This quote also relates to the ideas of direct and indirect coaching introduced earlier in the chapter. Similarly, but with a particular focus on politics as well as social factors, Potrac and Jones (2009) have further argued that coaching is 'as much about careful personal negotiation, orchestration, and manipulation, as about improving the performance of individuals or the team' (p. 566). Based upon these assertions, social and politically oriented researchers have argued that environmental complexity means that accurately modelling the coaching process is neither viable nor desirable. Additionally, Thompson *et al.* (2013) have stated that '[social] context is not just a passive backdrop to action. Rather, action both shapes and is shaped by context, making both mutually determinative' (p. 13). Notably, the importance of social context is also emphasized by many leadership theories presented in this book (e.g. multidimensional model; contingency theory), where greater emphasis is placed upon *how* actions are delivered rather than *what* actions are delivered.

Returning to a knowledge perspective, research that stresses the importance of social and political contexts (and argues that the coaching process cannot be accurately modelled) raises the suggestion that effective coaching may be driven by 'gut feeling' and instinct; or *tacit knowledge*. Tacit knowledge is considered to be that which is implicitly acquired via everyday experiences (i.e. the coach is not consciously aware that they have acquired it) and is difficult to articulate after it has been applied (i.e. coaches aren't often consciously aware of why they acted in a certain way: 'I just did it!') (Sternberg, 2003). However, as *expert* coaches have been shown to possess more knowledge of their domain than novices (or those who are less expert), such tacit knowledge and 'coaching automaticity' is not the product of any innate 'gift' but rather a detailed *declarative* knowledge base (i.e. understanding of the 'whys/why nots' of coaching). Indeed, we have yet to meet any expert coach who has little prior coaching experience or who has not continuously reflected in and on this experience! As the second author has stated in prior work, 'many of the coach's actions appear instinctive but are actually based on a complex interaction of knowledge and memory of similar situations, honed by years of experience and reflection' (Nash and Collins, 2006, p. 472).

UNDERSTANDING AND ENHANCING COACH EFFECTIVENESS THROUGH PROFESSIONAL JUDGEMENT AND DECISION MAKING

Given the dynamic and complex environments in which coaches must work, as well as the need to assess, manipulate and respond to evolving and unique contexts, expert coaching will therefore be underpinned by a professional judgement and decision making (PJDM) approach to both personal development (largely indirect) and performance (largely direct) factors. PJDM reflects the choices and chains of decision making by coaches that relate to assessing issues that require attention, identifying and evaluating different solutions, selecting suitable courses of action, and continually monitoring and modifying these courses of action. Indeed, as coaching is a context-dependent decision making process that must handle 'shades of grey' rather than 'black and white' situations and challenges, a focus on PJDM presents a logical, constructive and impactful route for understanding and enhancing coach effectiveness. Significantly, this approach does not overlook or downplay the pedagogical, social and political elements of coaching. Instead it acknowledges that all of these facets play a key role in shaping the coaching process but in an integrated (not isolated) way. In this manner, coach decision making (and ultimate effectiveness) requires a joint consideration of pedagogical principles against the prevailing (and anticipated) social and political context. To amalgamate pedagogical, social and political approaches to coaching, Abraham and Collins (2011) therefore outlined a new

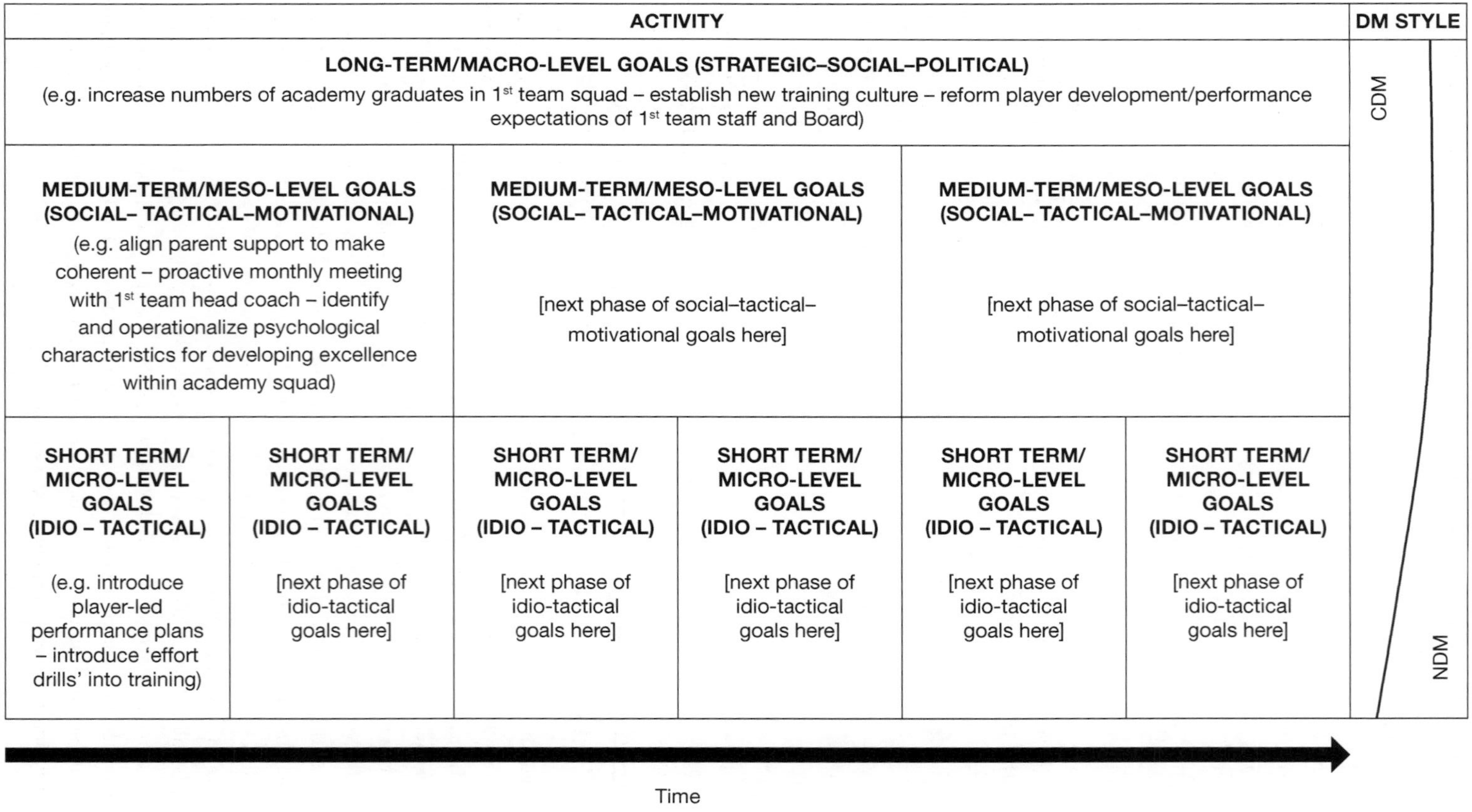
ACTIVITY
DM STYLE
LONG-TERM/MACRO-LEVEL GOALS (STRATEGIC–SOCIAL–POLITICAL)
(e.g. increase numbers of academy graduates in 1st team squad – establish new training culture – reform player development/performance expectations of 1st team staff and Board)
CDM
MEDIUM-TERM/MESO-LEVEL GOALS (SOCIAL– TACTICAL–MOTIVATIONAL)
(e.g. align parent support to make coherent – proactive monthly meeting with 1st team head coach – identify and operationalize psychological characteristics for developing excellence within academy squad)
MEDIUM-TERM/MESO-LEVEL GOALS (SOCIAL– TACTICAL–MOTIVATIONAL)
[next phase of social–tactical–motivational goals here]
MEDIUM-TERM/MESO-LEVEL GOALS (SOCIAL– TACTICAL–MOTIVATIONAL)
[next phase of social–tactical–motivational goals here]
SHORT TERM/ MICRO-LEVEL GOALS (IDIO – TACTICAL)
(e.g. introduce player-led performance plans – introduce 'effort drills' into training)
SHORT TERM/ MICRO-LEVEL GOALS (IDIO – TACTICAL)
[next phase of idio-tactical goals here]
SHORT TERM/ MICRO-LEVEL GOALS (IDIO – TACTICAL)
[next phase of idio-tactical goals here]
SHORT TERM/ MICRO-LEVEL GOALS (IDIO – TACTICAL)
[next phase of idio-tactical goals here]
SHORT TERM/ MICRO-LEVEL GOALS (IDIO – TACTICAL)
[next phase of idio-tactical goals here]
SHORT TERM/ MICRO-LEVEL GOALS (IDIO – TACTICAL)
[next phase of idio-tactical goals here]
NDM
Time

Figure 12.1 *Simplified model outline to 'scaffold' coaching practice and research.*

Source: Abraham and Collins (2011).

model to 'scaffold' coaching practice and research. Figure 12.1 offers a simplified version of this model.

Supporting adaptive expertise (or the ability to perform effectively, flexibly and innovatively in unstructured and unpredictable situations, Tozer *et al.*, 2007), Figure 12.1 outlines the structure for a multifaceted and multilevel form of coach planning and execution that is underpinned by *nested thinking* (cf. Abraham and Collins, 2011; Martindale and Collins, 2012). As part of this integrated approach, coaches are encouraged to prepare and deliver coherent actions across the micro- (e.g. day to day), meso- (e.g. month to month) and macro- (e.g. year to year) level of their behaviour. In this way, any day to day decisions and actions are *simultaneously* locked into targets/plans for that week, which are locked into targets/plans for that month, which are themselves locked into targets/plans for that quarter, year and so on. In short, the key point is that optimum 'in situ' decisions and actions (i.e. those made in the 'here and now' *and* shaped by social and political conditions) will be those that work to previously established and coherent short, medium and long term agendas. Focusing on one of these agendas alone will, more often than not, result in reduced efficiency and effectiveness (even though this might not be instantly apparent – think of coaches who have achieved notable early success but then stuck to this 'winning formula' instead of anticipating and preparing for later challenges). In this vein, Abraham and Collins (2011) have described how effective in situ decision making arises from deliberate and extended 'off-line' analysis, critical planning, cognitive experimentation (cf. Schön, 1987), detailed evaluations and critical reflection that focuses on the development of declarative understanding. Effective coaching (and coach leadership) is therefore characterized by the use of both naturalistic (i.e. quick and cue/feeling-based) *and classical* decision making (i.e. the deliberate and slowed down process that explores a range of different options to then select the most logical, structured and impactful option for action). Importantly, use of both classical and naturalistic decision making applies to *every* element of the coaching role (i.e. pedagogical, social and political). Promoting a systematic approach that is structured around broad conceptual ideas (i.e. the 'scaffolding' concept mentioned above) rather than prescriptive actions (i.e. do this, then that, then this), nested action therefore enables coach flexibility but contextualised against clear pedagogical, social and political objectives; or, as described by Kahneman and Klein (2009), 'skilled intuition' (note the difference from just 'intuition'!).

Of course, this is not to say that nested plans should be rigidly and arrogantly adhered to once they have been initially developed (leaders who would be described by Tetlock, 2005, as 'hedgehogs' and behaviour considered as 'complexity absorbing' by Ashmos *et al.*, 2000). Indeed, the challenges of coaching are so complex and dynamic that a continual revision and adjustment of these plans is pivotal (requiring a leadership style that Tetlock, 2005, describes as 'fox-like' and behaviour considered as 'complexity adapting' by Ashmos *et al.*, 2000). Additionally, engaging in experimentation rather than simply copying and pasting previously successful decisions or actions is also vital (Schön, 1991). In short, the really effective coach is almost always looking for better ways to do it. Only the imminent challenge of a major competition inhibits this drive and, positively for the upcoming performance, creates a stability from which high level achievement can spring.

161

EXCELLENCE IN PRACTICE – EXEMPLAR SKILLS TO SUPPORT COACH LEADERSHIP

Building on the theory presented thus far, we now highlight some (not all!) key skills that can help to make nested coaching work (and thereby enable fox-like/complexity adapting leaders). These are *multidirectionality, emotional intelligence, socio-political awareness* and *micro-political literacy, context manipulation*, and a *broad behavioural repertoire*. As this chapter aims to offer a general overview of coaching and raise some broad implications for coach leadership, we provide brief examples of these skills in action within each subsection rather than through one case study.

MULTIDIRECTIONALITY

Given the importance of context in decision making, including social/interpersonal components, recent research has begun to illuminate the merits of a *multidirectional* orientation when leading performers and teams (in either an individual or team sport environment). Indeed, while much coaching research has focused on coaching as a one-way process and, more recently, on the relationship between coach and performers (e.g. Hampson and Jowett, 2014), other work has pointed to the need for (and benefits of) a 360-degree approach (Cruickshank and Collins, 2012; 2014; Cruickshank *et al.*, 2014). In the case of coaching, leading performers will require additional considerations of those who operate *alongside* the coach (e.g. assistant coaches, sport science and medicine support staff), *above* the coach (e.g. head coach, team manager or the Board of Directors) and *in parallel* to the coach (e.g. parents, fans, the media). For example, take the following excerpt from Thompson *et al.* (2013) regarding a fitness coach who struggled to establish himself within a professional football team:

> While Adam was clearly influenced by context, he nevertheless consciously attempted to influence the structures in which he operated. . . . In order to deal with his vulnerability and to protect his professional interests, Adam sought to create working conditions where the quality of his collegial and professional interactions would allow him to fulfil his role in an effective and meaningful manner. . . . Hence, he tried to develop functional relationships with the Manager, the senior physiotherapist and the goalkeeping coach; those he identified as the critical reality makers within the environment.

Pointing to the use of micro-political action (more on this below), this quote clearly conveys how coaching effectiveness can be supported and validated (or perhaps undermined; see Collins and Collins 2011) by those who are not the primary target of the coach's technical knowledge (i.e. performers). The need for a multidirectional orientation is particularly apparent in coaching roles within performance sport. Indeed, it is well established that parents play a crucial role in performer development and that the media carry major influence within elite sport environments (Bloom, 1985; Kristiansen *et al.*, 2011). In this way, a multidirectional perspective acknowledges the power, agency and interaction of *all* other stakeholders within the specific and broader coaching environment; and that this power, agency and interaction constrains the actions available to the coach. It also works to ensure that coaches continually acquire social and political information that constantly shapes and refines their macro, meso and micro plans (as per the nested approach described earlier). As an immediate and simple implication, leaders will have more impact when (consistent) messages are sent through a variety of routes.

EMOTIONAL INTELLIGENCE

Given the role of emotion in shaping the nature and development of interpersonal relationships and group functioning, recent work has pointed to the benefits of emotional intelligence (EI) in coaches (Latimer et al., 2007; Meyer and Fletcher, 2007; Thelwell et al., 2008; Chan and Mallett, 2011a; Barlow and Banks, 2014). Indeed, EI has been found to promote effective coping with challenges and tensions (e.g. Jordon et al., 2002; Jordon and Troth, 2002) and has been conceptualised as both a useful trait and a specific ability. In terms of the former, EI is considered to be related to stable personality and behavioural dispositions rather than intelligence as it is conventionally defined (i.e. cognitive ability) (Petrides and Furnham, 2000). Alternatively, EI has also been conceptualised as the ability to detect emotions, their meanings and relationships, and to then use these skills as a basis for reasoning and problem-solving (Mayer and Salovey, 1997). More specifically still, managing the interaction between emotion and cognition is supported by four integrated 'branches' (p. 10):

- the ability to perceive accurately, appraise and express emotion
- the ability to access and/or generate feelings when they facilitate thought
- the ability to understand emotion and emotion knowledge
- the ability to regulate emotions to promote emotional and intellectual growth.

Considered in these terms, EI revolves around the perception, monitoring, employment and management of emotions in oneself and others and is therefore built upon self-awareness (Griffin and Moorhead, 2007; Haime, 2011). Indeed, without the ability to recognise and regulate one's own responses (through either reappraisal or emotion suppression: Grandey, 2000; Gross and Thompson, 2007; Augustine and Hemenover, 2009), coaches will struggle to consistently select the best option or delivery style when interacting with their followers – particularly in times of conflict or tension. With a lack of sufficient EI, they may also be less confident in applying the best option or delivery style (Thelwell et al., 2008; Hwang et al., 2013).

While sport-specific research in coaching EI is still in its early stages, with more work conducted on leaders within non-sport environments, it has long been acknowledged that effective coaching (especially indirect coaching) requires the ability to understand and control emotions (Hanson and Gould, 1988; Gould et al., 2002). Indeed, it is a highly face valid assertion that coaches should possess the ability to appraise and apply a variety of situation-specific emotional responses (e.g. when facing conflict with a performer during a training session). Given that effective coaching relies on interpersonal and social awareness, the 'soft' skill of EI offers a valuable route for improving sports performers'/teams' learning and performance. Incidentally, recent work has noted the benefits of intra- and inter-personal emotion abilities and regulation strategies (i.e. monitoring and managing the emotions of

163

oneself and others) across *all* levels of a sport organization (covering performers, coaches, team management, non-sport performance personnel: Wagstaff *et al.*, 2012). While our focus in this chapter is on the general merits of EI and not its outcomes, it is important to note that effective emotion regulation does not mean that all experienced emotions are positive in nature. Indeed, negative emotions (e.g. anger) *may* be beneficial in certain contexts (Hanin, 2011); just as socially undesirable behaviour might be more beneficial than socially desirable behaviour in certain contexts (something that we will come onto later in the chapter).

In sum, and given that effective decision making requires a sound understanding of interpersonal dynamics, a high level of EI can help coaches to focus the lens through which they perceive their environment, explore the rationale for action and then make effective performance-impacting choices (Chan and Mallett, 2011b). Indeed, without this ability (or trait), interactions with others will be somewhat constrained and critical opportunities for promoting 'emotional insight' and 'emotional contagion' in one's followers missed.

SOCIO-POLITICAL AWARENESS AND MICRO-POLITICAL LITERACY

Linked to emotional intelligence, another key skill of effective sport coaching lies in the ability to read and respond to social and political conditions. Indeed, as leading any level of sports performer and team can be a socially complex and contested task, the ability to evaluate and deploy actions against broader socio-political constraints and objectives has been forwarded as a core feature of planning and executing coherent behaviour (Abraham and Collins, 2011; Collins and Cruickshank, 2012; Cruickshank and Collins, 2014). With links to Hogan and Hogan's (2002) notion of socio-political intelligence, Potrac and Jones (2009) and then Thompson *et al.* (2013) have shed particular light on the need for socio- or 'micro-political literacy'; the skill needed to read and integrate oneself into the 'micro-political landscape'. Consider this further extract from Thompson *et al.* (2013, p. 14) on the fitness coach mentioned earlier:

> Adam's stigmatisation appeared to partly result from his inability to read the social frames within which action occurs . . . [i.e. the often unconscious structures that guide the perception of reality]. . . . Adam then, appeared to misconstrue or ignore the regularities and rules that guided contextual practice, and the meanings such rules held for the staff at Hollington F.C.. . . . He had not understood or correctly read the implicit, taken-for-granted forms of knowledge that give order to everyday interactions. This proved to be a costly error in light of the pressurised, unstable and often paranoid world of professional football.

Emphasising yet again the need for more than sport and role-specific technical knowledge, we have also found repeated support for micro-political literacy in our own research in elite team leadership. For example, a Head Coach of a UK professional football team noted how their failure to convey appropriate political sensitivity led to their eventual sacking:

> [To upgrade] all three [training] pitches would cost something like £65,000 . . . [and] it was decided [by the Board] to do one pitch. . . . Yet they built one of the corners

164

up of the [stadium] as a media center and . . . restaurant for £1m. . . . I don't see the logic in it . . . and I made my feelings known . . . I'm not saying that cost me, but maybe . . . banging on about [it] was something that didn't help.

(Cruickshank and Collins, 2014)

Given the pervasiveness of social and political issues, such as this example, coaches have therefore been advised to critically evaluate the broader socio-political goals of their practice (e.g. 'managing upwards' to one's line/top manager to secure or sustain resources that enable programme development). In this way, coaches can then take greater control of their socio-political environment rather than simply react and tolerate the constraints imposed upon them; a skill now described in the following section.

CONTEXT MANIPULATION

Beyond awareness to prevailing contexts, coaching excellence is also reflected in the ability to proactively manipulate contexts in one's favour. More specifically, as performers (or any implicated stakeholder for that matter) will have an opinion on coach-led processes, as well as the opportunity to act on this opinion, expert coaches will work to minimise/control this potentially incessant (and performance-detracting) contest. Drawing upon ideas from behavioural economics (Thaler and Sunstein, 2009), some of our own recent work has revealed that coach effectiveness (in high performance environments at least) is linked to an ability to shape the context in which target individuals make decisions rather than directly confront or negotiate these decisions themselves (Cruickshank et al., 2013). In this way, the often tricky challenge of agreeing what is 'right' or 'wrong' for everyone can be somewhat avoided as individuals instead base their choices on what is perceived to be *normal* or *desirable* (rather than requested or demanded). For example, during a period of notable success, the management and coaching team at Leeds Carnegie rugby union team created physical, structural and psychosocial contexts that: a) encouraged players to make their own decisions with regard to engaging with performance-optimising or performance-impairing behaviour; but b) be more likely to engage the former (Cruickshank et al., 2013). Highlighting this approach, a specialist coach discussed how publicly presented performance data worked to increase performer work rate without any overt coach demand or request:

I had a board up there where . . . I'd put their tackle completion up, so it was all there black and white for everyone to see and that really generated a lot of interest. . . . I've heard a lot of blokes coming in and saying 'oh I'm only just one tackle off, I don't want to miss any this week I'll remember that'.

(Cruickshank et al., 2013, p. 282)

On a structural level, the same individual also described how the development of a balanced squad (rather than recruitment of a few 'superstars') promoted high performing behaviours:

There are . . . two good players competing for every position . . . so there are a lot of pressures on the players to make sure they are in peak physical condition . . .

165

they understood they were in a position where they could [drink alcohol if they wanted to] but they wouldn't get away with it.

(Cruickshank *et al.*, 2013, p. 283)

In sum, the proactive manipulation of context can work to create and, to an extent, control the coaching environment so that stakeholders are more likely to offer a safe level of contest. For many effective coaches, this is achieved through the design and application of cleverly designed drills that offer 'social encouragement' to a player towards a certain role or set of behaviours. The addition of indirect coaching interactions, as mentioned above, is less common but a valuable addition to shaping team behaviour.

BROAD BEHAVIOURAL REPERTOIRE

As effective coaching relies on the ability to read, manipulate and respond to context, it follows that coaches (should they wish to be considered *expert*: Nash et al., 2012) cannot rely on one leadership style alone. Indeed, one style will best match one particular context; not a range of contexts. We leave it to following chapters to fully illuminate some pertinent leadership styles for sports coaches and so focus here on a recent research development that emphasises the need for a broad behavioural repertoire.

More specifically, and challenging the dominance of 'bright' (or socially desirable) leadership behaviours (e.g. transformational theory; Bass, 1985), recent studies have highlighted the additional and integrated use and perceived benefits of 'dark' (or socially undesirable) behaviours (Hogan and Hogan, 2001). Before considering some of these behaviours in detail, and in keeping with the opening chapters of this book, it is useful to clarify the difference between dark side *behaviours* and dark side *traits*. Dark side *traits* have been described as those that occupy the mid point between 'normal' (e.g. Big Five) and pathological traits (Paulhus and Williams, 2002). As such, 'one might consider them personality quirks that do not greatly inhibit day-to-day functioning, but [that] may cause severely negative outcomes in particular circumstances; such as during leadership social interactions' (Harms et al., 2011, p. 496). Perhaps most simply, these traits are also 'viewed negatively by most individuals in society' (Judge et al., 2009, p. 864). Notably, however, dark side traits do not feature in destructive forms of leadership alone. Indeed, although less prevalent, they also feature in fundamentally constructive approaches. As an example, Davies (2004) has reported that the transformational style was associated with the dark side traits of *imaginative* (i.e. acting and thinking in creative and at times odd or unusual ways) and *colourful* (i.e. wanting to be noticed and the centre of attention).

Indeed, many organisational researchers agree that dark side traits in a leader can actually improve follower functioning and performance. As other examples, positive links have been reported between Machiavellianism and legislative development as well as hubris and innovation (Judge et al., 2009). In contrast to the negative impact that dark side *traits* may have when they are repeatedly displayed in overt behaviour (i.e. continual narcissistic acts), sport-specific evidence suggests that the use of short-lived and contextually appropriate dark side *behaviours* can bolster leader effectiveness and performer/group success (Fletcher and Arnold, 2011; Bennie and O'Connor, 2012; Collins and Cruickshank, 2012; Elberse and Dye, 2012; Cruickshank et al., 2014). Interestingly, these findings match those that indicate that, in some scenarios, bright traits can actually be ineffective or even counterproductive (Judge et al., 2009).

Treating coaching as an innately complex and contested activity, the use of dark side behaviours by coaches is perhaps unsurprising. Indeed, we have already touched upon the micro-politics that coaches must engage in, often involving much 'face work' to promote personal value, power, and respect among peers and performers (Potrac *et al.*, 2002; Jones *et al.*, 2004; Jones, 2006). Our recent investigations with head coaches (and other leaders) of elite sports teams have also pointed to the use of other dark side behaviours (Cruickshank and Collins, 2014). Table 12.1 provides examples of these behaviours (note that their 'darkness' is borne from the view of the followers or targets of coach action).

Table 12.1 *Dark side behaviours*

Dark side behaviour	Definition	Exemplar quote
Machiavellian behaviour	Manipulative, deceitful, cunning and exploitative acts to further personal interests	[Introducing more conditioning work for the players] came . . . at the same time as Ryan Giggs' [yoga] DVD . . . [So I just] made a point of, 'have you seen this?' . . . Three or four players [then] came to see my analyst . . . and he got the DVD . . . [Then when] even the most ardent of [cynics] . . . sees four then six or seven people doing it . . . and getting results, ultimately something is going to click. . . . So from having three or four in the gym before training all of a sudden eight or nine were in [without overt demands].
Sceptical behaviour	Cynical, distrustful and doubting others' true intentions	[For] developing a good team . . . you can start through the [senior players]. . . . With some senior players [however] . . . it's your old enemy isn't it; keep your friends close but . . . keep your bloody enemies even closer! . . . [Failing to do so] may well have been a mistake that I made at [previous team] and perhaps is something that I've learned from.
Social dominance behaviour	Preference for hierarchy, achievement and control, as well as projection as a highly and consistently competent figure	Sometimes you don't want [players] to question everything, you just want them to do what we want them to do because we are the ones that have spent the hours looking at film and deciding the best way [to approach a game]. . . . There might have been times where we really encouraged their participation . . . but we probably just needed to tell them [at other times], 'this is the way we are doing it; end of!'
Performance-focused ruthlessness behaviour	'No compromise' approach to the promotion of the team or group's vision, values and standards	[Young modern players are] moaning away behind the scenes, and that's what you're going to get these days. . . . Society's made it, for every young man or young person, to have an excuse for failing; there is an excuse for everything now. There's a syndrome for people being lazy, rude. You come from a broken family? I don't give a >*. . . . I come from X; people getting stabbed and smacking each other so don't give me that >*. I've never been in trouble in my life, and all my mates have never been in trouble with the police.

Of course, and as per the consistent message through this chapter, use of dark leadership depends on making the right decision: in short, *any* style has to be appropriate and targeted rather than just following a prescription or an example from someone else.

SUMMARY

As we hope to have emphasised throughout this chapter, coaching is a highly complex and dynamic activity. Additionally, we have also stressed that the coaching process involves much more than developing and refining the technical and tactical skills of sports performers and teams. Indeed, through the need to consider and address a host of other factors, most notably those of a social and political nature, coaching is a multidimensional task that relies on the ability to make coherent and impactful decisions across the multiple levels of practice. In this way, and reflecting its potential to account for all of these key features, a professional judgement and decision making approach has been forwarded as the most appropriate and parsimonious for guiding the work of both coaching researchers and practitioners (Abraham and Collins, 2011). In particular, nested thinking can be used to explain and support coach effectiveness by providing a means to develop well-considered systematic plans that guide both long term/macro-level strategies and in situ processes. Shifting from *what* coaches have to do towards *how* they can best achieve this, we then described some key skills that revolved around understanding and managing the complex and dynamic contexts of coaching. While a host of skills not mentioned here are also important, such as reflective practice (Gilbert and Trudel, 2001), we chose to focus in particular on *multidirectionality*, *emotional intelligence*, *socio-political awareness* and *micro-political literacy*, *context manipulation* and a *broad behavioural repertoire*. We hope that our illumination of these skills provides a foundation on which readers can now consider the content and messages of the following chapters.

REVIEW QUESTIONS

1   What are some of the core differences between coaching requirements in participation and performance domains? And what other differences might exist but haven't been discussed here?

2   How do the models 'of' and 'for' coaching differ between each other and what are the limitations of both?

3   How does a focus on professional judgement and decision making provide a unifying focus for coaching researchers and practitioners?

4   You are the coach of a professional soccer club's under 14 squad and have decided that, even though your assistant coach disagrees, you need to improve players' effort in training – how might you use the exemplar skills outlined in this chapter to achieve this goal?

REFERENCES

Abraham, A. and Collins, D. 2011. Taking the next step: New directions for coaching science. *Quest* 6, pp. 366–384.

Abraham, A., Collins, D. and Martindale, R. 2006. The coaching schematic: Validation through expert coach consensus. *Journal of Sports Sciences* 24(6), pp. 549–564.

Ashmos, D. P., Duchon, D. and McDaniel, J. R. R. 2000. Organisational responses to complexity: The effect on organisational performance. *Journal of Organizational Change Management* 13, pp. 577–595.

Augustine, A. A. and Hemenover, S. H. (2009). On the relative effectiveness of affect regulation strategies: A meta-analysis. *Cognition and Emotion* 23, pp. 1181–1220.

Barlow, A. and Banks, A. P. 2014. Using emotional intelligence in coaching high-performance athletes: A randomized controlled trial. *Coaching: An International Journal of Theory, Research and Practice* 7(2), pp. 132–139.

Bass, B. M. 1985. *Leadership and performance beyond expectations.* New York: Free Press.

Bennie, A. and O'Connor, D. 2012. Perceptions and strategies of effective coaching leadership: A qualitative investigation of professional coaches and players. *International Journal of Sport and Health Science* 10, pp. 82–89.

Bloom, B. S. (1985) *Developing talent in young people.* New York: Ballantine.

Borrie, A. 1996. Coaching science. In: Reilly, T. ed. *Science and soccer.* London: E and F N Spon, pp. 243–258.

Chan, J. T. and Mallett, C. J. 2011a. The value of emotional intelligence for high performance coaching. *International Journal of Sports Science and Coaching* 6, pp. 315–328.

Chan, J. T. and Mallett, C. J. 2011b. The value of emotional intelligence for high performance coaching: A response to commentaries. *International Journal of Sports Science and Coaching* 6, pp. 351–355.

Collins, D. and Collins, J. 2011. Putting them together: Skill packages to optimize team/group performance. In: Collins, D., Button, A. and Richards, H. eds. *Performance psychology: A practitioner's guide*, pp. 361–380.

Collins, D. and Cruickshank, A. 2012. 'Multidirectional management': Exploring the challenges of performance in the World Class Programme environment. *Reflective Practice* 13, pp. 455–469.

Collins, D. and Cruickshank, A. 2014. Take a walk on the wild side: Exploring, identifying, and developing consultancy expertise with elite performance team leaders. *Psychology of Sport and Exercise.* doi: 10.1016/j.psychsport.2014.08.002.

Côté, J., Salmela, J. and Russell, S. 1995a. The knowledge of high performance gymnastic coaches: Competition and training considerations. *The Sport Psychologist* 9, pp. 76–95.

Côté, J., Salmela, J., Trudel, P., Baria, A. and Russell, S. 1995b. The coaching model: A grounded assessment of expert gymnastic coaches knowledge. *Journal of Sport and Exercise Psychology* 17, pp. 1–17.

Cruickshank, A. and Collins, D. 2012. Culture change in elite sport performance teams: Examining and advancing effectiveness in the new era. *Journal of Applied Sport Psychology* 24, pp. 338–355.

Cruickshank, A. and Collins, D. 2014. Illuminating and applying 'the dark side': Insights from elite team leaders. *Journal of Applied Sport Psychology.* Advance online publication, doi: 10.1080/10413200.2014.982771.

Cruickshank, A., Collins, D. and Minten, S. 2013. Culture change in a professional sports team: Shaping environmental contexts and regulating power. *International Journal of Sports Science and Coaching* 8, pp. 271–290.

Cruickshank, A., Collins, D. and Minten, S. 2014. Driving and sustaining culture change in Olympic sport performance teams: A first exploration and grounded theory. *Journal of Sport and Exercise Psychology* 36, pp. 107–120.

Cushion, C. J., Armour, K. M. and Jones, R. L. 2006. Locating the coaching process in practice: Models 'for' and 'of' coaching. *Physical Education and Sport Pedagogy* 11, pp. 83–99.

d'Arrippe-Longueville, F., Fournier, J.F. and Dubois, A. 1998. The perceived effectiveness of interactions between expert French judo coaches and elite female athletes. *The Sport Psychologist* 12, pp. 317–332.

Davies, M. 2004. Prediction of transformational leadership by personality constructs for senior Australian organizational executive leaders. Unpublished dissertation, Faculty of Health Science, Griffith University, Queensland, Australia.

Elberse, A. and Dye, T. 2012. Sir Alex Ferguson: Managing Manchester United. *Harvard Business School*, Case 513–051.

Fairs, J. R. 1987. The coaching process: the essence of coaching. *Sports Coach* 11(1), pp. 17–19.

Fletcher, D. and Arnold, R. 2011. A qualitative study of performance leadership and management in elite sport. *Journal of Applied Sport Psychology* 23, pp. 223–242.

Franks, I., Sinclair, G., Thomson, W. and Goodman, D. 1986. Analysis of the coaching process. *Science, Periodical, Research Technology and Sport* 1, pp. 1–12.

Gilbert, W. D. and Trudel, P. 2001. Learning to coach through experience: Reflection in model youth sport coaches. *Journal of Teaching in Physical Education* 21, pp. 16–34.

Gould, D., Guinan, D., Greenleaf, C. and Chung, Y. 2002. A survey of U.S. Olympic coaches: Variables perceived to have influenced athlete performances and coach effectiveness. *The Sport Psychologist* 16, pp. 229–250.

Grandey, A. A. 2000. Emotion regulation in the workplace: a new way to conceptualize emotional labour. *Journal of Occupational Health Psychology* 5, pp. 59–100.

Griffin, R. W. and Moorhead, G. 2007. *Organizational Behavior: Managing People and Organizations*. New York: Houghton Mifflin Company.

Gross, J. J. and Thompson, R. A. 2007. Emotion regulation: Conceptual foundations. In: Gross, J. J. ed. *Handbook of emotion regulation*. New York: Guilford Press, pp. 3–24.

Haime, J. 2011. The value of emotional intelligence for high performance coaching: A commentary. *International Journal of Sports Science and Coaching* 6, pp. 337–340.

Hampson, R. and Jowett, S. 2014. Effects of coach leadership and coach–athlete relationship on collective efficacy. *Scandinavian Journal of Science and Medicine in Sports* 24, pp. 454–460.

Hanin, J. 2011. The value of emotional intelligence for high performance coaching: A commentary. *International Journal of Sports Science and Coaching* 6, pp. 341–344.

Hanson, W. and Gould, D. 1988. Factors affecting the ability of coaches to estimate their athletes' trait and state anxiety levels. *The Psychologist* 2, pp. 298–313.

Harms, P. D., Spain, S. M. and Hannah, S. T. 2011. Leader development and the dark side of personality. *The Leadership Quarterly* 22, pp. 495–509.

Hogan, R. and Hogan, J. 2001. Assessing leadership: A view from the dark side. *International Journal of Selection and Assessment* 9, pp. 40–51.

Hogan, R. and Hogan, J. 2002. Leadership and sociopolitical intelligence. In Riggio, R. E., Murphy, S. E. and Pirozzolo, F. J. eds. *Multiple intelligences and leadership*. San Francisco, CA: Jossey-Bass, pp. 75–88.

Hwang, S., Feltz, D. L. and Lee, J. D. 2013. Emotional intelligence in coaching: Mediation effect of coaching efficacy on the relationship between emotional intelligence and leadership style. *International Journal of Sport and Exercise Psychology* 11(3), pp. 292–306.

Jones, R. 2006. Dilemmas, maintaining 'face' and paranoia: An average coaching life. *Qualitative Inquiry* 12(5), pp. 1012–1021.

Jones, R. L., Armour, K. M. and Potrac, P. 2004. *The cultures of coaching*. London: Longman.

Jordan, P. J. and Troth, A. C. 2002. Emotional intelligence and conflict resolution: Implications for human resource development. *Advances in Developing Human Resources* 4, pp. 62–79.

Jordan, P. J., Ashkanasy, N. M. and Charmine, E. J. 2002. Emotional intelligence as a moderator of emotional and behavioral reactions to job insecurity. *Academy of Management Review* 27, pp. 361–372.

Judge, T. A., Piccolo, R. F. and Kosalka, T. 2009. The bright and dark side of leader traits: A review and theoretical extension of the leader trait paradigm. *The Leadership Quarterly* 20, pp. 855–875.

Kahneman, D. and Klein, G. 2009. Conditions for intuitive expertise: A failure to disagree. *American Psychologist* 64(6), pp. 515–526.

Kristiansen, E., Hanstad, D. V. and Roberts, G. C. 2011. Coping with the media at the Vancouver Winter Olympics: 'We all make a living out of this'. *Journal of Applied Sport Psychology* 23, pp. 443–458.

Latimer, A. E., Rench, T. A. and Brackett, M. A. 2007. Emotional intelligence: A framework for examining emotions in sport and exercise groups. In: Beauchamp, M. and Eys, M. eds. *Group dynamics advances in sport and exercise psychology: Contemporary themes.* New York: Routledge, pp. 3–24.

Lyle, J. W. B. 2002. *Sports coaching concepts: A framework for coaches' behaviour.* London: Routledge.

McClean, J. C. and Chelladurai, P. 1995. Dimensions of coaching performance: Development of a scale. *Journal of Sport Management* 9, pp. 194–207.

Martindale, A. and Collins, D. 2010. But *why* does what works work? A response to Fifer, Henschen, Gould, and Ravizza. *The Sport Psychologist* 24, pp. 113–116.

Martindale, A. and Collins, D. 2012. A professional judgment and decision making case study: Reflection-in-action research. *The Sport Psychologist* 26, pp. 500–518.

Mayer, J. D. and Salovey, P. 1997. What is emotional intelligence? In Salovey, P. and Sluyter, D. eds. *Emotional development and emotional intelligence: Implications for educators.* New York: Basic Books, pp. 3–31.

Meyer, B. B. and Fletcher, T. B. 2007. Emotional intelligence: A theoretical overview and implications for research and professional practice in sport psychology. *Journal of Applied Sport Psychology* 19, pp. 1–15.

Nash, C. and Collins, D. 2006. Tacit knowledge in expert coaching: Science or art? *Quest* 58, pp. 465–477.

Nash, C., Martindale, R., Collins, D. and Martindale, A. 2012. Parameterising expertise in coaching: Past, present and future. *Journal of Sports Sciences* 30, pp. 985–994.

Paulhus, D. L. and Williams, K. 2002. The dark triad of personality: Narcissism, Machiavellianism, and psychopathy. *Journal of Research in Personality* 36, pp. 556–568.

Petrides, K. V. and Furnham, A. 2000. On the dimensional structure of emotional intelligence. *Personality and Individual Differences* 29, pp. 313–320.

Potrac, P. and Jones, R. 2009. Power, conflict and cooperation: Toward a micropolitics of head coaching. *Quest* 61, pp. 223–236.

Potrac, P., Jones, R. L. and Armour, K. 2002. 'It's all about getting respect': The coaching behaviours of a top-level English football coach. *Sport, Education and Society* 7(2), pp. 183–202.

Schön, D. 1987. *Educating the reflective practitioner.* San Francisco, CA: Jossey-Bass.

Schön, D. 1991. *The reflective practitioner: How professionals think in action.* New York: Arena.

Sherman, C., Crassini, B., Maschette, W. and Sands, R. 1997. Instructional sports psychology: A reconceptualisation of sports coaching as instruction. *International Journal of Sports Psychology* 28(2), pp. 103–125.

Sternberg, R. J. 2003. *Wisdom, intelligence, and creativity synthesized.* New York: Cambridge University Press.

Tetlock, P. 2005. *Expert political judgment: How good is it? How can we know?* Princeton, NJ: Princeton University Press.

Thaler, R. H. and Sunstein, C. 2009. Libertarian paternalism. *The American Economic Review* 93(2), pp. 175–179.

Thelwell, R. C., Lane, A. M., Weston, N. J. V. and Greenlees, I. A. 2008. Examining relationships between emotional intelligence and coaching efficacy. *International Journal of Sport and Exercise Psychology* 6, pp. 224–235.

Thompson, A., Potrac, P. and Jones, R. (2013). 'I found out the hard way': Micro-political workings in professional football. *Sport, Education and Society*, advance online publication, doi: 10.1080/13573322.2013.862786.

Tozer, M., Fazey, I. and Fazey, J. 2007. Recognising and developing adaptive expertise within outdoor and expedition leaders. *Journal of Adventure Education and Outdoor Learning* 7, pp. 55–75.

Wagstaff, C., Fletcher, D. and Hanton, S. 2012. Positive organizational psychology in sport: An ethnography of organizational functioning in a national sport organization. *Journal of Applied Sport Psychology* 24, pp. 26–47.

Chapter 13

Sport coach leadership models

Paul Cummins and Jarrod Spencer

CHAPTER OBJECTIVES

After completing this chapter you should be able to:

1 understand the pertinent leadership theories in the complex sport coaching domain;
2 discuss a wide range of sport coach leadership models and how these differ in terms of their emphasis, strengths and limitations;
3 explain the commonalities within numerous models of sport coach leadership;
4 describe some key competencies that can help coaches to lead effectively in the dynamic environments within which they operate.

KEY TERMS

■ relational models
■ athlete centred models
■ group centred models
■ coaching effectiveness models

INTRODUCTION

This chapter is based on an extensive review of the sport coaching leadership literature and it investigates the past theories and models of leadership in sport coaching from a theoretical approach. Recent pertinent leadership models are discussed in detail and coaching effectiveness is reviewed with regard to measurement outcomes.

Past research in sport and coaching suggests that coaches have a significant role and influence on their athletes, in particular on youth athletes, mainly through the attitudes, values and beliefs they emphasise, the behaviours and actions they model, the goals and targets they set for their players, and the overall environment and culture they seek to create. Research on coaching behaviours emerged over 30 years ago with a specific focus on coach–athlete interactions within sports participation, and subsequent athletic psychosocial development and past studies investigated coaching behaviours and the frequency and timing of coaching behaviours mainly through observational methods; delivering instruction, punishment and praise.

Sport is an excellent setting in which one can research the behaviours of leaders and the dimensions of leadership. This may be because sport performance (successes and failures) are accurately measurable, sports teams provide a neat sample size that can provide both scope and depth of investigation, and leadership behaviours are critical and widely relied upon within sport at every level. Methods of investigation include field studies, lab experiments and qualitative interviews. One must stress the importance of field studies relating group performance and morale to behavioural data on leaders, and that both the greater importance of a leader's behaviour to followers, and the increased time for interactions that occur in a field setting may produce stronger relationships than what had been obtained in the lab (Lavallee et al., 2008).

Coaching effectiveness and coach leadership in sport research has varied in its use of methodologies over the years of investigation to date; however, the conceptual approaches to coaching and leadership effectiveness are categorised into two broad groups: those based on theoretical models and those based on a grounded theory approach. The pertinent theoretical models are presented and discussed in this chapter, with particular attention given to more recent theoretical approaches; the servant leadership model, the authentic leadership model and the transformational leadership model.

THEORETICALLY BASED RESEARCH

The most significant theoretical leadership effectiveness models in the sport coaching field to date include the multidimensional model of leadership proposed by Chelladurai (1978, 1990, 2007), the cognitive-mediational model of leadership (Smoll and Smith, 1989) and the motivational model of the coach–athlete relationship (Mageau and Vallerand, 2003). More recent theoretical contributions to the sport coaching leadership literature include leadership models applied to the sport setting such as the transformational model of leadership (Charbonneau et al., 2006; Smith et al., 2013), the servant leadership model (Rieke et al., 2008), the altruistic leadership model (Miller and Carpenter, 2009) and the authentic leadership model (Luthans and Avolio, 2003).

Leadership, as a process of social influence, is the most important factor in sport team dynamics (Kao and Cheng, 2005). Coaching leadership is the main social influence in the interaction of sports team building (Smith and Smoll, 1997; Yukelson, 1997). The leadership models applied to the sport coach domain naturally converge under the four following overarching leadership approaches: relational, athlete-centred, group-centred and coaching effectiveness. Multiple models have been designed within these approaches to varying degrees of success (see Table 13.1). Below is a description of each approach followed by an outline of the most pertinent sport coach leadership models utilised to date with reference to their added value to the sport coaching field.

RELATIONAL MODELS

Relational approaches seek to explore and understand the sport coaching leadership process through the dyadic coach–athlete lens and include the altruistic leadership model (Miller and Carpenter, 2009), the transactional model (Carthen, 2006), the motivational model (Mageau and Vallerand, 2003), the emotional intelligence model (Chan and Mallet, 2009), and the athlete–coach relationship model (Lorimer and Jowett, 2009).

The altruistic model of leadership

Altruism is defined as a motivational state with the ultimate goal of increasing another's well-being (Batson and Leonard, 1987). Upon deconstructing this statement with reference to a simple definition of leadership (e.g. getting things done through others), and with the understanding that people will not effectively follow a leader in getting things done unless their own well-being is increased in some form, then altruism is a key component to effective leadership. Altruism has been examined with reference to sportsmanship and volunteering within general sports literature; however, few studies have been conducted that investigate the altruistic motivations of sport coaches. Miller and Carpenter (2009) investigated the altruistic model of leadership within the sport coaching field through a case-study analysis where Jim Tressel (Head Coach of the Ohio State American Football team) was interviewed at length about the altruistic leadership techniques that have proved successful over his lengthy tenure as coach.

The transactional leadership model

Transactional leadership identifies the leader as the catalyst for follower expectations, goals, and the provision of recognition and rewards when a task is completed (Bass, 1985). Trans-actional leadership provides the pathway for contingent reinforcement where the leader and follower agree on the necessary path to achieve the reward and avert punishment (Bass, 1985; Bass and Avolio, 1994; Burns, 1978). In sport, transactional leadership offers a cognitive framework that helps to explain an athlete's willingness to subject their body to injury (Carthen, 2006). Carthen (2006) explored the advent of a transactional leadership paradigm in sports antiquity with a focus on athletes' reactions to types of intrinsic and extrinsic motivation in sport such as external influence, preparation, training, coaching and establishing a path to victory or defeat. This research indicated that an athlete's adherence or rejection of contingent reinforcement served as a road map to follower motivation and goal attainment (Bass, 1985) and that sport and society are inextricably connected (Carthen, 2006). In today's working and sport society, there is real-world evidence that transactional leadership is

175

an important component, especially in professional sport, where extrinsic motivation is heightened and activated through external monetary reward. Nevertheless, other models of leadership in sport that tend to operate at higher levels of human needs (e.g. social belonging, self-actualisation) such as the transformational approach seem to be more effective in providing long-term and sustainable effective leadership results.

The motivational model of the coach–athlete relationship

The motivational model of the coach–athlete relationship incorporates a hierarchical perspective on intrinsic and extrinsic motivation as well as Deci and Ryan's (1985) cognitive-evaluation theory. The Mageau and Vallerand (2003) model explains that three factors (coach's personal orientation, the coaching context, and the coach's perceptions of the athlete's behaviour and motivation) determines the degree to which the coach exhibits autonomy-supportive behaviours towards and with his/her athletes. Mageau and Vallerand (2003) suggest that the combination of a) coach autonomy-supportive behaviours (e.g. behaviours that support athlete autonomy/decision-making), b) the structure set by the coach (e.g. practices, routines, limits and standards) and c) the level of athlete engagement affects athlete's perceptions of competence, autonomy and relatedness, which in turn establish athlete's level of intrinsic and self-determined extrinsic motivation. This model suggests that effective coaching behaviour includes supporting athlete's perceptions of autonomy, providing structure for athletes in the sport setting, and demonstrating involvement in athlete's welfare (e.g. encouragement, emotional support).

Upon further investigation, if one looks at this model from a traditional leadership perspective, a link forms with a transformational leadership approach leading to effective coaching. Specifically, intellectual stimulation is defined as the ability of a leader to challenge followers, as well as incorporating their opinions into the decision-making process (Bass, 1999). This is closely associated with effective coaches demonstrating autonomy-supportive behaviours within the motivational model of the coach–athlete relationship. In addition, individualised consideration refers to the ability of a leader to be aware of followers' needs (Bass, 1999), a concept that is connected to the level of coach engagement and involvement with their athletes. Finally, transformational leaders exert idealised influence through acting as role models and cultivating admiration, trust and respect in their subordinates (Bass, 1999). This is related to Mageau and Vallerand's (2003) establishment of structure to help guide athletes towards team and individual goals. Transformational leadership models applied to sport coaching is discussed later in this chapter.

The emotional intelligence model of leadership

The emotional intelligence (EI) construct refers to an individual's ability to effectively manage the interplay between emotion and cognition and sport coaches are required to lead and manage multiple human elements associated with enabling high performance (Mallett, 2010). Given the dynamic nature of sport and the real-time adaptability necessary for success within this complex domain (Cushion, 2007), a coach requires strong leadership to guide the coach–team–performance relationship (Lyle, 2002). Chan and Mallet (2011) presented a review of emotional intelligence applied to the leadership field that suggested that coach-leaders with low EI may have poor interpersonal skills and the inability to develop a trustworthy and inspiring relationship with their staff and athletes. Thus EI appears to be a valuable component for high-performance coach-leaders as it contributes to effective leadership (Humphrey, 2002). Nevertheless, there is also evidence that points to successful coaches with limited EI, thus further investigation is required to examine the efficacy of EI levels as a predictor of effective coach leadership.

The coach–athlete relationship model

The coach–athlete relationship has been an important area of research in the sport coach leadership field for many years as it is a highly dynamic factor in both athletic and coaching performance. Smith *et al.* (1979) were the pioneers of research on the coach–athlete relationship when they embarked on a study guided by a meditational model of coach–athlete interactions in which the core assumptions were that coaching behaviours interacted with athlete perceptions and recall which then resulted in athlete evaluative reactions and consequential behaviour: coach behaviours – athlete perception and recall – athletes' evaluative reactions. Recent research in this area has focused on investigating the nature and significance of the coach–athlete relationship within the context of the interpersonal constructs of closeness, co-orientation and complementarity (the 3 Cs) as identified as key operational components within the coach–athlete relationship dyad. Jowett and Cockerill (2003) interviewed 12 Olympic medallists about their athletic relationship with their coach. Findings from this study demonstrated that feelings of closeness (e.g. trust and respect), thought of co-orientation (e.g. common goals) and complementary roles (e.g. coach–athlete role structure in practice) marked the positive athletic relationships of the Olympic medallists to their respective coaches. Negative relational aspects also emerged from the interview process; however, the impact of the coach–athlete relationship on the success achieved was evident through the qualitative process (Jowett and Cockerill, 2003). The authors concluded that the nature of the coach–athlete relationship plays an important role in athlete development both as a person and as a performer. Such research has highlighted the importance of the coach–athlete relationship in effective coach-leadership and significantly, the quality of the coach–athlete relationship will inform the level of interpersonal knowledge a coach has of their athletes, thus leading to improved leader effectiveness (Vella *et al.*, 2010).

ATHLETE-CENTRED MODELS

Athlete-centred approaches are focused predominantly on the athletes as integral and inclusive cogs in the leadership process, both in how they perceive their coach leaders to be, and the impact that the leadership process has on them as performers. Athlete-centred leadership approaches include the servant leadership model (Rieke *et al.*, 2008), the athlete satisfaction model (Riemar and Chelladurai, 1995), the self-determination model (Hollembeak and Amorose, 2005), the self-enhancement model (Smoll *et al.*, 1993) and the autonomy-supportive model (Gagne *et al.*, 2003).

SERVANT LEADERSHIP IN SPORT

Servant leadership is defined by the core constructs of trust, humility and service to others (Vella *et al.*, 2010). Like many other leadership models, servant leadership emerged from within the organisational context (Greenleaf, 1977) and is a leadership approach based on teamwork and community, involving others in decision making, displaying ethical and caring behaviour and enhancing personal growth of subordinates while improving the varying and quality of institutions (Spears, 1998). A servant leader in essence inverts the traditional leadership pyramid model (where leaders are at the top and subordinates at the bottom) to where servant leaders are at the bottom and are responsible for giving subordinates clear roles/job descriptions and then serving the subordinate in achieving what the role requires. Servant leaders place other people's needs, aspirations and interests above their own and the result, theoretically, is a work/team environment where relationships are cultivated, everyone is valued, standards are upheld and productivity enhanced (Greenleaf, 1977).

Servant leadership applied to sport coaching effectiveness

Rieke *et al.* (2008) explored the suitability of the servant leadership model in increasing sport coaching effectiveness and found that athletes preferred the servant leader coaching style to more traditional styles. In a prior study, Hammermeister *et al.* (2008) assessed the impact that servant leader coaching behaviour had on athletes' intrinsic motivation (intrinsic motivation inventory: IMI, Ryan, 1982), mental toughness (Ottawa mental skills assessment tool-3: OMSAT-3, Durand-Bush and Salmela, 2001) and sport satisfaction (athlete satisfaction questionnaire: ASQ, Riemer and Chelladurai, 1998) using a sample of 251 collegiate basketball athletes. This initial study suggested that the servant leadership model was viable for use in sport settings.

The revised servant leadership profile for sport (RSLP-S)

In the follow-up study Rieke *et al.* (2008) examined a sample of 195 high-school basketball athletes to assess the relationship between servant leader coach behaviours and numerous sport variables such as intrinsic motivation, sport satisfaction, mental skills and sport performance. The researchers used the revised servant leadership profile for sport (RSLP-S) to measure athlete perceptions of their coach's servant leadership behaviour. The RSLP-S represents three servant leader constructs: a) trust/inclusion; b) humility and c) service. The results of this follow-up study showed that athletes who perceived their coach to possess servant leader qualities also displayed higher intrinsic motivation, were more task oriented, were more satisfied, were mentally tougher and performed better than athletes coached by non-servant leaders. This study also reported findings that suggested athletes' preferred coaches who displayed servant leader behaviours than those who did not, specifically on two of the three servant leader sub-scales (trust/inclusion and service). Despite study limitations such as the limited athlete participant sample (high-school basketball) and the cross-sectional nature of this investigation, this research provided valuable insight into a new leadership paradigm's (servant leadership) potential applicability and success within the sport environment.

178

The athlete satisfaction model

Athlete satisfaction is an effective measure of coach leadership given that the satisfaction levels and well-being of each athlete is a critical outcome of constructive sport leadership and effective sport coaching. House (1971) suggested that athlete satisfaction is influenced by the leader exhibiting behaviours appropriate to the characteristics of the task and, specifically, structure established by a leader serves to regulate and clarify path–goal relationships when tasks are varied and interdependent (i.e. as in most sport teams). Thus, a leader's structuring behaviour will have a significant impact on athlete levels of coordination, satisfaction and performance. Riemar and Chelladurai (1995) explored the following two important areas within the sport setting: a) the differences between the offensive and defensive personnel of football teams in preferred leadership, perceived leadership and satisfaction with leadership and b) the relationship among preferred and perceived leadership, their congruence and satisfaction with leadership. Two hundred and one American football athletes were assessed through a quantitative survey, and findings demonstrated that defensive positioned players preferred and perceived greater amounts of democratic behaviour, autocratic behaviour and social support than the offensive positioned players. In addition, the congruence of preferred and perceived leadership in the social support leadership dimension was shown to enhance athlete satisfaction; however, perceived leadership (e.g. actual leadership behaviours) in both the training and instruction and positive feedback dimensions were stronger determinants of satisfaction with leadership than both the preferred and congruence of preferred/perceived leadership in these dimensions. Ultimately, perceived leadership behaviours by athletes have a significant effect on athlete satisfaction levels and this tends to vary in line with the components (e.g. congruence among preferred and perceived leader behaviours, the preferences among athletes, and the requirements of the situation) of the multidimensional model of leadership (Chelladurai, 1978, 1990, 1993; Chelladurai and Carron, 1978).

The self-determination model

Hollembeak and Amorose (2005) used the self-determination theory (SDT) to explore whether perceived competence, autonomy and relatedness mediated the relationships between perceived coaching behaviours and athletes' intrinsic motivation (IM). SDT (Deci and Ryan, 1985; Ryan and Deci, 2000, 2002) specifies that the need for competence (e.g. to perceive our behaviour as competent), autonomy (e.g. to perceive our thoughts and behaviour as freely chosen) and relatedness (e.g. to perceive we are connected to those around us) are fundamental to humans. According to SDT, humans are thus drawn to choose activities that meet these three fundamental needs and therefore people are intrinsically motivated to participate in activities that support one's perceptions of personal competence, autonomy and relatedness. Therefore, SDT suggests that anything that impacts the needs of competence, autonomy and relatedness can ultimately impact intrinsic motivation (Hollembeak and Amorose, 2005). To explore SDT within the sport setting, Hollembeak and Amorose (2005) administered surveys to 280 college athletes measuring perceived coaching behaviours based on the leadership sports scale (e.g. training and instruction, positive feedback, social support, autocratic and democratic behaviour). Findings indicated that all of the coaching behaviours other than social support significantly predicted perceived competence, autonomy and/or relatedness which predicted athletes' intrinsic motivation (Hollembeak and Amorose, 2005). Results also showed that only perceived autocratic and democratic behaviours had a significant effect on IM. Given that the role of the sport coach as a leader has been deemed extremely important in motivating athletes (Horn, 2002), this research supports SDT as a very useful component in effective sport coach leadership.

The self-enhancement model

Smoll et al. (1993) examined the impact of coaching behaviours on athletes' self-enhancement processes. Self-enhancement refers to the increase in self-esteem levels and was mediated in this study through coach training that focused on two self-enhancement components: a) coach supportiveness and b) instructional effectiveness. Following coach training, the authors set up an experiment that assessed 152 youth baseball players based on whether the players had either a) the self-enhancement trained coaches or b) the control group of coaches. Following post-study athlete interviews, findings suggested that the trained coaches differed from the controls in player-perceived behaviours (Smoll et al., 1993). Specifically, trained coaches were evaluated more positively by their athletes, the athletes who were coached by the trained coaching group reported to have more fun, and their teams also exhibited a higher level of inter-team attraction. Despite such positive results, there was no significant difference found between either group's win–loss performance records. Nevertheless, in youth sports the key area of focus is participation, task mastery and enjoyment, and findings are consistent with the self-esteem enhancement model in that young athletes with low self-esteem who played for the trained coaches showed significant increases in general self-esteem when compared to the young low self-esteem athletes in the control group. Such valuable research supports the self-enhancement model of leadership as an effective tool for use by coaches, especially in the early stages of athlete development.

The autonomy-supportive model of leadership

Autonomy support is a component of the motivational climate in sport (youth sport most significantly) that may promote athletes' internalisation of behaviours and attitudes (Conroy and Coatsworth, 2007). Conroy and Coatsworth (2007) conducted a non-experimental study that examined the psychometric properties of the Autonomy-Supportive Coaching Questionnaire (ASCQ) through survey administration to a sample of 165 youth swimming athletes. Athletes in the study also completed a psychological satisfaction survey and results demonstrated that the ASCQ provided a valid assessment of youth athlete perceptions of autonomy-supportive coaching and that it positively predicted athlete satisfaction. In a further study, the effects of autonomy-supportive coaching methods on youth athletes were explored and results indicated that coaches' autonomy support, particularly via process-focused praise, predicted youth competence need satisfaction and relatedness need satisfaction in the coaching relationship (Coatsworth and Conroy, 2009). Such findings suggest that the quality of the coaching climate experienced by youth athletes is an important predictor of the psychological developmental benefits of sport participation and the autonomy-supportive model of coach leadership can positively influence the coaching quality of youth athletes.

GROUP-CENTRED MODELS

Despite the current gap in the sport leadership literature defined as the lack of research applied to understanding the sport coaching leadership process on a group level, group centred approaches are minimal within the sport domain. Apart from the team cohesion model (Williams and Widmeyer, 1991) and the organisational citizenship model (Aoyagi et al., 2008), there has been limited exploration into sport coach leadership from a group-centred perspective. The premise of group-centred leadership is to emphasise group interactions and, more specifically, how the leadership process works within the group setting.

Team cohesion model

Widmeyer and Williams (1991) conducted research to examine the sport coaching variables that resulted in greater team cohesion. It was hypothesised that team cohesion was related to team size, total satisfaction, similarity of experience, coaches' efforts to foster cohesion, prior performance outcome, having a team goal, total communication and prior liking (Widmeyer and Williams, 1991). The authors assessed 85 female intercollegiate golfers for levels of cohesion (measured using the group environment questionnaire, GEQ) in relation to the aforementioned nine variables. Findings showed that all nine variables predicted a significant amount of team cohesion with total satisfaction being the highest predictor of team cohesion.

The organisational citizenship model

Organisational citizenship behaviour (OCB) has been frequently applied to the organisational setting (Dalal, 2005; Kidder and Parks, 2001; Organ et al., 2006) and is defined as individual behaviour that is discretionary, not directly or explicitly recognised by the formal reward system, and that in the aggregate promotes the effective functioning of the organisation (Organ, 1988). The three components central to the OCB construct are a set of behaviours that a) are discretionary, are not part of the job description, and are performed by employees as a result of personal choice, b) go above and beyond that which is an enforceable requirement of the job description and c) contribute positively to overall organisational effectiveness. Based on previous OCB research in the organisational literature, the multidimensional model of leadership (Chelladurai, 1978), the conceptual framework of team cohesion (Carron and Hausenblas, 1998) and the model of athlete satisfaction (Riemar and Challadurai, 1997) were selected as theoretically sound antecedents to be associated with OCB in sport (Aoyagi et al., 2008). Aoyagi et al. (2008) explored OCB in a sport setting using a sample of 193 collegiate athletes and findings supported preliminary evidence for OCB as a unique and meaningful construct in sport.

COACHING EFFECTIVENESS MODELS

Coaching effectiveness leadership approaches are based on examining how effective coaches are leading typically through specified and predetermined outcome measures (e.g. win–loss record, efficacy, competence, athlete experience etc.). Coaching effectiveness is a key issue in practice and research (Horn, 2002). Thus coaching effectiveness leadership models are the most abundant of the leadership in sport frameworks and include the multidimensional model of leadership (Chelladurai, 1984), the cognitive-mediational model of coach leadership (Smoll and Smith, 1989), the transformational leadership model (Bass, 1985; Callow et al., 2009; Charbonneau et al., 2001; Rowold, 2006; Vallee and Bloom, 2005), the coaching model (Côté et al., 1995), the authentic leadership model (Luthans and Avolio, 2003), the fitness leader behaviour model (Loughead et al., 2008) and multiple models termed as coaching effectiveness models (Boardley et al., 2008; Horn, 2008; Côté and Gilbert, 2009).

The multidimensional model of leadership

Chelladurai (1978, 1990, 2007) constructed the multidimensional model of leadership to provide a framework for the specification and identification of effective leadership behaviour in specific sport situations. Chelladurai proposed that the specific leadership behaviours that produced desired performance outcomes were a function of three aspects of leader behaviour: the actual behaviour exhibited by the coach, the leader behaviour preferred by the athletes, and the type of leader behaviour required in the situational context. Chelladurai explained that each of these three constructs is driven by antecedent factors (e.g. coach characteristics and situational requirements will inform coach leadership behaviours, athlete characteristics and situational factors will determine the leader behaviour desired by the athletes, and the sporting context and group characteristics will drive the requirements of the situation). Chelladurai hypothesised that positive outcomes of group performance and member satisfaction is a result of the level of congruence between the three aspects of leader behaviour. The multidimensional model of leadership introduced by Chelladurai (1984) is one of the most commonly used models of leadership in sports coaching and is discussed in further detail later in this chapter.

The cognitive-mediational model of leadership

Smoll and Smith's (1989) cognitive-mediational model of leadership gave consideration to the relationships among situational, cognitive, behavioural and individual difference variables (Horn, 2002, p. 241). This model proposed that coach behaviour was a function of both their own personal characteristics (e.g. goals, motives, habits, personality) and contextual factors (e.g. nature of sport, level of competition). Smoll and Smith (1989) suggested that within their coach leadership model, the behaviours exhibited at all times by the coach are interpreted on an individual basis by each athlete. Thus, athlete's evaluations of the coach are a function of both their own personal characteristics (e.g. age, sex, personality) and the situational factors evident at the time (e.g. nature of sport, level of competition). The cognitive-mediational model of coach leadership suggests that cognitive processes and individual difference variables will mediate the relationship between coach behaviour and athlete outcomes in addition to the specific situational variables that are of influence concurrently (Smoll and Smith, 1989).

182

TRANSFORMATIONAL LEADERSHIP IN SPORT

Transformational leadership is viewed as an ability of a leader to elevate the interest of his or her followers and to foster their commitment and energy towards the group and its goals (Bass, 1990). Transformational leadership is particularly apparent in the organisational field and past research describes transformational leaders as having the ability to promote a cooperative working environment, foster a culture of trust, give regular feedback, provide solutions through times of crises and implement a participative decision-making process. Within sport coaching, transformational leaders were seen to provide not just a strict 'top–bottom' hierarchy, but also a relationship where a 'transformation' occurred in both directions (Armstrong, 2001). Armstrong (2001) continued to explain in a non-empirical article that coaches educated their athletes in understanding life lessons in addition to sport knowledge and that while winning was considered no less important, a large emphasis was placed on fair play, total group effort and honesty.

Vallee and Bloom (2005) inadvertently provided through this research an initial step in connecting transformational leadership styles to coaching. The four categories that emerged from this qualitative investigation (coaches' attributes, individual growth, organisational skills and vision) appeared similar to the four characteristics of transformational leadership (e.g. inspirational motivation, idealised influence, intellectual stimulation and individual consideration; Bass, 1999) and other research on transformational leadership (e.g., Armstrong, 2001; Bass, 1990; Bass and Avolio, 1994; Graham, 1987; Sashkin and Burke, 1990). Research on transformational leadership has mostly been found in the fields of business, management, industry, spirituality, politics, education, health care and military (e.g. Bass, 1990, 1998). Bass and Avolio (1994) explained that there are four 'Is' that characterise a transformational leader: inspirational motivation, idealised influence, intellectual stimulation and individualised consideration. Each component is presented below.

Inspirational motivation

Inspirational motivation is the leader's ability to envision the future, articulate a vision, sell the vision to the group, and gain commitment from the followers towards a specific vision (Bass, 1999). Vallee and Bloom's (2005) study revealed expert coaches as visionaries, motivators, goal-setters and organised leaders who were able to gain achievement and success by gaining commitment and enthusiasm from their followers, and having them buy into the vision. A clear relationship exists between inspirational motivation (an ability of a trans-formational leader) and the expert coaches investigated in the above study, and the idea of creating a vision as a coach is paramount in forming the foundation to then lead in a transformative manner.

Idealised influence

Transformational leaders act as role models and cultivate both admiration and respect in their subordinates (Bass, 1999). This tendency was reflected in Vallee and Bloom's (2005) study through the Coach Attributes category, where expert coaches described role model

183

qualities as necessary to influence their followers such as cultivating the coach–athlete relationship as key in gaining respect and enjoyment of activity, leading by example through coach's personality characteristics and determining high-performance goals for the team. Expert coaches worked very hard at developing healthy personal relationships with their players based on trust, respect, communication and care for the person (Vallee and Bloom, 2005).

Intellectual stimulation

Intellectual stimulation was defined as the ability of a leader to challenge followers, as well as incorporating their opinions into the decision-making process (Bass, 1999). Achieving member buy-in leads to ownership and maximal performance, and is a very important aspect to transformational leadership. Expert coaches within Vallee and Bloom's (2005) study offered a strong match to the intellectual stimulation component of transformational leadership through both the Individual Growth and Organisational Skills categories. The Individual Growth category referred to expert coach's ability to empower players, involve them in the decision-making process and promote player's leadership and responsibility, while the Organisational Skills category involved challenging players to reach higher levels of achievement through creative and effective training sessions (Vallee and Bloom, 2005).

Individualised consideration

Individualised consideration refers to the ability of a leader to be aware of followers' needs (Bass, 1999). Previous research on expert coaches found similarities between individualised consideration and the Individual Growth category, where expert coaches gave specific attention to every team member, were respectful of personal differences and were concerned with empowering each athlete as an individual in addition to as an athlete (Vallee and Bloom, 2005). The ability of a coach to view each athlete as more than just an athlete, and coach the individual to be the best person they can be both on and off the floor is an apparent philosophy in many successful coaches (e.g. John Wooden, Jim Tressell). Providing individual consideration and catering for the needs of each athlete is consistent with the positive outcomes of altruistic leadership and also serves to increase the strength of the coach–athlete relationship.

AUTHENTIC LEADERSHIP IN SPORT

Not much attention has been given to authentic leadership as applied within the sports realm. Nevertheless, it appears to be a model of leadership that will define future leadership research in most domains along with other innovative and holistic approaches (e.g. social identity theory of leadership). Given the positive results yielded from very minimal authentic leadership research in the sport domain, more exploration in the area may prove beneficial to the sport leadership literature, specifically from a sport coaching perspective.

Authentic leadership

Past research concludes that authenticity consists of a range of mental and behavioural processes that explain how people discover and construct a core sense of self, and how this

184

core self is maintained across situations and over time (Kernis and Goldman, 2006). Four themes are prevalent within the literature relating to individuals' authentic functioning of 1) self-understanding, 2) openness to objectively recognising their desirable and undesirable self-aspects, 3) actions and 4) orientation towards interpersonal relationships. Based on this research, past authentic leadership literature has identified four key components of authenticity: 1) awareness, 2) unbiased processing, 3) behaviour and 4) relational orientation (Kernis and Goldman, 2006).

The awareness component refers to an individual's trust in and knowledge of one's feelings, thoughts, motives and values while the unbiased processing component refers to the ability of an individual to remain objective and accept their positive and negative attributes. Authentic leaders will behave according to their true preferences, values and needs rather than action to please others, secure rewards or avoid punishments, and the relational orientation component refers to achieving and valuing truthfulness and openness in one's close relationships. Throughout its history, defining what an authentic leader is has evolved according to the research conducted. A recent definition of authentic leadership states that an authentic leader 1) is self-aware, humble, always seeking improvement, aware of those being led and looks out for the welfare of others, 2) fosters high degrees of trust by building an ethical and moral framework and 3) is committed to organisational success within the construct of social values (Whitehead, 2009, p. 850).

The authentic leadership questionnaire

Building upon the four components identified in Kernis and Goldman's (2003; 2006) work Walumbwa et al. (2008) developed and validated the authentic leadership questionnaire (ALQ). The ALQ contains 16 items and four subscales to form a composite authentic leadership score. The ALQ measures four subscales that build upon the original components: 1) balanced processing (three items), 2) internalised moral perspective (four items), 3) relational transparency (five items) and 4) self-awareness (four items). Past research investigating the effects of authentic leadership within the organisational context show that this recent leadership approach has a positive impact on follower attitudes and behaviours, team performance, leader satisfaction, job satisfaction and team or organisational commitment (Jensen and Luthans, 2006; Walumbwa et al., 2008).

Authentic leadership in the sports domain

Given the recent emergence of the authentic leadership model within the leadership literature, its application to contexts outside of the organisational management domain is limited. Thus, there is minimal research on the usefulness and applicability of an authentic leadership approach within the sport coaching domain. Much past sport leadership research has focused on behavioural theory, so similar to the social identity approach, stressing other variables impacting on the complex leadership process (e.g. such as group dynamics, social context or the character of leaders) would provide a more valuable and well-rounded insight into the leadership process as a whole. Investigating authentic leadership in the context of sport coaching would involve studying a sport coach's fundamental character and value and such exploration

185

may help minimise some of the negative sport events such as game-fixing, illegal fundraising, illegal recruiting and embezzlement. In addition, based on the results from its application in the organisational field, authentic leaders may increase an athlete's satisfaction with the sport coach as a leader, may increase their satisfaction with playing their sport and may increase their team commitment.

Despite the limited focus and application of authentic leadership to the sport domain, some research would suggest that this model could be a valuable approach in furthering our understanding of sport leadership and more specifically how to be an effective sport coach. A recent study aimed to explore the structural relationship among sports team leaders' authentic leadership, athletes' satisfaction with the leader, athletes' job satisfaction and their team commitment in order to build more positive and healthy sport teams and enhance their effectiveness as leaders (Kim, 2013 – NASSM dissertation). This study utilised survey method to assess 414 athletes across a range of sports. Findings indicated that sport team leaders' authentic leadership had a positive direct effect on athletes' satisfaction with the leader, their job satisfaction and their team commitment (Kim, 2013 – NASSM dissertation). Another recent dissertation's results suggested that sports teams may benefit from training in authentic leadership, given that it predicts higher levels of trust, team cohesion and group performance (Houchin, 2011 – UMI Dissertations Publishing). Most interestingly, a recent review of the application of coach leadership models to coaching practice (Vella *et al.*, 2010) suggested that future research may be to commence testing theories of leadership that incorporate self-awareness and self-management constructs, implying authentic leadership incorporates such constructs. The theory of authentic leadership has been proposed as the future of leadership-theory building by experts in the field (Avolio *et al.*, 2009).

Other important theoretical leadership models in sport coaching

In addition to the theoretical models outlined above, other theoretically based models on coaching effectiveness include Duda's (2001) model which provides a mechanistic perspective as to how and why coaching behaviours affect athlete's psychosocial development. Duda's (2001) model incorporated elements from both the mediational model of leadership (Smoll and Smith, 1989), the multidimensional model of leadership (Chelladurai, 1978, 1990, 2007) and achievement goal theory (Ames, 1992; Dweck, 1989; Nicholls, 1984, 1989). The coach–athlete relationship is central to effective coach leadership and the four 'C' model (closeness, commitment, complementarity and co-orientation) explores and describes the quality of the coach–athlete interpersonal relationship (Jowett and Cockerill, 2002; Jowett and Ntoumanis, 2004). Other researchers have also examined the dynamics of the intricate interpersonal relationships found in sport such as the aforementioned coach–athlete relationship, the parent–athlete relationship and the parent–coach relationship (e.g. Gould *et al.*, 2002; Poczwardowski *et al.*, 2002).

FRAMING THE PERTINENT SPORT COACH LEADERSHIP MODELS

Given the numerous leadership approaches and models that exist within the sport coaching domain (as presented in Table 13.1), it is necessary and helpful to frame each within the sport

186

Table 13.1 *Review of pertinent leadership model(s)/approaches*

Model/ Approach	Framework	Focus	Author(s)	Method	Sample size
Multi-dimensional model of leadership	Coaching effectiveness	Coaching behaviours	*Chelladurai and Saleh (1980);* Chelladurai (1984)	*Quantitative survey, factor analysis*	485 athletes
Cognitive-mediational model of coach leadership	Coaching effectiveness	Coach characteristics/ coach context	Smoll and Smith (1989)		
Transforma-tional model of leadership	Coaching effectiveness	Coach characteristics/ athlete outcomes	*Smith et al. (2013);* Rowold (2006); Callow *et al. (2009);* Bass (1985); Vallee and Bloom (2005); Charbonneau *et al. (2001)*	*Quantitative survey*	199 athletes *(student ultimate frisbee)*
Servant leadership	Athlete-centred	Athlete characteristics/ outcomes	Rieke *et al.* (2008)	*Quantitative survey*	195 athletes *(high-school basketball)*
Coaching effectiveness models	Coaching effectiveness	Coach behaviours/ athlete outcomes	*Boardley et al. (2008);* Becker (2009); Horn (2008); Côté and Gilbert (2009); Côté *et al.* (2010)	*Quantitative survey*	166 athletes *(rugby union)*
Altruistic leadership model	Relational/ athlete-centred	Coach behaviours/ athlete outcomes/ characteristics	*Miller and Carpenter (2009)*	*Case study*	1 *(head coach)*
Transactional model	Relational	Coach behaviours/ athlete outcomes/ characteristics	*Rowold (2006);* Carthen (2006)	*Quantitative survey*	186 athletes *(martial arts students)*
Motivational model	Relational	Athlete outcomes/ characteristics	*Mageau and Vallerand (2003)*	*Review*	*Multiple samples*
Emotional intelligence model	Relational	Athlete outcomes/ characteristics	*Chan and Mallet (2009; 2011)*	*Review*	*N/A*

continued . . .

Table 13.1 Continued

Model/ Approach	Framework	Focus	Author(s)	Method	Sample size
The coaching model	Coaching effectiveness	Coaching context/ behaviours	Côté et al. (1995)	Qualitative interview	17 expert gymnast coaches
Athlete–coach relationship model	Relational	Athlete outcomes/ characteristics	Jowett and Cockerill (2003)	Qualitative interview	12 Olympic medallists
Athlete satisfaction model	Athlete-centred	Athlete outcomes/ characteristics	Riemer and Chelladurai (1995); Bebetsos and Theodorakis (2003)	Quantitative survey	201 athletes (American football)
Team cohesion model	Group-centred	Intra-team communication/ member motivation	Williams and Widmeyer (1991); Gardner et al. (1996)	Quantitative survey	83 athletes (student-athlete female golfers)
Self-concordance model	Athlete-centred	Goal striving/ coach autonomy support	Smith et al. (2007)	Quantitative survey	218 athletes (British athletes)
Self-enhancement model	Athlete-centred	Self-enhancement/ coach supportiveness/ instructional effectiveness	Smoll et al. (1993); Smith and Smoll (1990)	Experimental design	18 coaches & 152 youth athletes (baseball)
Self-determination model	Athlete-centred	Coach behaviours/ athlete outcomes/ characteristics	Chin, Khoo and Low (2012); Hollembeak and Ambrose (2005)	Quantitative survey	630 athletes (track & field)
Authentic leadership model	Coaching effectiveness	Coach behaviours/ athlete outcomes/ characteristics	Luthans and Avolio (2003)	Review	N/A

continued . . .

Table 13.1 Continued

Model/ Approach	Framework	Focus	Author(s)	Method	Sample size
Organisational citizenship behaviour model	Group-centred	Coach behaviour/ athlete outcomes/ group dynamics	Aoyagi et al. (2008)	Quantitative survey	193 student-athletes (range of sports)
Fitness leader behaviour model	Coaching effectiveness	Coach behaviours	Loughead et al. (2008)	Quantitative survey	151 participants (physical activity/ fitness)
Autonomy-supportive model	Athlete-centred	Athlete outcomes/ characteristics	Coatsworth and Conroy (2009); Gagne et al. (2003)	Quantitative survey	165 youth athletes (swimming)

Source: Vella et al. (2010).

coaching context and then further explore the commonalities between these pertinent models. In a recent review of the sports coaching leadership literature, Vella et al. (2010) summarised the frameworks around which the models of coach leadership converge. According to past research in the area of sports coaching and leadership, these frameworks accurately represent the primary focus of numerous coaching leadership models:

1   the coaching context, including player age, gender, goals, sport and competition level;
2   the coach's personal characteristics, which include professional, intrapersonal and interpersonal knowledge, values, beliefs and goals;
3   athlete outcomes, which have been summarized as including the four broad areas of competence, confidence, connection and character (Côté and Gilbert, 2009);
4   athlete characteristics, which include perceptions, beliefs and attitudes;
5   coaching behaviours, which are the fundamental drivers of athlete outcomes.

A variety of coach leadership models can be categorised within separate frameworks, and based on an extensive review of the literature; Table 13.1 represents a review of pertinent leadership model(s)/approaches, their distinguishable framework, the primary focus according to Vella et al.'s (2010) summary, and the method and study sample size used for the first selected model-representative study (*italicised* in the above table).

189

SUMMARY

Multiple leadership models exist to help explain the sport coaching process with reference to effective leadership capabilities. The numerous approaches differ in their expectations, delivery and outcomes (e.g. relational, coaching effectiveness, athlete-centred, group-centred); however, there is a general consensus within the literature that both the process of leadership and the process of sport coaching are a) similar in their makeup and thus work in synergy with one another, b) dependent on coach leader style/characteristics, follower/athlete characteristics, the coaching/leadership context, and the quality of leader-follower (coach-athlete) relationship, and c) complex and dynamic social processes. The natural connection between organisational leadership approaches and the sport coach setting has led to a recent surge of research that has applied the latest organisational leadership approaches to the sport setting with a focus on whether desirable measurable outcomes can result. The servant leadership model, the authentic leadership model, and the transformational leadership model are good examples of organisational models that have arisen in an attempt to further explain the leadership process in sport coaching. Nevertheless as of yet no one model has managed to encapsulate every aspect of the complex sport coach leadership process. The social identity theory of leadership (discussed in Chapter 14) may prove useful in helping to explain from a macro-group perspective the complexity of the sport coach leadership process, thus helping to position the value of the numerous models discussed in this chapter.

REVIEW QUESTIONS

1 Explain the key differences between the four main theoretical approaches within the sport coaching leadership domain: a) Relational Approach; b) Athlete-Centred Approach; c) Group-Centred Approach; and d) Coaching Effectiveness Approach.

2 Discuss the emphasis, strengths and limitations of the altruistic model, the athlete satisfaction model, the team cohesion model and the multidimensional model of leadership in sport coaching.

3 Discuss the ways in which organisational leadership theories seem to be applicable to the sport coaching domain.

4 Describe and explain three models of leadership that originated in the organisational domain and have proved to be beneficial within the sport coaching domain.

5 What sport coach leadership theories discussed in this chapter are most applicable to your experience to date and explain how this is the case.

REFERENCES

Aoyagi, M. W., Cox, R. H. and McGuire, R. T. (2008). Organisational citizenship behaviour in sport: Relationships with leadership, team cohesion, and athlete satisfaction. *Journal of Applied Sport Psychology*, 20, 25–41.

Ames, C. (1992). Achievement goals, motivational climate, and motivational processes. In G. C. Roberts (ed.), *Motivation in sport and exercise* (pp. 161–176). Champaign, IL: Human Kinetic.

Armstrong, S. (2001). Are you a 'transformational' coach. *Journal of Physical Education, Recreation and Dance*, 72(3), 44–47.

Avolio, B. J., Walumbwa, F. O. and Weber, T. J. (2009) Leadership: Current theories, research, and future directions. *Annual Review of Psychology*, 60, 421–449.

Bass, B. M. (1985). *Leadership and Performance Beyond Expectations*. New York: Free Press.

Bass, B. M. (1990). From transactional to transformational leadership: Learning to share the vision. *Organizational dynamics*, 18(3), 19–31.

Bass, B. M. (1998). *Transformational leadership: Industry, military, and educational impact*. Mahwah, NJ: Erlbaum.

Bass, B. M. (1999). Two decades of research and development in transformational research. *European Journal of Work and Organisational Psychology*, 8, 9–32.

Bass, B. M. and Avolio, B. J. (1994). *Improving organisational effectiveness through transformational leadership*. Thousand Oaks, CA: Sage.

Batson, C. D. and Leonard, B. (1987). Prosocial motivation: Is it ever truly altruistic? *Advances in Experimental Social Psychology*, 20, 65–122.

Bebetsos, E. and Theodorakis, N. (2003). Athletes' satisfaction among team-handball players in Greece. *Perceptual and Motor Skills*, 97, 1203–1208.

Becker, A. J. (2009). It's not what they do, it's how they do it: Athlete experiences of great coaching, *International Journal of Sports Science and Coaching*, 4, 93–119.

Boardley, I. D., Kavussanu, M. and Ring. C. (2008). Athletes' perceptions of coaching effectiveness and athlete-related outcomes in rugby union: An investigation based on the coaching efficacy model. *The Sport Psychologist*, 22, 269–287.

Burns, J. M. (1978). *Leadership*. New York: Harper & Row.

Callow, N., Smith, M. J., Hardy, L., Arthur, C. A. and Hardy, J. (2009). Measurement of transformational leadership and its relationship with team cohesion and performance level. *Journal of Applied Sport Psychology*, 21, 395–412.

Carron, A. V. and Hausenblas, H. A. (1998) *Group dynamics in sport* (2nd edn). Morgantown, WV: Fitness Information Technology.

Carthen, J. D. (2006). War, warrior heroes and the advent of transactional leadership in sports antiquity. *Sport Journal*, 9(2), 6.

Chan, J. T. and Mallet, C. J. (2009). *How developing emotional intelligence can develop effective sports leadership*. Evolution of the Athlete Coach Education Conference, Queensland, Australia.

Chan, J. T. and Mallet, C. J. (2011). The value of emotional intelligence for high performance coaching. *International Journal of Sport Science and Coaching*, 6(3), 315–328.

Charbonneau, D., Barling, J. and Kelloway, K. E. (2001). Transformational leadership and sports performance: The mediating role of intrinsic motivation. *Journal of Applied Social Psychology*, 31, 1521–1534.

Chelladurai, P. (1978). A contingency model of leadership in athletics. Unpublished doctoral dissertation, University of Waterloo, Canada.

Chelladurai, P. (1984) Discrepancy between preference and perception of leadership behaviour and satisfaction of athletes in varying sports. *Journal of Sport Psychology*, 6, 27–41.

Chelladurai, P. (1990). Leadership in sports: A review. *International Journal of Sport Psychology*, 21, 328–354.

191

Chelladurai, P. (1993). Leadership. In R. N. Singer, M. Murphey and L. K. Tennant (eds), *Handbook of research on sport psychology* (pp. 647–671). New York: Macmillan.

Chelladurai, P. (2007). Leadership in sports. In G. Tenenbaum and R. C. Eklund (eds), *Handbook of sport psychology* (pp. 113–135). Hoboken: NJ: John Wiley & Sons.

Chelladurai, P. and Carron, A. V. (1978). *Leadership.* CAPHER, Sociology of Sport Monograph Series A. Calgary, AB: University of Calgary.

Chelladurai, P. and Saleh, S. (1980). Dimensions of leader behavior in sports: Development of a leadership scale. *Journal of Sport Psychology, 2,* 34–45.

Chin, N. S., Khoo, S. and Low, W. Y. (2012). Self-determination and goal orientation in track and field. *Journal of Human Kinetics, 33,* 151–161.

Coatsworth, J. D. and Conroy, D. E. (2009). The effects of autonomy-supportive coaching, need satisfaction, and self-perceptions on initiative and identity in youth swimmers. *Developmental Psychology, 45,* 320–328.

Conroy, D. E. and Coatsworth, D. J. (2007). Assessing autonomy-supportive coaching strategies in youth sport. *Psychology of Sport and Exercise,* 8(5), 671–684.

Côté, J. and Gilbert, W. D. (2009). An integrative definition of coaching effectiveness and expertise. *International Journal of Sports Science and Coaching, 4,* 307–323.

Côté, J., Salmela, J., Trudel, P., Baria, A. and Russell, S. (1995). The coaching model: A grounded assessment of expert gymnastic coaches' knowledge. *Journal of Sport and Exercise Psychology, 17,* 1–17.

Côté, J., Bruner, M., Erickson, K., Strachan, L. and Fraser-Thomas, J. (2010). Athlete development and coaching. In J. Lyle and C. Cushion (eds), *Sports coaching: Professionalisation and practice* (pp. 63–83). Edinburgh: Churchill Livingstone Elsevier.

Cushion, C. J. (2007). Applying sport psychology philosophies, principles and practices onto the gridiron: A commentary. *International Journal of Sport Sciences and Coaching,* 1(4), 351–352.

Dalal, R. S. (2005). A meta-analysis of the relationship between organizational citizenship behavior and counterproductive work behavior. *Journal of Applied Psychology,* 90(6), 1241–1255.

Deci, E. L. and Ryan, R. M. (1985). *Intrinsic motivation and self-determination in human behavior.* New York: Plenum Press.

Duda, J. L. (2001). Achievement goal research in sport: Pushing the boundaries and clarifying some misunderstandings. In G. C. Roberts (ed.), *Advances in motivation in sport and exercise* (pp. 129–182). Leeds: Human Kinetics.

Durand-Bush, N. and Salmela, J. H. (2001). The development of talent in sport. In R. N. Singer, H. A. Hausenblas and C. Janelle (eds), *Handbook of sport psychology* (2nd edn, pp. 269–289). New York: John Wiley.

Dweck, C. S. (1989). Motivation. In A. Lesgold and R. Glaser (eds), *Foundations for a psychology of education* (pp. 87–136). Hillsdale, NJ: Erlbaum.

Gagne, M., Ryan, R. M. and Bargmann, K. (2003). Autonomy support and need satisfaction in the motivation and well-being of gymnasts. *Journal of Applied Sport Psychology, 15,* 372–390.

Gould, D., Greenleaf, C., Chung, Y. and Guinan, D. (2002). A survey of U.S. Atlanta and 131 Nagano Olympians: Variables perceived to influence performance. *Research Quarterly for Exercise and Sport,* 73(2), 175–186.

Graham, J. W. (1987). Transformational leadership: Fostering follower autonomy, not automatic followership. In J. G. Hunt (ed.), *Emerging leadership vistas.* Boston, MA: Lexington Books.

Greenleaf, R. K. (1977). *Servant leadership.* Mahwah, NJ: Paulist Press.

Hammermeister, J. J., Burton, D., Pickering, T., Chase, M., Westre, K. and Baldwin, N. (2008). Servant leadership in sport: A concept whose time has arrived. *International Journal of Servant Leadership, 4,* 185–215.

Hollembeak, J. and Amorose, A. J. (2005). Perceived coaching behaviours and college students' intrinsic motivation: A test of self-determination theory. *Journal of Applied Sport Psychology, 17,* 20–36.

Horn, T. (2002). Coaching effectiveness in the sport domain. In T. Horn (ed.), *Advances in sport psychology* (2nd edn, pp. 309–354). Champaign, IL: Human Kinetics.

Horn, T. S. (2008). Coaching effectiveness in the sport domain. In T. S. Horn (ed.), *Advances in sport psychology* (3rd edn, pp. 239–268). Champaign, IL: Human Kinetics.

Houchin, G. (2011). Authentic leadership in sports teams. The University of Tennessee at Chattanooga, ProQuest, UMI Dissertations Publishing. 1492316.

House, R. J. (1971). A path-goal theory of leader effectiveness. *Administrative Science Quarterly*, 16, 321–338.

Humphrey, R. H. (2002). The many faces of emotional leadership. *The Leadership Quarterly*, 13(5), 493–504.

Jensen, S. M. and Luthans, F. (2006). Entrepreneurs as authentic leaders: Impact on employees' attitudes. *Leadership and Organization Development Journal*, 27, 646–666.

Jowett, S. and Cockerill, L. (2002). Incompatibility in the coach–athlete relationship. In I. Cockerill (ed.), *Solutions in sport psychology* (pp. 16–31). Andover: Thomson Learning.

Jowett, S. and Cockerill, L. (2003). Olympic medallists' perspective of the athlete–coach relationship. *Psychology of Sport and Exercise*, 4(4), 313–331.

Jowett, S. and Ntoumanis, N. (2004). The Coach–Athlete Relationship Questionnaire (CART-Q): Development and initial validation. *Scandinavian Journal of Medicine and Science in Sports*, 14, 245–257.

Kao, S. F. and Cheng, B. S. (2005). Assessing sport team culture: Qualitative and quantitative approaches. *International Journal of Sport Psychology*, 36, 22–38.

Kernis, M. H. and Goldman, B. M. (2003). Stability and variability in self-concept and self-esteem. In M. R. Leary and J. P. Tangney (eds), *Handbook of self and identity* (pp. 106–127). New York: Guilford Press.

Kernis, M. H. and Goldman, B. M. (2006). A multicomponent conceptualization of authenticity: Theory and research. In M. P. Zanna (ed.), *Advances in experimental social psychology* (vol. 38, pp. 283–357). San Diego, CA: Academic Press.

Kidder, D. and Parks, J. (2001). The good soldier: Who is s(he)? *Journal of Organizational Behavior*, 22(8), 939–959.

Kim, S. H. (2013). Effectiveness of authentic leadership in the context of sports. 2013 North American Society for Sport Management Conference (NASSM 2013), Austin TX (oral presentation), 31 May 2013.

Lavallee, D., Williams, J. M. and Jones, M. V. (2008) *Key studies in sport and exercise psychology*. New York: McGraw-Hill.

Lorimer, R. and Jowett, S. (2009). Empathic accuracy in coach–athlete dyads who participate in team and individual sports. *Psychology of Sport and Exercise*, 10, 152–158.

Loughead, T. M., Patterson, M. M. and Carron, A. V. (2008). The impact of fitness leader behavior and cohesion on an exerciser's affective state. *International Journal of Sport and Exercise Psychology*, 6, 53–68.

Luthans, F. and Avolio, B. J. (2003). Authentic leadership development. In K. S. Cameron, J. E. Dutton and R. E. Quinn (eds), *Positive organizational scholarship* (pp. 241–258). San Francisco, CA: Berrett-Koehler.

Lyle, J. (2002). *Sports coaching concepts: A framework for coaches' behaviors*. London: Routledge.

Mageau, G. A. and Vallerand, R. J. (2003). The coach–athlete relationship: A motivational model. *Journal of Sport Sciences*, 21, 883–904.

Mallett, C. J. (2010). High performance coaches' careers and communities. In J. Lyle and C. Cushion (eds), *Sport coaching: Professionalism and practice* (pp. 119–133). London: Elsevier.

Miller, L. M. and Carpenter, C. L. (2009). Altruistic leadership strategies in coaching: A case study of Jim Tressel of the Ohio State University. *Strategies*, 22, 9.

Nicholls, J. G. (1984). Achievement motivation: Conceptions of ability, subjective experience, task choice and performance. *Psychological Review*, 91, 328–346.

Nicholls, J. G. (1989). *The competitive ethos and democratic orientation*. Cambridge, MA: Harvard University Press.

Organ, D. W. (1988). *Organizational citizenship behavior: The good soldier syndrome*. Lexington, MA: Lexington Books.

Organ, D. W., Podsakoff, P. M. and MacKenzie S. P. (2006). *Organizational citizenship behavior: Its nature, antecedents, and consequences*. London: Sage.

Poczwardowski, A., Barrot. J. E. and Peregoy, J. J. (2002). The athlete and coach: Their relationship and its meaning. *International Journal of Sport Psychology*, 33(1), 98–115.

Rieke, M., Hammermeister, J. and Chase, M. (2008). Servant leadership in sport: A new paradigm for effective coach behaviour. *International Journal of Sports Science and Coaching*, 3, 227–239.

Riemer, H. and Chelladurai, P. (1995). Leadership and satisfaction in athletics. *Journal of Sport and Exercise Psychology*, 17, 276–293.

Rowold, J. (2006). Transformational and transactional leadership in martial arts. *Journal of Applied Sport Psychology*, 18, 312–325.

Ryan, R. M. (1982). Control and information in the intrapersonal sphere: An extension of cognitive evaluation theory. *Journal of Personality and Social Psychology*, 43, 450–461.

Ryan, R. M. and Deci, E. L. (2000). Self-determination theory and the facilitation of intrinsic motivation, social development, and well-being. *American Psychologist*, 55, 68–78.

Ryan, R. and Deci, E. (eds), (2002). *Handbook of self-determination research*. Rochester, NY: University of Rochester Press.

Sashkin, M. and Burke, W. W. (1990). Understanding and assessing organizational leadership. In K. E. Clark and M. B. Clark (eds), *Measures of leadership* (pp. 297–325). Greensboro, NC: Center for Creative Leadership.

Smith, M. J., Arthur, C. A., Hardy, J., Callow, N. and Williams, D. (2013) Transformational leadership and task cohesion in sport: The mediating role of intrateam communication. *Psychology of Sport and Exercise*, 14(2), pp. 249–257.

Smith, R. E. and Smoll, F. L. (1997). Coach-mediated team building in youth sports. *Journal of Applied Sport Psychology*, 9, 114–132.

Smith, R. E., Smoll, F. L. and Curtis, B. (1979). Coach effectiveness training: A cognitive-behavioral approach to enhancing relationship skills in youth sports coaches. *Journal of Sport Psychology*, 1, 59–75.

Smoll, F. L. and Smith, R. E. (1989). Leadership behaviours in sport: A theoretical model and research paradigm. *Journal of Applied Sport Psychology*, 19, 1522–1551.

Smoll, F. L., Smith, R. E., Barnett, J. J. and Everett, J. J. (1993). Enhancement of children's self-esteem through social support training for youth sport coaches. *Journal of Applied Psychology*, 78(4), 602–610.

Spears, L. C. (ed.). (1998). *Insights on leadership: Service, stewardship, spirit and servant-leadership*. New York: John Wiley & Sons.

Vallee, C. N. and Bloom, G. A. (2005). Building a successful university program: Key and common elements of expert coaches. *Journal of Applied Sport Psychology*, 17, 179–196.

Vella, S. A., Oades, L. G. and Crowe, T. P. (2010). The application of coach leadership models to coaching practice: Current state and future directions. *International Journal of Sports Science and Coaching*, 5(3), 425–434.

Walumbwa, F. O., Avolio, B. J., Gardner, W. L., Wernsing, T. S. and Peterson, S. J. (2008). Authentic leadership: Development and validation of a theory-based measure. *Journal of Management*, 34, 89–126.

Whitehead, G. (2009). Adolescent leadership development: Building a case for an authenticity framework. *Educational Management Administration and Leadership*, 37, 847–872.

Williams, J. M. and Widmeyer, N. W. (1991). The cohesion-performance outcome relationship in coaching sport. *Journal of Sport and Exercise Psychology*, 13(4), 364–371.

Yukelson, D. (1997). Principles of effective team building interventions in sport: A direct services approach at Penn State University. *Journal of Applied Sport Psychology*, 9, 73–96.

Chapter 14

Organisational leadership approaches in sport coaching

Tony Cassidy

CHAPTER OBJECTIVES

After completing this chapter you should be able to:

1   understand some of the ideas in the development of leadership theories;
2   discuss the relative strengths and weaknesses of different leadership theories;
3   understand the emerging consensus around leadership as a social interaction;
4   discuss the overlap between leadership theories in work organisations and sport coaching.

KEY TERMS

■   trait theory
■   situational leadership theory
■   servant leader theory
■   leaders and followers
■   social identity theory

INTRODUCTION

Leadership is one of the most important factors in determining worker behaviour in terms of performance, motivation and commitment, and a century of research in psychology has tried to explicate its anatomy and aetiology (Avolio *et al.*, 2009). Style of leadership will form the context for any work-based interaction and will be reflected in the general culture of the organisation. It is little wonder then that its applicability to the field of sport, particularly to team sport and sport coaching, has become a major focus in sport psychology (Chelladurai, 2007).

In terms of work organisations, leadership is embedded in management structures and the terms leader and manager have been presumed to equate (Yukl, 2007). This is a rather unfortunate, unfounded and damaging presumption that is now widely challenged. However, it means that much of the traditional research on leadership at work has taken as its subject matter the behaviour and experience of managers. Leadership has been viewed from different angles throughout the history of work and organisational (W/O) psychology. Early theories focused on the personal qualities of the leader based on the assumption that leaders are born not made. Other theories argued the opposite and focused on how the situation influenced leadership behaviour. The more recent approach presents an interactional perspective based on the person-in-context model of Lewin (1951). Lewin argued that behaviour is a function of the person, the environment and the interaction between the two, a philosophy that is expressed in his famous equation $B=f(P.E)$. The contingency model of leadership suggests that skills and abilities are important but will be contingent upon appropriate situational factors. Essentially, the evolution of theoretical perspectives on leadership at work has paralleled the person–situation debate in psychology generally, and it is important to assess this debate in evaluating the arguments (Sternberg and Vroom, 2002).

LEADERSHIP AS A TRAIT

When we want to understand leadership it is inevitable that we first look at the leader and herein lay the first limitation of early leadership research. The observation that great leaders possess certain admirable qualities lulls the casual thinker into assuming that they were born with these qualities, thereby ignoring a wealth of evidence to the contrary, and thus the 'Great Man' theory of leadership that dominated early thinking in the field. Throughout history there have been numerous examples of famous and infamous individuals who have stood out from the pack and been conferred with the title leader. Yet it does not take much depth of exploration to recognise that while they were all leaders they often differed substantially from each other in many important ways. However, the label is sufficient for us to accentuate their similarities and underestimate their differences. This is a fundamental tenet of social identity theory which is arguably the most effective theory of leadership currently available. The focus on 'innate' qualities led to the selection of people for management roles based on characteristics such as intelligence, motivation and dominance. The theory was then defended by reference to the fact that managers tend to be more intelligent, dominant and motivated than their followers – not a surprising finding given the selection process.

However, concern for worker satisfaction with the growth of the human relations movement led to the questioning of the person-based leadership theories (Taneja et al., 2011). There are many problems in using general measures of intelligence or personality as predictors of work performance. On one hand the measures themselves are often questionable and on the other their predictive validity has been shown to be very poor. The assumptions behind person based theories of leadership were also shown to be unfounded in that the leaders of history can often be seen as being dependent on the situational context for their success. The example often used is that Winston Churchill was a great war-time leader but not so effective during peace time.

One might rightly assume that studying great leaders would provide us with an understanding of leadership but that has not been the case (Stogdill, 1974; Yukl, 1989). There are two main problems, a) defining good or great leadership and b) separating the qualities that define good leadership from those that are incidental. Good leadership is generally defined in terms of outcomes, e.g. winning a war, making a large profit in business, or winning a league in sport. These are all complex processes and while we might identify traits or personal qualities that observably coexist with moments of success, it is almost impossible to demonstrate that a causal relationship exists. Proponents of the trait approach talk about charisma and charismatic leaders but are faced with the same difficult to answer question, i.e. what is charisma? However, we will not dismiss the fact that great leaders are perceived as having special qualities as the social identity theory provides a mechanism for explaining both the content and the source of such qualities. One cannot deny that great sports coaches display exceptional qualities associated with leadership, but were they born with these qualities, did they attain them through learning, or perhaps a more important recent question, were these qualities attributed to them by their team members (i.e. their followers).

LEADERSHIP AS A ROLE

The disappointing performance of trait theories led to a focus on situational influences in the evolution of the leadership role, with theorists committing the all too frequent error in the development of theory, throwing the baby out with the bath water. Bales (1950; 1970) contributed to the situational approach through his studies of the process of group formation using interaction process analysis (IPA) (not to be confused with the recently developed qualitative method of Interpretative Phenomenological Analysis also known as IPA). He observed that at the forming stage the first role generally observed is that which he called the task specialist. This is the person who gives direction and helps others to focus on the task. This is clearly a leadership role. At this stage the task specialist is best liked by other members. However, as the group moves into the storming stage another role is observed, that of the socio-emotional specialist. This is the person who tries to keep the peace by helping members to reach compromise and generally focuses on the emotional aspect of the interaction. At this stage liking switches to the socio-emotional specialist. This is another leadership role. Initially Bales suggested that they were separate roles that would be performed by different people. Later research shows that both roles can be performed by one person, and that the most effective leader will be able to switch from one to the other. Numerous studies using different methods have confirmed these two essential elements of leadership – i.e. person focus and task focus. The essential mistake in this tradition was to focus too much on the role and the person, rather than on the social interaction which is where the real insight was to be gained.

For example, Halpin and Winer (1957) at Ohio State University factor analysed ratings on 1500 adjectives describing leaders and found that two broad factors could account for most of the variance. These were labelled consideration (C: a focus on the person) and initiating structure (IS: a focus on the task). Blake and Mouton (1964) combined these two dimensions to devise their Managerial Grid which reflects four different styles of management, a) high C and high IS, b) high C and low IS, c) low C and high IS, and d) low C and low IS. The manager who was high on both dimensions was shown to be most effective in terms of both performance and worker satisfaction.

197

Katz *et al.* (1950) at Michigan University looked at effective and ineffective managers as determined by their performance. They then looked at differences in behaviour between the two groups. They found that the effective managers tended to be person centred or focused and to use a more general type of supervision reflecting a trust in their workers. The ineffective managers tended to be task focused and use a close supervision style. While these studies and others show clear and consistent replication of the two dimensions they really provide a description of leadership behaviour rather than an explanation. In addition, the dimensions are assumed to reflect characteristics of the person rather than the situation.

FROM PERSON TO CONTINGENCY MODELS

Leadership research changed direction during the 1960s with the move to contingency models of leadership, which presented a more complex view fitting with developments generally in W/O psychology that provided a more complex model of people in the workplace.

Fiedler (1967) developed his leader-match theory of leadership that has been widely used, although also widely criticised, leading to a revision as the cognitive resource theory (Fiedler and Garcia, 1987). Fiedler started by getting a sample of managers to identify the person they had least preferred to work with in the past, their least preferred co-worker. They were then asked to rate this person on 18 bipolar dimensions (e.g. pleasant – unpleasant). Fiedler used these ratings to identify the manager's style using the rationale that if they rated the person positively they were person centred and if not they were task centred. One criticism of this is that while positive ratings of a least preferred co-worker could be argued to indicate a person focus, the negative ratings do not necessarily indicate a task focus.

Although a key element of Fiedler's leader-match theory is the characteristics of the leader and his two dimensions do agree with the dimensions that have been identified by previous theorists, he went on to look at how those characteristics interact with the situation within which leadership is observed. He identifies three dimensions of the situation that are important.

1   *Leader-member relations*: The quality of the relationship between the leader and the group members in terms of how much the leader is trusted, respected, and has the confidence of workers.
2   *Task structure*: Whether the task is structured or unstructured.
3   *Position power*: The power of the leader to control things such as hiring, firing, discipline, promotions and salary.

Using the three situational dimensions produces eight different situations that range from favourable to unfavourable for the leader.

The rationale is that trade-offs occur between the situational dimensions. One might link this to the different types of power. Where relations are very good power is likely to be seen as legitimate or referent and more acceptable to group members. However, where relations are bad and the leader has control over rewards, power is more likely to be seen as coercive. The latter situation is likely to produce high levels of dissatisfaction and may be associated with what is perceived as a bullying culture. There is some evidence to support Fiedler's model, particularly in training programmes for managers; however, it does not really capture

198

the essence of an interactional model of leadership since it focuses on the matching of particular styles to particular situations. It does not allow for the changing nature of work situations and the need for managers to be able to quickly switch styles. Fiedler and Garcia (1987) revised the leader-match theory with their cognitive resources theory. This revision adds the dimensions of leader experience and leader intelligence and suggests that while leader intelligence can be an asset in favourable and moderately favourable situations, it is the leader's experience that pays off in unfavourable situations. Fiedler's work highlighted the importance and power of the social interaction in determining leader success, but stopped short of identifying the process of social categorisation and social identity involved.

Another approach to leadership in the contingency category was that of Vroom and Yetton (1973) and later of Vroom and Jago (1988). Over this period of time a group of workers led by Vroom developed what is known as the decision-making theory of leadership. The focus of this theory is on what is seen as the central task of leaders or managers in the workplace, i.e. their role in terms of decision making, and in particular their decision as to whether or not to involve subordinates in the decision-making process. The key elements of evaluation of the effectiveness of the decision-making process in the model are a) the level of acceptance and commitment subordinates show, and b) whether the decision results in effective task performance. Decision-making theory identifies five basic styles of leadership that range along a dimension from autocratic to democratic, and seven key situational features. From this, the theorist's developed a complex tree or flow chart that can help the manager to choose what style of leadership to adopt. Evidence tends to show that using the decision tree is effective in deciding how autocratic one can be and still engage subordinates. However, it is a very narrow model and generally felt to be too complex to be useful.

Both of Fiedler's and Vroom's models are very formulaic guides to the leadership process and both have been very useful for structuring training courses for managers. However, their ultimate effectiveness as models of leadership is questionable, largely because they are in fact models of managerial behaviour rather than leadership.

Yet another contingency model is the situational leadership theory (SLT) of Hersey and Blanchard (1977; 1982) which focuses on the relationship between leadership style and worker maturity. Worker maturity (or readiness) refers to how willing and able workers are to do the job required of them. In essence, this theory takes the four possible combinations of the two well established leadership styles, task-oriented or person-oriented, and produces four leadership styles labelled, *telling*, *selling*, *participating*, and *delegating*.

The SLT recognises that the leader needs to adapt their style to their workers as opposed to a process of matching as in Fiedler's theory. When reviewing a range of theories such as this, one is struck by the amount of common ground and one cannot help feeling that each contributes something to an overall model of leadership. All of the models in the role and contingency tradition have at their heart the two-dimensional task-oriented versus person-oriented dichotomy. Each theory in the contingency tradition adds another aspect of the situation. Fiedler adds the three situational variables of leader–member relations, task structure and position power, and in the later Cognitive Resource Theory (CRT; Fiedler and Garcia, 1987) adds the variables of leader intelligence and experience. Vroom adds the decision-making steps, and Hersey and Blanchard add the concept of worker maturity. There is evidence to support each model, which suggests that all of the concepts identified play a role in describing

199

or explaining leadership behaviour to some extent. One of the problems with the research in the field of organisational psychology is that there has been a tendency to substitute a manager for a leader and while these models are proposed as models of leadership behaviour or leadership style, in effect the evidence and the models are based on a manager's behaviour or style. A number of organisational theorists have moved away from this model and draw a distinction between leadership and management. For example Warr (1987) suggests that there is an important distinction between managers and leaders in that managers '*do things right*' whereas leaders '*do the right thing*'. In other words leaders envision and inspire their followers whereas managers tend to implement existing processes and procedures. The difference between managers and leaders is sometimes linked to the distinction between transactional and transformational leadership. Transactional leadership models could incorporate many of the models that we have already looked at and are based on the notion of leadership as being a transaction between the leader and her subordinates. Transformational leadership on the other hand transforms followers through the inspirational actions of the leader (Charbonneau *et al.*, 2001). The distinction between managers and leaders raises doubts about whether the research thus far has really told us anything at all about leadership and brings us right back to the questions that we started with and the 'great man' approach of the 1940s. We face again the notion of the charismatic leader. The notion of charisma, while elusive in terms of definition and measurement, sits very neatly with lay theories that see leaders as having some special quality that sets them apart. The problem with this of course is that we may be attributing this charisma to the individual because we see them in situations of status and in admiring their success we attribute it to their special personal qualities. Our experience of the current spate of reality television that shows where lay people are turned into celebrities before our eyes should make us aware that even the most non distinct people cast into the public gaze can take on the cloak of stardom.

Attempts have been made to define charisma and because it is one of those concepts that we all recognise but find hard to describe, definitions have not come easily. One model identifies five characteristics of the charismatic leader: *the ability to articulate a vision*; *willingness to take risks in pursuit of the vision*; *sensitivity to environmental and resource constraints*; *sensitivity to the needs of followers*; *unconventional behaviour* (Robbins, 2001). Charismatic leaders are often seen as heroic individuals who have the strength of character and the willingness to challenge or to put themselves in the line of fire, who command and give loyalty, and have the ability to provide individualised support and encouragement so that all feel valued.

The term charisma was introduced by Weber (1921) as something that was conferred on leaders by followers and brings us back to an important aspect of the process only touched on by some of the theories discussed so far, i.e. the role of followers in leadership. Hollander (1958) made the simple but important point that successful leadership cannot occur without dedicated followers and over a decade went on to introduce and argue the case for *followership* in leadership research (Hollander, 2008). The essence of the case is that to understand leadership we must understand the interdependent relationship between leaders and followers, between leaders and groups. One thing that traditional models of management or leadership have tended to ignore, or to at best only partially grasp, is the true relationship between the manager or the leader and the group. This is where social identity theory and self-categorisation theory can help us to move beyond the individualistic approach of identifying characteristics either of the individual or the situation and then trying to add them together to form some model of leadership at a group level, to a more fundamental understanding of leadership as a function of a group rather than as a characteristic of the person.

Lord *et al.* (1982) introduced leadership categorisation theory which argues that leadership is essentially determined by followers' perceptions of the leader in terms of categories of appropriate leadership behaviour. These categories or prototypes of leadership are dependent on the expectations of followers and it is just a short step from there to recognising that followers' expectations will be largely determined by group norms. This is probably as far away as we can get from the 'great man' theories because it normalises leadership as a process in which leadership is conferred by followers onto the person who best meets their expectations. Thus anyone has the possibility of becoming a leader. Leadership categorisation theory was undoubtedly influenced by perhaps the greatest theory to emerge in social psychology in the last hundred years, i.e. social identity theory. It was developed by Henri Tajfel and formulated by Tajfel and Turner (1979) as a group level, non-reductionist, European theory to explain inter group behaviour. Tajfel was concerned with group rather than individual influence. This was something initially suggested by LeBon (1896) in terms of group mind. LeBon was trying to explain mob behaviour observed in the Paris riots of 1890. He suggested that some sort of group or mob mind developed which he used to explain the mindless violence that is often witnessed in these sorts of situation. Floyd Allport (1924) rejected this, saying that only individual consciousness can exist and the notion of some sort of abstract mob consciousness just was not reality. However, the notion that group or crowd behaviour was something more than just the summation or average of individual behaviours continued to be debated. Asch (1952) used the analogy of the chemical combinations in water (H_2O). Water is just hydrogen and oxygen – yet it is totally different from either. Tajfel proposed the notion of social identity and elaborated the distinction between personal and social identity. He argued that the difference is that in group situations, where the group is important to us or salient, we are acting in terms of our social identity which generates and justifies different behaviours. He talked about groups in our mind, or an internalisation of our group identity. His explanation for the development of social identity was based on some very basic psychological processes, beginning with categorisation and moving through social comparison to a sense of distinct social identity. The theory was developed to explain prejudice (inter group attitudes) but it is now recognised as a general theory of group behaviour. The research background was based on studies using the minimal group paradigm and an outline of the findings will help in understanding the theory.

THE MINIMAL GROUP PARADIGM

This was developed by Rabbie and Horowitz (1969) in order to investigate how little, if any, competition was necessary for ethnocentrism and prejudice to develop. They took children who had not previously met each other and randomly allocated them to four groups of four children. Each group was given a colour label; children were just told, for example, you are in the blue group and you are in the green group. Thus, there was no basis for group identification, hence the term minimal group. The groups were divided by screens from each other. Two groups were allocated to the experimental condition and two to the control condition. In the experimental condition children were told they would get a reward depending on their performance, in the control condition no rewards were offered. The screens were then removed and each child read out details about themselves as instructed. They were then rated both by their own group (in group) and the other group (out group). In group members were rated highest despite the fact that there was no objective reason for this. While this ethnocentrism was stronger in the experimental condition, it also occurred to a significant level in the control condition. This suggests that even in non competitive conditions ethnocentrism occurs. Tajfel *et al.* used the minimal group paradigm to further investigate this. In the study they demonstrated that mere categorisation is sufficient to elicit in group favouritism. An example of the type of study is one where children were allocated to two groups on the basis of their alleged preference for one or other of two abstract artists (Klee and Kandinsky). The actual identities of group members were kept secret by the use of code numbers. Children were then given booklets in which they were asked to allocate money to two group members at a time. The children knew only which group they themselves belonged to and the group membership of the two to whom they had to allocate money. Children were never asked to allocate money to themselves. Over 70 per cent clearly favoured their own group. This tendency to maintain the differential in favour of the in group has been consistently demonstrated in experiments and has also been observed in behaviours such as pay negotiations where settlements are often accepted by trade unions that maintain differentials even where this may actually mean taking the lower of several options for their members. While many criticisms may be levelled at these studies, particularly concerning their ecological validity, they do demonstrate some form of group behaviour in situations where there are no real reasons for such to occur. The problem then was to explain these findings.

SOCIAL IDENTITY THEORY

Tajfel and his colleagues explained the findings outlined above in terms of social identity theory, which is based on some very basic psychological processes and essentially describes the process whereby we move from individuals in groups, to groups in the individual. The process begins with the very basic human need to categorise, i.e. categorisation. We see seven discrete bands of colour in the rainbow despite the fact that it is really a continuum of light of different wavelengths. Our cognitive processes categorise in order to simplify perception. This process is the basis of all information processing whether the information is about physical objects or other people. Categorising other people or social categorisation is the initial part of the development of social identity. In order to clarify our categories we accentuate similarities and differences. Thus when we have identified seven possible categories of colour in the rainbow we accentuate similarities between wavelengths within a colour and accentuate differences between wavelengths in different colours, thus seeing seven distinct bands. Tajfel and Wilkes (1963) demonstrated that participants who were judging line length exaggerated the differences between and similarities within categories when shorter and longer lines were placed in discrete categories. We do the same with people. The accentuation effect is related to and influenced by the second process, social comparison (Festinger, 1954). There is broad acceptance in social psychology that much of reality is socially constructed. In other words we confirm our view of the world through feedback from and comparison with the behaviour and opinions of others. A range of approaches in social psychology are based on this social constructivist philosophy. Social learning theory (Bandura, 1977) and symbolic interactionism (Mead, 1934; Blumer, 1969) are examples. In fact there are a range of theories that parade under the banner of the dramaturgical perspective and that span both social psychology and sociology. This approach uses the analogy of actors on a stage to understand social interaction and originated in the work of the sociologist Goffman (1959).

These theories all acknowledge the role of social comparison in human behaviour. In fact there is an argument that even our emotional experience is determined by social comparison. A classic series of studies by Schachter and Singer (1962) demonstrate this. They divided participants into several experimental and control groups. Some were given injections of adrenalin, some were given placebos. Some of those who were given the adrenalin were informed that they should expect a surge of physiological arousal, while others were not told what to expect. This last group were placed in different surroundings. Some sat in a waiting room with confederates who acted angrily about something they read in a newspaper. Others were placed with confederates who laughed and appeared generally happy. Participants were later interviewed about their experience. The interesting aspect was that those not told what to expect, who were with the angry confederate, reported feeling angry and hostile, while those with the happy confederate reported feeling happy and elated. The consistency of this effect demonstrates how we rely on cues from others in situations where physiological arousal is ambiguous. Similar findings have been reported from studies of the development of relationships.

In terms of social identity theory social comparison operates to help us place ourselves and others in social groups. Social categorisation and social comparison work together to construct groups in our mind that are significant to us; this then determines our behaviour in terms of groups. In other words having categories of people in our mind based on comparison between them and between them and ourselves we begin to act in terms of the values and norms of the groups with which we personally identify. Comparison between and within categories of people are based on salient characteristics and the accentuation effect leads to the exaggeration of difference between and similarities within groups. The groups with which we tend to identify ourselves are referred to as the in groups and other groups are generally called the out groups. The exaggeration of differences between and similarities within leads to what is referred to as social psychological distinctiveness. In other words we begin to stereotype individuals in terms of group characteristics and to see out group members as not only socially distinct but also psychologically distinct from in group members.

This is the basis of the development of prejudice since these groups have now become groups in our mind and we begin to act in terms of group or social identity rather than in terms of personal (or individual) identity. Tajfel argued that we can see personal identity and social identity as two ends of a continuous dimension (or continuum) and that behaviour will be located somewhere along that continuum. In fact it is often very difficult to identify behaviour that is totally located at the personal identity end. As a general theory of the operation of psychological processes in the development of group identities, social identity theory has had widespread and growing support. It suggests that social groups are inevitable because they allow individuals to satisfy their needs for order, structure, simplification, and predictability – in fact, the need to exercise power and control over their experience. The development

203

of a positive social identity is a major motivating factor. Some would argue, the main factor, as exemplified in the quote: 'the pursuit of reputation in the eyes of others is the overriding preoccupation of human life' (Harré, 1979, p. 3).

While the main focus of the above has been in explaining how we come to hold negative attitudes of out groups, the theory also demonstrates how we come to hold positive attitudes towards our in groups and hence a sense of in group cohesion and conformity to in group norms. This has immediate relevance to teams and it is a truism that in team sports it is only when the 'team' moves from a collection of individuals to operating as a team that they become effective. As a team, performance will often outstrip the average of ability of team members, for example, when a lower league team beats premiership teams in the FA cup. Arguably, in team sport the 'manager' or 'coach' who can lead their players to perform as a team will be a success.

The processes that occur within groups as we see from social identity theory are closely interlinked with relationships between groups. The relationships between groups are extremely important in work organisations since they generally need to communicate and cooperate in order for the organisation to function effectively. Barriers to communication and cooperation need to be understood in order to improve the processes. However, in team sports those very processes that prevent teams at work from cooperating will enhance sport teams in competition with each other. This is perhaps nowhere as clearly illustrated as in a classic series of studies by Sherif et al. (1961). Sherif et al. studied groups of boys at summer camp at Robbers Cave under various situations involving competition. The main finding was that competition leads to intensification of categorisation, stereotyping, prejudice, and both motivation and effort to win. In these studies, groups that became used to winning tended to rest on their laurels and became 'fat and happy', while groups constantly losing became 'lean and hungry' with increased motivation to win; an easily recognisable phenomenon in team sports, which presents the leader with new challenges in maintaining the motivation of a winning team.

Despite what can now be seen as the obvious utility of a social identity theory of leadership, it was only formulated at the turn of the century (Haslam, 2001; Hogg, 2001), drawing together ideas from leadership categorisation theory and the work of Tajfel and Turner among others. After a decade of ground breaking research by its main proponent Alex Haslam and colleagues it is now proclaimed as the new psychology of leadership (Haslam et al., 2011). This theory explains the emergence of leadership as a group process through increasing social identity salience, social prototypes, social attraction, and attributions (Hogg, 2001). A consequence of social identity formation and self-categorisation is depersonalisation, whereby people are no longer perceived as persons but rather as prototypes of in group or out group characteristics. Prototypes are arrived at through stereotyping on the basis of group categories. The most prototypical in group member will be the person who is perceived by other group members as the closest fit to their own attitudes, beliefs, and aspirations (Haslam et al., 1995). The most prototypical member acquires their ability to influence group members because they are the most socially attractive group member (Hogg, 2001). As the member begins to be perceived as the most prototypical and therefore more socially attractive, they attract more attention and attributional processes play a role. The attribution bias operates towards attributing the attractive prototypical behaviours to internal characteristics and hence the leader is bestowed with charisma. The basic premises of the social identity theory of leadership were tested in a series of laboratory and field studies (Fielding and Hogg, 1997;

204

Hains *et al.*, 1997; Turner and Haslam, 2001). These researchers showed that perceived leadership effectiveness was closely linked to perceived prototypicality and social attractiveness.

Just as with social identity in general, perceptions of prototypicality are context dependent (Haslam, 2001); the definition of prototypical behaviour will depend on the situation within which the group operates at a given time. Haslam (2001) uses the analogy of a stand-up comedian to illustrate the way in which effective organisational leadership works from a social identity perspective. The comedian adapts to the tastes and attitudes of the audience in developing a rapport which then allows them to move forward in interaction to explore new territory. The social identity approach does not dispense with the concept of a charismatic leader; rather it helps to explain how charisma is attributed through perceived prototypicality and social attraction. The essence of charisma in this view is having the social and interpersonal skills to adapt to group perceptions of typicality and to manipulate those perceptions in various ways. According to social identity theorists, an established leader can maintain prototypicality in the face of changing contexts by attempting to redefine the prototype to serve the self and disadvantage others (Hogg, 2001). This is usually done by finding a way to re-emphasise the existing prototype, scapegoating deviants, denigrating selected out groups, or a combination of all three. One can see this at work regularly in the political arena where the threatened leader produces a new strategy based on the prototypical principles of the party, undermining deviants within his/her own party, and making an attack on the failure of the opposition parties to tackle the issue. The concepts and constructs that underpin the other leadership models discussed can be incorporated and explained within the social identity perspective and it goes beyond previous theory to provide a group level model of both process and content.

We have come a long way in leadership theory from the very simple personality trait theories of the early twentieth century. Theories no longer focus on the leader but are rather broader, encompassing followers and contexts, and leadership is viewed as 'dyadic, shared, relational, strategic, global, and a complex social dynamic' (Avolio *et al.*, 2009, p. 423). Researchers are just beginning to look at the social identity theory of leadership in sport coaching (Cassidy *et al.*, 2014). However, one theory of leadership that arguably has the potential to be integrated with social identity theory, and that has been applied to sport coaching, is servant leadership theory (Greenleaf, 1977). The growth in positive psychology along with the move towards more focus on followers in leadership theorising coinciding with more concern for worker well-being created the ideal context for servant leadership to come of age (van Dierendonck, 2011).

> The Servant-Leader is servant first. . . . It begins with the natural feeling that one wants to serve, to serve first. Then conscious choice brings one to aspire to lead. . . . The best test, and difficult to administer is this: Do those served grow as persons? Do they, while being served, become healthier, wiser, freer, more autonomous, and more likely themselves to become servants? And, what is the effect on the least privileged in society? Will they benefit, or at least not further be harmed?
>
> (Greenleaf, 1977, p. 7)

The words of Greenleaf, though not based on empirical evidence, provide as a good a definition of servant leadership as can be gleaned from the empirical evidence that has

205

since provided support for it (Laub, 1999; Patterson, 2003; Russell and Stone, 2002; van Dierendonck, 2011). Van Dierendonck describes ten dimensions of servant leadership. These are (1) listening, emphasizing the importance of communication and seeking to identify the will of the people; (2) empathy, understanding others and accepting how and what they are; (3) healing, the ability to help make whole; (4) awareness, being awake; (5) persuasion, seeking to influence others relying on arguments not on positional power; (6) conceptualisation, thinking beyond the present-day need and stretching it into a possible future; (7) foresight, foreseeing outcomes of situations and working with intuition; (8) stewardship, holding something in trust and serving the needs of others; (9) commitment to the growth of people, nurturing the personal, professional, and spiritual growth of others; (10) building community, emphasising that local communities are essential in a persons' life. These would appear to also be central to social identity theory of leadership.

Recent research has extended to the consideration of servant leadership as a potentially appropriate model of leadership within the sport coaching context. Servant leadership is defined by the core constructs of trust, humility, and service to others (Vella *et al.*, 2011). Rieke *et al.* (2008) explored the suitability of the servant leadership model in increasing sport coaching effectiveness and found that athletes preferred the servant leader coaching style to more traditional styles. The results of this study showed that athletes who perceived their coach to possess servant leader qualities also displayed higher intrinsic motivation, were more task oriented, more satisfied, were mentally tougher, and performed better than athletes coached by non-servant leaders. In a prior study, Hammermeister *et al.* (2008) assessed the impact that servant leader coaching behaviour had on athletes' intrinsic motivation (intrinsic motivation inventory: IMI, Ryan, 1982), mental toughness (Ottawa mental skills assessment tool -3: OMSAT-3, Durand-Bush and Salmela, 2001) and sport satisfaction (athlete satisfaction questionnaire: ASQ, Riemer and Chelladurai, 1998) using a sample of 251 collegiate basketball athletes. This initial study suggested that the servant leadership model was viable for use in sport settings.

In the follow-up study Rieke *et al.* (2008) examined a sample of 195 high-school basketball athletes to assess the relationship between servant leader coach behaviours and numerous sport variables such as intrinsic motivation, sport satisfaction, mental skills, and sport performance. The researchers used the revised servant leadership profile for sport (RSLP-S) to measure athlete perceptions of their coach's servant leadership behaviour. The RSLP-S represents three servant leader constructs: a) trust/inclusion; b) humility; and c) service. The results of this follow-up study showed that athletes who perceived their coach to possess servant leader qualities also displayed higher intrinsic motivation, were more task oriented, more satisfied, were mentally tougher, and performed better than athletes coached by non-servant leaders. This study also reported findings that suggested athletes' preferred coaches who displayed servant leader behaviours than those who did not, specifically on two of the three servant leader sub-scales (trust/inclusion and service). Despite study limitations, such as the limited athlete participant sample (high-school basketball) and the cross-sectional nature of this investigation, this research provided valuable insight into a new leadership paradigm's (servant leadership) potential applicability and success within the sport environment.

Servant leader theory is joined in this new age of leadership theorising by authentic leadership theory (George, 2003; Luthans and Avolio, 2003). Past research concludes that authenticity consists of a range of mental and behavioural processes that explain how people discover and construct a core sense of self, and how this core self is maintained across situations and over time (Kernis and Goldman, 2006). Four themes are prevalent within the literature relating to individual's authentic functioning of: 1) self-understanding, 2) openness to objectively recognising their desirable and undesirable self-aspects, 3) actions, and 4) orientation towards interpersonal relationships. Based on this research, past authentic leadership literature has identified four key components of authenticity: 1) awareness, 2) unbiased processing, 3) behaviour, and 4) relational orientation (Kernis and Goldman, 2006). Despite the limited focus and application of authentic leadership to the sport domain, some research would suggest that this model could be a valuable approach in furthering our understanding of sport leadership and more specifically how to be an effective sport coach. A recent review of the application of coach leadership models to coaching practice (Vella et al., 2011) suggested that future research may be to commence testing theories of leadership that incorporate self-awareness and self-management constructs, implying authentic leadership incorporates such constructs.

Although these theoretical perspectives are often presented as unique and novel they are in fact overlapping and based on a long history of social research. We can go back to Bales (1950) on group formation and the evolution of a leadership role to find the germ of an idea that is central to these modern theories. In fact the germ was probably first demonstrated in Mayo's (1933) Hawthorne studies – essentially, that the success of a leader is largely dependent on whether they are fully acceptable to their followers. Another well-established strand of relevant research is around participative decision making as demonstrated in the work of Vroom and Yetton (1973). This idea is to be found best expressed in the writings of Lewin (1947) and is simply that if you really want to change behaviour and ensure that the changes stick you need to enable people to feel that they have played a significant role in making the decision to change in the first place. The conclusion from this is that a leader will only be acceptable if people feel they have to some extent chosen that leader. Without going through every single past theory it can be argued that social identity, authentic leadership, and servant leadership theories integrate the key conclusions of the trait, role, cognitive resources, decision-making, and situational leader theories in regard to leadership behaviour and effectiveness. The key elements of these past theories have been refined through the lens of the manager versus leader debate so that what remains is relevant to leadership.

In order to help explain why a chosen leader might be most effective we return to the social identity theory of leadership (Haslam et al., 2011). In essence, a chosen leader will reflect the central attitudes and values of group members, i.e. they will be the most prototypical members. Prototypicality reflects how representative a member is of their group identity (e.g. group values, norms, attitudes) and evidence shows that the higher the perceived prototypicality levels the more influence that person has on a group level (Fielding and Hogg, 1997; Platow and van Knippenberg, 2001). Prototypical members espouse the shared core values and attitudes that in turn reflect the ethical and moral stance of the group and the reality of the social world that they inhabit. Hence, a prototypical leader will be perceived as authentic. Additionally as the prototypical member will be perceived to pursue the aims and aspiration of the group they will be seen as serving the group. This helps explain why a servant leader will be accepted and successful.

REVIEW QUESTIONS

1   What can sport coaching learn from organisational theories of leadership?

2   What are the limitations of equating management with leadership in understanding theories of leadership?

3   Do trait approaches of leadership have anything useful to contribute to current leadership debates?

4   Why is it essential to consider leadership as a social interaction?

REFERENCES

Allport, F. (1924) *Social Psychology*. Boston, MA: Houghton Mifflin.

Asch, S. E. (1952). *Social Psychology*. Englewood Cliffs, NJ: Prentice Hall.

Avolio, B. J., Walumbwa, F. O., and Weber, T. J. (2009). Leadership: Current theories, research, and future directions, *Annual Review of Psychology*, 60, 421–449.

Bales, R. F. (1950) *Interaction Process Analysis: A Method for the Study of Small Groups*. Cambridge, MA: Addison-Wesley.

Bales, R. F. (1970) *Personality and Interpersonal Behavior*. New York: Holt, Rinehart, & Winston.

Bandura, A. (1977). Social learning theory. *The Journal of Communication*, 28, 12–29.

Blake, R., and Mouton, J. (1964). *The Managerial Grid: The Key to Leadership Excellence*. Houston, TX: Gulf Publishing.

Blumer, H. (1969). *Symbolic Interactionism: Perspective and Method*. Englewood Cliffs, NJ: Prentice Hall.

Cassidy, T., Cummins, P., Breslin, G., and Stringer, M. (2014). Perceptions of coach social identity and team confidence, motivation and self-esteem. *Psychology*, 5, 1175–1184.

Charbonneau, D., Barling, J., and Kelloway, E. K. (2001). Transformational leadership and sports performance: The mediating role of intrinsic motivation. *Journal of Applied Social Psychology*, 31, 1521–1534.

Chelladurai, P. (2007). Leadership in sports. In G. Tenenbaum and R. C. Eklund (eds), *Handbook of Sport Psychology*. Hoboken, NJ: John Wiley & Sons, 113–135.

Durand-Bush, N., and Salmela, J. H. (2001). The development of talent in sport. In R. N. Singer, H. A. Hausenblas, and C. Janelle (eds), *Handbook of Sport Psychology* (2nd edn). New York: John Wiley, 269–289.

Festinger, L. (1954). A theory of social comparison processes. *Human Relations*, 7(2), 117–140.

Fiedler, F. E. (1967) *A Theory of Leadership Effectiveness*. New York: McGraw-Hill.

Fiedler, F. E. and Garcia, J. E. (1987) *New Approaches to Leadership: Cognitive Resources and Organizational Performance*. New York: John Wiley & Sons.

Fielding, K. S., and Hogg, M. A. (1997). Social identity, self-categorisation, and leadership: A field study of small interactive groups. *Group Dynamics: Theory, Research, and Practice*, 1, 39–51.

George, B. (2003). *Authentic Leadership: Rediscovering the Secrets to Creating Lasting Value*. New York: John Wiley & Sons.

Goffman, I. (1959). *The Presentation of Self in Everyday Life*. New York: Doubleday.

Greenleaf, R. K. (1977). *Servant Leadership*. Mahwah, NJ: Paulist Press.

Hains, S. C., Hogg, M. A., and Duck, J. M. (1997). Self-categorization and leadership: Effects of group prototypicality and leader stereotypicality. *Personality and Social Psychology Bulletin*, 23, 1087–1100.

Halpin, A. W., and Winer, B. J. (1957). A factorial study of the leader behavior descriptions. In R. M. Stogdill and A. E. Coons (eds), *Leader Behavior: Its Description and Measurement*. Columbus, OH: The Ohio State University, Bureau of Business Research, Monograph No. 88.

Hammermeister, J. J., Burton, D., Pickering, T., Chase, M., Westre, K., and Baldwin, N. (2008). Servant leadership in sport: A concept whose time has arrived. *International Journal of Servant Leadership*, 4, 185–221.

Harré, H. Rom. (1979). *Social Being: A Theory for Social Psychology*. Oxford: Blackwell.

Haslam, S. A. (2001). *Psychology in Organisations: The Social Identity Approach*. London: Sage.

Haslam, S. A., Reicher, S., and Platow, M. J. (2011). *The New Psychology of Leadership: Identity, Influence, and Power*. Hove: Psychology Press.

Haslam, S. A., Oakes, P. J., McGarty, C., Turner, J. C., and Onorato, S. (1995). Contextual changes in the prototypicality of extreme and moderate outgroup members. *European Journal of Social Psychology*, 25, 509–530.

Hersey, P., and Blanchard, K. H. (1977). *Management of Organizational Behavior: Utilizing Human Resources* (3rd edn). Englewood Cliffs, NJ: Prentice Hall.

Hersey, P., and Blanchard, K. H. (1982) *Management of Organizational Behavior* (4th edn). Englewood Cliffs, NJ: Prentice Hall.

Hogg, M. A. (2001). A social identity theory of leadership. *Personality and Social Psychology Review*, 5(3), 184–200.

Hollander, E. P. (1958). Conformity, status, and idiosyncrasy credit. *Psychological Review*, 65 (2): 117–127.

Hollander, E. P. (2008). *Inclusive Leadership: The Essential Leader–Follower Relationship*. New York: Routledge.

Katz, D., Maccoby, N., and Morse, N. C. (1950). *Productivity, Supervision and Morale in an Office Situation*. Ann Arbor, MI: Survey Research Centre.

Kernis, M. H., and Goldman, B. M. (2006). A multicomponent conceptualization of authenticity: Theory and research. *Advances in Experimental Psychology*, 38, 283–356.

Laub, J. (1999). Assessing the servant organization: Development of the servant organizational leadership (SOLA) instrument. *Dissertation Abstracts International*, 60(2), 308.

LeBon, G. (1896). *The Crowd: A Study of the Popular Mind*. London: T. Fisher Unwin.

Lewin, K. (1947). Frontiers of group dynamics: Concept, method and reality in social science, social equilibria, and social change. *Human Relations*, 1, 5–41.

Lewin, K. (1951). *Field Theory in Social Science: Selected Theoretical Papers*. London: Tavistock.

Lord, R. G., Foti, R. J., and Phillips, J. S. (1982). A theory of leadership categorization. In J. G. Hunt, U. Sekaran, and C. Schriesheim (eds). *Leadership: Beyond Establishment Views*. Carbondale, IL: Southern Illinois University Press, 104–121.

Luthans, F., and Avolio, B. J. (2003). Authentic leadership development. In K. S. Cameron, J. E. Dutton, and R. E. Quinn (eds), *Positive Organizational Scholarship*. San Francisco, CA: Berrett-Koehler, 241–258.

Mayo, E. (1933). *The Human Problems of an Industrial Civilization*. Cambridge, MA: Harvard.

Mead, G. H. (1934). *Mind, Self and Society*. Chicago, IL: University of Chicago Press.

Patterson, K. (2003). Servant leadership: A theoretical model. In S. Adjiboloos (ed.), *Proceedings of the Servant-Leadership: The Human Factor in Shaping the Course of History and Development*. Lanham, MD: American University Press, 69–110.

Platow, M. J., and van Knippenberg, D. (2001). A social identity analysis of leadership endorsement: The effects of leader ingroup prototypicality and distributive intergroup fairness. *Personality and Social Psychology Bulletin*, 27, 1508–1519.

Rabbie, J. M., and Horowitz, M. (1969). Arousal of ingroup–outgroup bias by a chance win or loss. *Journal of Personality and Social Psychology*, 13(3), 269–277.

Rieke, M., Hammermeister, J., and Chase, M. (2008). Servant leadership in sport: A new paradigm for effective coach behaviour. *International Journal of Sports Science and Coaching*, 3, 227–239.

Riemer, H. A., and Chelladurai, P. (1998). Development of the athlete satisfaction questionnaire. *Journal of Sport and Exercise Psychology*, 20, 127–156.

Robbins, S. (2001). *Organizational Behavior* (9th edn). Englewood Cliffs, NJ: Prentice Hall.

Russell, R. F., and Stone, A. G. (2002). A review of servant leadership attributes: Developing a practical model. *Leadership and Organization Development Journal*, *23*, 145–157.

Ryan, R. M. (1982). Control and information in the intrapersonal sphere: An extension of cognitive evaluation theory. *Journal of Personality and Social Psychology*, 43, 450–461.

Schachter, S., and Singer, J. (1962). Cognitive, social and physiological determinants of emotional state. *Psychological Review*, 69, 379–399.

Sherif, M., Harvey, O. J., White, B. J., Hood, W. R., and Sherif, C. W. (1961). *Intergroup conflict and cooperation: The Robbers Cave experiment (Vol. 10)*. Norman, OK: University Book Exchange.

Sternberg, R. J., and Vroom, V. (2002). Theoretical letters: The person versus the situation in leadership. *Leadership Quarterly*, 13, 301–323.

Stogdill, R. M. (1974). *Handbook of Leadership*. New York: Free Press.

Tajfel, H., and Wilkes, A. L. (1963). Classification and quantitative judgment. *British Journal of Psychology*, 54, 101–114.

Tajfel, H., and Turner, J. (1979). An integrative theory of inter-group conflict. In W. Austin, and S. Worscehl (eds), *The Social Psychology of Inter-group Relations*. Monterey, CA: Brooks/Cole, 33–47.

Tajfel, H., Billig, M. G., Bundy, R. P., and Flament, C. (1971). Social categorization and intergroup behaviour. *European Journal of Social Psychology*, 1, 149–177.

Taneja, S., Pryor, M. G., Humpheries, J. H., and Toombs, L. A. (2011). Where are the new organization theories? Evolution, development and theoretical debate. *International Journal of Management*, 28(3), 959–978.

Turner, J. C., and Haslam, S. A. (2001). Social identity, organisations, and leadership. In M. E. Turner (ed.), *Groups at Work: Advances in Theory and Research*. Hillsdale, NJ: Erlbaum, 25–65.

Van Dierendonck, D. (2011). Understanding servant leadership. *RSM Insight*, 7(3), 7–9.

Vella, S. A., Oades, L. G., and Crowe, T. P. (2011). The role of the coach in facilitating positive youth development: Moving from theory to practice. *Journal of Applied Sport Psychology*, 23(1), 33–48.

Vroom, V. H., and Yetton, P. W. (1973). *Leadership and Decision Making*. Pittsburgh, PA: University of Pittsburgh Press.

Vroom, V. H., and Jago, A. G. (1988). *The New Leadership: Managing Participation in Organizations*. Englewood Cliffs, NJ: Prentice Hall.

Warr, P. (1987). *Work, Unemployment, and Mental Health*. Oxford: Clarendon Press.

Weber, M. (1921/1968). *Economy and Society*. (G. Roth, C. Wittich, eds, G. Roth, C. Wittich, trans.) New York: Bedminster Press.

Yukl, G. (1989). Managerial leadership: A review of theory and research. *Journal of Management*, 15(2), 251–289.

Yukl, G. (2007). *Leadership in Organisations* (6th edn). Upper Saddle River, NJ: Prentice Hall.

Chapter 15

Measuring leadership in sport coaching

Robert Vaughan

CHAPTER OBJECTIVES

After completing this chapter you should be able to:

1 provide a brief overview of two of the more popular models of leadership;
2 describe two methods of how we measure leadership in sport coaching;
3 detail some of the main operationalisations or instruments of leadership;
4 be familiar with recent advances in sport leadership measurement.

KEY TERMS

- factor analysis
- internal consistency
- operationalisation
- reliability
- test–retest reliability
- validity

INTRODUCTION

The sport domain involves many important interactions and processes between athletes and coaches. Of specific concern in this chapter is the assessment of attributes, antecedents and consequences of sport leadership measurement. Much of the leadership research has concentrated on the multidimensional model (Chelladurai, 1990) or the mediational model of leadership (Smoll *et al.*, 1978) in order to conceptualise leadership. Each model has been operationalised differently by the measures proposed to measure them and will be discussed with reference to conceptual issues surrounding measurement, e.g. validity and reliability. As noted in earlier chapters, leadership can be generally defined as the behavioural process of influencing individuals and groups towards set goals (Barrow, 1977). Additionally, newer theories of leadership highlight the importance of success in leadership and include the positive impact that individuals can have on group dynamics relative to a team objective (Loehr, 2005, p. 155). These points raise one of the most critical issues in research measurement: how are the variables of a particular model operationalised? The measurement of these variables will directly influence the applicability of theory and practice (Chelladurai and Riemer, 1998). Furthermore, a requisite of theory development is the testability of the proposed model, and should therefore include an appropriate method of measurement and evaluation. Accordingly, a key feature of this chapter will be to comprehensively describe the measures of leadership theories and to evaluate the psychometrics of those measures. Note, it would not be possible to evaluate all measures of leadership. Therefore, a systematic approach to discussing the most extensively researched instruments will be proposed with directions to alternatives offered.

MEASUREMENT ISSUES

The main aim of this chapter is to review measurement of leadership. The term measurement in science refers to the process of assigning numbers to objects according to predetermined rules (Meier, 1994). This task becomes difficult when the objects are abstract representations of variables. This next section will discuss some general measurement issues that will help clarify key terms found later in the chapter (for a full overview of psychometrics see Furr and Bacharach, 2014). Researchers study leadership using different methods but with the same goal of *operationalising* the construct. This refers to the process through which abstract concepts are translated into measureable variables (Sarantakos, 1993). Before specific aspects of reliability and validity, i.e. psychometrics, are discussed in relation to each leadership measure, a brief overview of what each refers to is appropriate. The term *reliability* is defined as the extent to which a questionnaire, test, observation or any measurement procedure produces the same results on repeated trials (Nunnally and Bernstein, 1994). In a word, it is the consistency of scores over time (*test–retest reliability*) or across raters/individuals (*internal consistency*). An example of reliability is the extent to which judges at the 2012 London Olympics ice skating event agree on the scores for each skater. Similarly, the degree to which participants' scores/responses on a leadership questionnaire remain constant over time and across individuals is also a sign of reliability. It is important to understand that a measure can be reliable but not be valid. For example, consider a scale that always weighs you as being 5 kilograms heavier than your actual weight. This scale – though invalid, as it incorrectly assesses weight – is perfectly reliable as it consistently weighs you as being 5 kilograms heavier than you actually are. Researchers are typically concerned with the internal consistency and retest reliability of a measure that indicates its stability across individuals and time respectively, as poor reliability limits comparability.

Researchers are also concerned with *validity*, which is defined as the extent to which the instrument measures what it purports to measure (Nunnally and Bernstein, 1994). With regard to research measurement, an example of poor validity would be a leadership questionnaire that asked questions gauging diet, exercise intensities and facility satisfaction, i.e. items that do not directly measure leadership. There are many different types of validity, including: content validity, face validity, criterion-related validity (or predictive validity), construct validity, factorial validity, concurrent validity, convergent validity and divergent (or discriminant) validity. However, many of these are beyond the scope of this chapter (for a full review of reliability and validity see Coaley, 2009). Nonetheless, this text will be concerned with the factorial validity of leadership measures which refers to a specific statistical technique that can be used to estimate the dimensionality of a questionnaire and, most importantly, replicate the original dimensions hypothesised.

It should be remembered that psychometric support is a never ending process with no conclusive answer. This is the case for most construct variables due to the variability of human behaviour. As an alternative, researchers propose increasing bodies of literature that either support or reject the construct, to which then informative decisions can be made. It is for this reason that no recommendations will be made with regard to leadership measure, as it will become evident later on that evidence for several competing measures exist. Also, it is important to remember that the ability to answer a research question is only as good as the instruments utilised. A well-developed instrument will better provide better data which will increase confidence in your findings. Therefore, researchers will have to decide what theory/ type of leadership they want to measure and tailor their study to the merits of that operationalisation and acknowledge its limitations accordingly.

MEDIATIONAL MODEL OF LEADERSHIP

The mediational model of leadership (Smoll and Smith, 1989) focuses on the cognitive and affective mechanisms and the individual difference variables of athletes, and how these mediate the relationship between leadership behaviours, its antecedents and consequences. The model emphasises these factors along with situational variables in a three component structure consisting of coach behaviours, player perception and recall, and the player's evaluative reactions. It was hypothesised that evaluations of coach's behaviour would be mediated by the meaning an athlete attributes to that behaviour. The model postulates that cognitive and affective processes serve as filters between coaching behaviours and athlete's attitude towards the coach and sport experience. Moreover, a coach's perception of a player's attitude mediates the relationship between a coach's behaviour and a player's evaluative reaction to those behaviours. Furthermore, the model allows for reciprocal interactions between variables in conjunction with the normal mediator relationships (Smoll and Smith, 1989). A display of the model is presented in Figure 15.1.

COACHING BEHAVIOUR ASSESSMENT SYSTEM

Smith and Smoll developed an observational method to measure leadership behaviour according to their mediational model. The athlete's perceptions and recall of leader behaviour and affective reactions to the sport experience are usually measured using structured interviews; whereas coach's perceptions of their own behaviour are typically assessed by questionnaire.

213

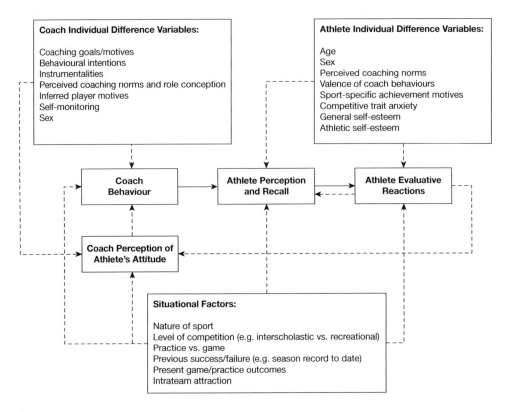

Figure 15.1 *Mediational model of leadership behaviours in sport and hypothesized relationships among situational, cognitive, behavioural and individual difference variables.*

Source: adapted from Smoll and Smith (1989).

The questionnaire operationalises the behaviour through single item sub-scales. Smith and Smoll coined their observational instrument the Coaching Behaviour Assessment System (CBAS). The instrument was developed over several years observing youth coaches and driven by social learning theories. Transcripts were analysed using content analysis from which 12 categories emerged to form the scoring system. These 12 categories were reinforcement, non-reinforcement, mistake-contingent encouragement, mistake-contingent technical instruction, punishment, punitive technical instruction, ignoring mistakes, keeping control, general technical instruction, general encouragement, organisation, and general communication (Smith *et al.*, 1977). Findings indicated that the system encompassed the majority of coaching behaviours, that it could distinguish individual differences in behaviours, and that the measure could be easily utilised in field research (Chelladurai and Riemer, 1998). The 12 coaching behaviour categories can be grouped as either reactive, i.e. an immediate response to player/team behaviour, or spontaneous, i.e. initiated by the coach independently of previous action. The reactive sub-factor contains responses to desirable performances, mistakes and misbehaviours; whereas the spontaneous sub-factor includes game related or irrelevant behaviours. The CBAS is an observational measure of coach's actual behaviour, gauging the frequency a coach displays one of the 12 behaviours. Normally, the observation is conducted by one or more individuals during competitive, e.g. games, or non-competitive, e.g. training, scenarios.

COACHING BEHAVIOUR ASSESSMENT SYSTEM RELIABILITY

The naturalistic basis of the scoring system of the CBAS creates unique difficulties in assessing the psychometrics of the instrument. However, efforts have been made to improve its reliability. For example, the authors created a training program for individuals utilising the measure which included a comprehensive overview of the manual, instruction for using the scoring system with video footage, tests on knowledge of the categories, practice scoring of video footage, and consistency checks of field use (Smith et al., 1983). Furthermore, empirical investigation has assessed the relevant reliability of the coding system; specifically, the extent of agreement between raters, i.e. the correlation between the observers coding the coach's behaviour or correlation between the same observer over time. Smith et al. (1977) reported an agreement of 97.8 per cent between 31 trainee raters on 48 coaching behaviours observed on video recordings. Furthermore, Smith et al. (1983) reported a 90 per cent agreement between trainees and expert observers. Other researchers (Chaumeton and Duda, 1998; Horn, 1984) have reported median inter-rater reliability adopting Cohen's (1960) methods ranging from .68 to .96. Unfortunately, investigations adopting these methods have not always reported reliability estimates (Wandzilak et al., 1988). Furthermore, the guidelines proposed by the authors have not always been adhered to. For example, pass rates on the coder tests have varied, as has time spent training to use the instrument (Sherman and Hassan, 1986). Furthermore, some research has failed to report any information regarding coder training (Krane et al., 1991). Finally, Smoll and Smith (1989) have stressed the importance that coaches are not aware of being observed. Naturally, this has issues regarding the legitimacy of observations, e.g. through social desirability, with coaches modifying behaviour to be viewed more positively. These issues make it difficult to agree consensus on the instrument's reliability.

COACHING BEHAVIOUR ASSESSMENT SYSTEM VALIDITY

As mentioned, the CBAS relies largely on qualitative procedures in its creation and assessment. Some of these procedures lack clarity and detail in the literature, e.g. the methods used to create the 12 categories (Chelladurai and Riemer, 1998). For example, the number of coaches utilised in the original observation in the conception of the 12 categories is not provided in the original text. These deficits create difficulties in evaluating the validity of the instrument. This is contrary to Patton's (1990) call for stringency in reporting details of qualitative investigation for the purposes of evaluation. Nonetheless, examples of content validity exist in the literature. Smoll and Smith (1989) noted that the 12 categories of the CBAS can be observed in nonathletic samples. Furthermore, the 12 categories can be classified as positive and negative, which are the two broad types of communication that exist in small groups (Bales and Slater, 1955). Furthermore, the CBAS includes all the categories included in the Leadership Scale for Sport (Chelladurai and Saleh, 1980). Chelladurai (1993) suggests that the CBAS is a comprehensive operationalisation of leadership behaviour, therefore suggesting that it possesses content validity. Similar to the assessment of reliability, the authors suggest that validity can be accurately appraised by adopting a triangulation of observers. One of the most common methods of assessing a measures validity is through conducting a *factor analysis* on a given set of data. Factor analysis is a statistical method used to describe variability among observed and correlated variables, e.g. items in a questionnaire, in terms of a potentially lower number of unobserved variables called factors (Nunnally and Bernstein, 1994). The construct validity of a measure is supported if the factor structure is replicated from the data (confirmatory techniques) or if the theory the measure is based on emerges (exploratory techniques). A consistent replication of an instruments factor structure is a meaningful estimate of both construct validity and reliability. Research investigating the factor structure of the CBAS has provided mixed support with Smith and Smoll (1990) replicating the structure and Smith *et al.* (1983) reporting an alternative ten category structure. Comparison of these studies should yield similar results as the same theory is being tested. However, the discrepancies between the numbers of categories can be partially explained by the differences in techniques used to replicate the structures. For example, the use of orthogonal rotation techniques that force categories to be uncorrelated may not be representative of coaching behaviours (Chelladurai and Riemer, 1998). Furthermore, remember that the goal of factor analysis is to reduce the amount of observed data to fewer factors. Therefore, the differences between the numbers of reported factors (or categories in the example of the CBAS) could be data driven depending on the characteristics of the sample data.

COACHING BEHAVIOUR ASSESSMENT SYSTEM REVIEW

The mediation model and related instrument provides a comprehensive description of actual leadership behaviour. The 12 category model theoretically encompasses the full range of coach's behaviour that has also been reported in other theories and measures. However, the subjectivity involved with single item observational measures is problematic. For example, issues surrounding subjectivity and differences in observer training make comparison across studies difficult. Thus, inferences on its reliability and validity are inconclusive. A list of some of the most commonly used observational measures is presented in Table 15.1.

THE MULTIDIMENSIONAL MODEL OF LEADERSHIP

The Multidimensional Model of Leadership combined several existing theories of leadership in order to conceptualise leadership behaviours and processes (Chelladurai, 1993). The model postulates that group performance and member satisfaction as outcomes/consequences are dependent on two clusters of related factors. The first cluster consists of three antecedent factors that influence leadership states, such as: situational characteristics, e.g. whether the opposition is weak or strong; leader characteristics, such as experience, personality, etc.; group member characteristics, including age, gender and experience of the members. As mentioned, there are three types of leader states in the second cluster: required behaviour, i.e. what the situation requires the leader to do; actual behaviour that details what the leader actually does, which depends on the situation, leader and member characteristics; and

Table 15.1 *Observational instruments utilised to measure coaching behaviour*

Instrument	What it measures	Coding categories	Authors
Coaching Behaviour Assessment System (CBAS)	Coaches' overt leadership behaviours during both practices and competitive events (can be used to assess coach behaviour towards teams or individual athletes)	12 coding categories divided into reactive and spontaneous coaching behaviours	Smith *et al.*, 1977
Arizona State University Observation Instrument (ASUOI)	Coaches' instructional and other behaviours in practice settings	14 categories of coaching behaviour, 7 of which are directly related to instruction	Lacy and Darst, 1989
Coaching Behaviour Recording Form	Coaches' behaviour in practices and competitive events	10–12 categories of coaching behaviour including performance feedback, instruction, encouragement and modelling	Tharp and Gallimore, 1976
Coach Analysis Instrument (CAI)	Coaches' verbal behaviour	Computer-based system that uses hierarchical form of event recording so that coaches' comments can be analysed at up to five levels: direction, focus, timing, delivery and emphasis	Franks *et al.*, 1988

preferred behaviour that refers to what the team members want the leader to do. Each of the antecedent factors can influence leadership states in different ways. For example, the demands created by situational characteristics require the leader to behave in certain ways to ensure that group goals are successfully achieved. However, this is not a unilateral process model with multiple antecedents affecting leadership states. For example, the situation and member characteristics will directly influence the required behaviour. Furthermore, the model predicts that performance and satisfaction will also influence actual behaviour (Chelladurai, 1993). A display of the model is presented in Figure 15.2.

LEADERSHIP SCALE FOR SPORTS

Chelladurai and Saleh (1980) constructed the Leadership Scale for Sports (LSS) in order to operationalise their multidimensional model. The instrument consists of 40 items scored on a 5-point Likert scale, according to their level of agreement with that phrase; always, often (about 75 per cent of the time), occasionally (about 50 per cent of the time), seldom (about

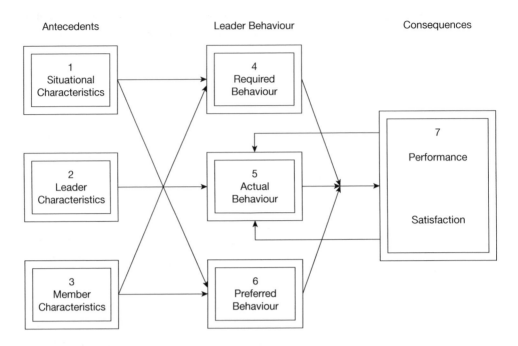

Figure 15.2 *Multidimensional model of leadership in sport displaying relationship between antecedents, behaviour and consequences.*

Source: adapted from Chelladurai (1993).

25 per cent of the time), and never. The scale attempts to operationalise five dimensions of leadership behaviour: one factor that is directly related to group tasks (training and instruction), two decision-making style factors (democratic and autocratic behaviour), and two motivational factors (rewarding behaviour and social support). The training and instruction dimension refers to coaching behaviour intended to improve athlete's performance by stressing and assisting intense training, providing specific skill, technique and tactical guidance, detailing relationships between members and managing the group's activities; it is comprised of 13 items. The democratic behaviour dimension details coaching behaviours that enable and encourage autonomy in decision making to members, and consists of nine items. The autocratic behaviour dimension states the independence displayed by group leaders in decision making, and contains five items. The social support dimension describes coaching behaviours that are characterised by emphasising relationships between members, a positive atmosphere and member well-being, and is comprised of eight items. Finally, the rewarding behaviour dimension refers to the coaching behaviours that reinforce good performances through recognition/rewards and consists of five items. The main tenet of the model is the congruency between the three states and the consequences, i.e. satisfaction and performance. This theorises that leaders will need to successfully manage and negotiate the demands posed by situations and members' preferences. The model provides two different feedback loops from satisfaction and performance to actual behaviour. The leader is likely to modify behaviour based on the relative attainment of the consequence variables.

The instrument was developed in two stages, with the first stage involving selecting items from other leadership questionnaires. This resulted in a 99 item questionnaire which was distributed to 160 physical education students and then factor analysed. The analysis revealed a five factor solution (as mentioned earlier) and was considered expressive and representative of coaching behaviours. The five factor solution consisted of 37 items that met the predetermined cut-offs for retention, i.e. high loading on one of the factors and low on the other four. In the second stage items were added to reflect behaviours such as teaching skills and tactics, and social support to conceptualise leader's group facilitation. This new version was distributed to 102 physical education students and 223 college athletes. The data was again subjected to factor analysis, however, the five factors were specified a priori. The findings, subjected to the same cut-offs as the developmental study, suggested that a 40 item instrument was most suitable for the five factors and currently represents the most current version of the scale. Also, the LSS is available in three formats: athletes' preference for coaching behaviour, athletes' perception of their coach's behaviour, and coaches' perception of their own behaviour. All three versions of the LSS are identical in terms of structure and wording of items. However, the scenario for participant's response is gauged from a different context. For example, in the 'athletes' preference' version, an athlete is asked to express how they would like a coach to behave towards them. In the 'athletes' perception' version, the athlete rates how their coach actually behaves. Finally, in the third version, 'coaches' perception', coaches provide a self-report evaluation of how often they behave in certain ways towards their players. The scale has also been modified for use with non-English speaking participants with the most recent translation being revised for Polish samples (Wałach-Biśta, 2013).

LEADERSHIP SCALE FOR SPORTS RELIABILITY

Chelladurai (1993) assessed the test–retest reliability of the five dimensions over a four week period during the initial validation of the LSS. The correlations reported were satisfactory for the developmental stage (Nunnally and Bernstein, 1994). The values reported were .72 for training and instruction, .82 for democratic behaviour, .76 for autocratic behaviour, .71 for social support and .79 for rewarding behaviour dimensions. A range of adequate internal consistency values has been reported in the literature ranging from .61 to .97 utilising different samples of athletes (Riemer and Chelladurai, 1995; Chelladurai and Riemer, 1998). As mentioned, there are three versions of the scale gauging leadership behaviour from a coach's perspective, an athlete's perception and athlete's preference. Typically, scales adopting the perceptions format report higher internal consistency scores. Both versions rely on athlete's subjectivity to recall; however, perceptions are generally thought of as more stable and will therefore remain more consistent compared to preferences (White et al., 1985). Nunnally and Bernstein have recommended a cut-off of .70 for satisfactory internal consistency/ reliability. However, some of the internal consistency scores for the LSS sub-scale fall below this cut-off, particularly the autocratic behaviour dimension. This may be due to mechanical reasons such as the differing number of items in each of the sub-scales which will have a direct effect on the average-item correlations. Furthermore, the autocratic behaviour dimension attempts to tap into two different leadership facets, e.g. two items are concerned with handling issues and two are concerned with how the coach addresses players; whereas the democratic behaviour dimension centres on items concerned with decision making. Thus the difference in facets tapped may explain why the autocratic behaviour dimension is typically lower. Chelladurai and Riemer (1998) recommend revising the autocratic behaviour dimension to include more items in order to more comprehensively represent autocratic leadership behaviours and to increase its average inter-item correlations.

LEADERSHIP SCALE FOR SPORTS VALIDITY

Chelladurai and Saleh (1980) claimed that the LSS possessed several examples of validity. The authors noted that content and criterion related validity was represented in the meaningful relationships observed between the dimensions and related areas and theories of leadership. For example, the training and instruction, rewarding behaviour and social support dimensions were evident in Porter and Lawler's (1968) model of leadership motivation, with each playing a significant role in motivation behaviours (Chelladurai, 1981). Empirical research has reported significant relationships between the consequence factors from the multidimensional model of leadership that the LSS operationalises, i.e. satisfaction and performance, and the five dimensions of the LSS (Garland and Barry, 1988; Horne and Carron, 1985; Riemer and Chelladurai, 1995; Weiss and Friedrichs, 1986). The authors also claim evidence for factorial validity is presented from the developmental samples that produced the same five factor solutions. Furthermore, several investigations have supported the five factor solution (Iordanoglou, 1990; Isberg and Chelladurai, 1990). However, there are a few methodological issues with Chelladurai and Saleh's factor analytic work. A relatively low amount of variance was explained in the validations studies, e.g. 39.3–55.8 per cent. What this means is that a significant portion of the data was unaccounted for in the five factor solution and therefore some coaching behaviours may not be represented in the model. Furthermore, the independence of each factor can be questioned as there is evidence of correlations of approximately .35 between items from different dimensions of the LSS (Riemer and Chelladurai, 1995). Also, there are examples of the five factor solution not being replicated from different data (Gordon, 1986; Summers, 1983). These discrepancies arise from the low amount of variance accounted for in the original data. As exploratory factor analytic techniques try to reduce the amount of variables, the low percentages accounted for may not be replicable in other samples. Furthermore, the original aim of trying to establish meaningful factors from data means that exploratory techniques or item-to-total correlations, as the technique of choice utilised by the authors, may have not been entirely appropriate. The items selected should have been subjected to confirmatory techniques in order to establish the suitability of the items' dimensionality. Chelladurai and Riemer (1998) revisited the original data employing confirmatory techniques and reported that the model could be considered valid. However, there was scope for improvement and, akin to reliability evaluations, the higher scores were found on the perception versions. It should be noted that stringent psychometric evaluation is important for a scales validation and later utility. However, precedence must always be given to the meaningfulness of the values, i.e. the model makes sense (Browne and DuToit, 1991). Although this requirement is purely subjective, it does provide support for the five factor solution. The LSS is also critiqued at the conceptual level, e.g. the original items were derived from leadership measures belonging to the business domains and may not be representative of the unique coaching behaviours observed in sport. Much of the LSS theory is based on transactional theories of leadership, whereas modern approaches to leadership are characterised by transformational leadership theories. The transformational theories are not readily represented in the LSS dimensions and may require reconfiguration in order to conceptualise dimensions such as reactive and adaptive behaviours (Chelladurai and Riemer 1998). Transformational leadership theories stress coaches need to motivate, empower and express confidence in members. Nonetheless, the interaction effects of the antecedents in the multidimensional model can be considered facilitative and partially transformational.

LEADERSHIP SCALE FOR SPORTS REVIEW

The multidimensional model of leadership and related instrument provide a systematic account of leadership based on several existing theories of leadership in non-sporting contexts. The five dimension model explains behaviour by highlighting possible antecedents that explain different types of coaching behaviour and thus group consequences. The authors of the leadership scale for sport have made efforts to psychometrically evaluate their operationalisation. However, methodological weaknesses surrounding their factor analytic work have questioned the psychometrics of the scale. Furthermore, issues surrounding the appropriateness and dimensionality of the five factor solution exist. Nonetheless, more contemporary approaches to evaluating the five factor solution are warranted as evidence has suggested the scale possesses adequate levels of reliability and validity. A list of some of the most commonly used questionnaire measures of coaching behaviour are presented in Table 15.2.

FUTURE DIRECTIONS AND CONTEMPORARY APPROACHES

Amorose and Horn (2000) reconceptualised the CBAS measures to construct the Coaching Feedback Questionnaire (CFQ). The CFQ attempts to quantify the mediational model from a quantitative perspective, operationalising their 16 item questionnaire. The 16 items tapped eight factors, which included: three categories of responses to players' performances and five categories reflecting errors reflected. Amorose and Horn claimed that these eight factors correspond to those of CBAS, particularly the reactive behaviours. Factor analysis and internal consistency assessment provided mixed support for the instrument's reliability and validity. Factor analysis suggested that three factors characterised the data with dimensions in positive and informative feedback, punishment orientated feedback and non-reinforcement/ignoring mistakes reported. However, the amount of explained variance was quite low. This may be due to the under-representation of eight factors in a 16 item instrument; Nunnally and Bernstein (1994) recommend that at least five items operationalise a dimension. Similarly, the same values are required for participants-to-items ratio. However, the internal consistency scores were satisfactory, ranging from .72 to .83 for the three factor solution. The CFQ may be preferred due to its brevity and psychometric evidence. However, it is not as representative of coaching behaviours as the original CBAS. Therefore, researchers will have to decide between an instrument with a much narrower range of application but promising psychometric evidence or a more comprehensive definition of coaching behaviours with little psychometric evidence.

221

Table 15.2 *Questionnaire instruments utilised to measure coaching behaviour*

Instrument	What it measures	Subscales	Authors
Leadership Scale for Sports (LSS)	Dimensions of leader behaviour: three versions have been developed to measure a) athletes' preferences for different types of coaching behaviour, b) athletes' perceptions of their coaches' behaviour, and c) coaches' self-evaluation of their own behaviour	1 Autocratic behaviour 2 Democratic behaviour 3 Training and instruction behaviour 4 Positive feedback behaviour 5 Social support behaviour	Chelladurai and Saleh (1980)
Decision-style questionnaires	How coaches make decisions in sport contexts: different versions have been developed to assess athletes' perceptions of their coaches' style and coaches' perceptions of their own style	Range of decision-making styles (e.g. autocratic, consultative, participative, delegative) that reflect the degree to which the coach allows athletes to participate in the decision-making process	Chelladurai and Arnott (1985)
Perceived Motivational Climate in Sport Questionnaire – 2 (PMCSQ-2)	Athletes' perceptions of the motivational climate that their coaches initiate or create in practice and game contexts	Each of two higher order factors – task-involving climate and ego-involving climate – has three sub-scales	Seifriz *et al.* (1992)
Coaches' Interpersonal Behavioural Style	Athletes' perceptions of their coaches' interpersonal behaviours towards and with them	1 Autonomy-supportive interpersonal style 2 Controlling interpersonal style	Bartholomew *et al.* (2010)
Coach Behaviour Questionnaire (CBQ)	Athletes' perceptions and evaluative reactions to both positive and negative coaching behaviours	1 Negative activation 2 Supportiveness and emotional composure	Kenow and Williams (1993)

continued . . .

Table 15.2 *Continued*

Instrument	What it measures	Subscales	Authors
Greek Coach-Athlete Relationship Questionnaire (GrCART-Q)	Coaches' and athletes' direct perspective of their interpersonal relationship: a modified GrCART-Q2 has been developed to assess athletes' and coaches' meta-perspective of the coach–athlete relationship	1 Closeness 2 Commitment 3 Complementarity	Jowett and Ntoumanis (2003)
Coaching Behaviour scale for Sport (CBS-S)	Coaching behaviours exhibited in training, competitive and organisational settings	Seven dimensions of coaching behaviour (e.g. physical training and planning, goal setting, personal rapport)	Côté *et al.* (1999)
Multifactor Leadership Questionnaire (MLQ-5X)	Individuals' perceptions of their leaders' attributes, behaviours and leadership styles	Nine leadership factors composed of five transformational factors, three transactional factors, and one non-leadership (laissez-faire) factor	Bass and Avolio (1997)

Zhang *et al.* (1997) modified the LSS to include more items and dimensions but retained the other features of the original instrument, e.g. three response formats and instructions. Zhang *et al.* retained the original five dimensions but added two further dimensions, group maintenance behaviour and situational consideration behaviour. Group maintenance behaviours categorise cohesion and coach–athlete improving behaviours. Situational consideration behaviours describe behaviours aimed at considering situational factors and setting goals for members and determining how they can achieve them. Zhang *et al.*(1997) developed the Revised Leadership Scale for Sport (RLSS) by employing experts to evaluate 240 items generated from interviews with college coaches. Three samples of athletes and coaches, i.e. 696 athletes on the preferred version, 661 on the perception version, and 206 coaches, were factor analysed. The results revealed that 60 items conceptualised six of the proposed dimensions with the group maintenance behaviour dimensions not emerging as a distinct factor as its items loaded on other factors. The internal consistency was also evaluated, which reported values above .80 for all factors except for the autocratic behaviour dimension. One major flaw of this line of research is that a comparison between the LSS and RLSS was not made. This would have enabled researchers to make a judgement on what was the most parsimonious operationalisation of coaching behaviour. Therefore, despite Zhang and colleagues' effort to combat the weaknesses of the LSS, these issues remain in their instrument albeit to a lesser degree.

223

SUMMARY

One approach in measuring coaching behaviour is through behaviour assessment of practice and game contexts either directly or using videotaped sequences. This approach utilises trained observers to assess coach behaviours using a systematic observation and recording device. The most commonly used system is the Coaching Behaviour Assessment System devised by Smoll et al. (1977) which provides a direct, observationally based assessment of 12 categories of coaching behaviour. The CBAS is aimed at operationalising the mediational model of leadership. The 12 categories can be broadly classified into two sets of behaviours: reactive (behaviours exhibited by a coach in response to a variety of player behaviours) and spontaneous (behaviours exhibited by a coach outside of responding to player behaviours). Mixed support has been provided for the instruments reliability and validity partially due to its naturalistic origins. However, due to the practical development of the instrument it theoretically provides one of the most comprehensive measures of actual coaching behaviour.

The multidimensional model of leadership has been conceptualised by the Leadership Scale for Sports. The LSS consists of five subscales, two of which measure the coach's motivational tendencies (social support and positive feedback), two of which measure the coach's decision-making style (autocratic and democratic), and one that measures the coach's instructional behaviour (training and instruction). The LSS has been through stringent assessments of its psychometric properties and these procedures have generally supported the reliability and validity of the LSS, although not conclusively. Furthermore, the authors note concern with regard to the autocratic subscale and have suggested further psychometric testing and instrument revision (Horn, 2008).

In conclusion, two of the most prominent leadership behaviour models and their respective instruments have been reviewed in terms of their theory and measurement, i.e. the Coaching Behaviour Assessment System of the mediational model of leadership (Smoll and Smith, 1989) and the Leadership Scale for Sport of the Multidimensional Model of Leadership (Chelladurai, 1993). Throughout this chapter specific attention was paid to the development, reliability, validity and measurement issues surrounding each scale. The psychometric evidence of both instruments warrant further research as both are consistently and theoretically measuring coaches' leadership behaviours. The most recent attempts at conceptualising the models have also experienced difficulties. This suggests that regressing back to theoretical underpinnings for further evaluation may be required. It may be possible that the advances in methodologies over the past few decades, e.g. advances in factor analytic techniques and availability of software packages to measure them, will enable leadership researchers to reach new conclusions regarding the models proposed. Once this has been undertaken, researchers could utilise the mixed methods framework deployed by Zhang et al. to operationalise a contemporary instrument of coaching behaviour. This would require harvesting expert opinion of leadership behaviour to generate items, and then subjecting this data to both exploratory and confirmatory factor analytic techniques. This could result in a more psychometrically sound measure of leadership being developed.

REVIEW QUESTIONS

1   Note the components of the mediational model and how the Coaching Behaviour Assessment System operationalises this?

2   What are some of the issues surrounding the psychometrics of the Coaching Behaviour Assessment System?

3   The multidimensional model is operationalised by the Leadership Scale for Sport. What are the five sub-scales and how are these sub-scales categorised?

4   Explain the utility of factor analysis in the development and validation of the Leadership Scale for Sport?

REFERENCES

Amorose, A. J., and Horn, T. S. (2000). Intrinsic motivation: Relationships with collegiate athletes' gender, scholarship status, and perceptions of their coaches' behavior. *Journal of Sport and Exercise Psychology, 22*, 63–84.

Bales, R. F., and Slater, P. (1955). Role differentiation in small decision-making groups. In P. Parsons and R. F. Bales (eds), *Family, socialisation, and interaction processes* (pp. 259–306). Glencoe, IL: Free Press.

Barrow, J. (1977). The variables of leadership: A review and conceptual framework. *Academy of Management Review, 2*, 231–251.

Bartholomew, K. J., Ntoumanis, N., and Thøgersen-Ntoumani, C. (2010). The controlling interpersonal style in a coaching context: Development and initial validation of a psychometric scale. *Journal of Sport and Exercise Psychology, 32*, 193–216.

Bass, B. M., and Avolio, B. J. (1997). *Full range leadership development: Manual for the Multifactor Leadership Questionnaire*. Palo Alto, CA: Mind Garden.

Browne, M. W., and DuToit, S. H. C. (1991). *Models for learning data*. In L. M. Collins and J. L. Horn (eds), *Best methods for the analysis of change* (pp. 47–68). Washington, DC: APA.

Chaumeton, N. R., and Duda, J. L. (1998). Is it how you play the game or whether you win or lose? The effect of competitive level and situation on coaching behaviours. *Journal of Sport Behavior, 11*(3), 157–174.

Chelladurai, P. (1981). The coach as motivator and chameleon of leadership styles. *Science periodical on research and technology in sport*. Ottawa, Canada: Coaching Association of Canada.

Chelladurai, P. (1990). Leadership in sports: A review. *International Journal of Sport Psychology, 21*, 328–354.

Chelladurai, P. (1993). *Leadership*. In R. N. Singer, M. Murphy, and L. K. Tennant (eds), *Handbook on research on sport psychology* (pp. 641–671). New York: McMillan.

Chelladurai, P., and Arnott, M. (1985). Decision styles in coaching: Preferences of basketball players. *Research Quarterly for Exercise and Sport, 56*(1), 15–24.

Chelladurai, P., and Riemer, H. A. (1998). Measurement of leadership in sport. In J. L. Duda (ed.), *Advances in sport and exercise psychology measurement* (pp. 227–253). Morgantown, WV: Fitness Information Technology.

Chelladurai, P., and Saleh, S. D. (1980). Dimensions of leader behaviour in sports: Development of a leadership scale. *Journal of Sport Psychology, 2*, 34–55.

Coaley, K. (2009). *An introduction to psychological assessment and psychometrics.* London: Sage.

Cohen, J. (1960). A coefficient of agreement for nominal scales. *Educational and Psychological Measurement, 20*(1), 37–46.

Côté, J. J., Yardley, J., Hay, W., Sedgwick, J., and Baker, J. (1999). An exploratory examination of the coaching behavior scale for sport. *Avante, 5*, 82–92.

Franks, I. M., Johnson, R. B., and Sinclair, G. D. (1988). The development of a computerized coaching analysis system for recording behavior in sporting environments. *Journal of Teaching in Physical Education, 8*, 23–32.

Furr, R. M., and Bacharach, V. R. (2014). *Psychometrics: An introduction.* London: Sage.

Garland, D. J., and Barry, J. R. (1988). The effects of personality and perceived leader behaviour on performance on collegiate football. *The Psychological Record, 38*, 237–247.

Gordon, S. (1986). Behavioral correlates of coaching effectiveness. Unpublished doctoral dissertation. University of Alberta, Canada.

Horn, T. S. (1984). Expectancy effects in the interscholastic athletic setting: Methodological considerations. *Journal of Sport Psychology, 6*, 60–76.

Horne, T., and Carron, A. V. (1985). Compatibility in coach–athlete relationships. *Journal of Sport Psychology, 7*, 137–149.

Iordanoglou, D. (1990). Perceived leadership in Greek soccer: A preliminary investigation. Unpublished paper, University of Manchester, Department of Education, Manchester, UK.

Isberg, L., and Chelladurai, P. (1990). The Leadership Sale for Sports: Its applicability to the Swedish context. Unpublished manuscript, University College of Falun/Borlange, Sweden.

Jowett, S., and Ntoumanis, N. (2003). The Greek Coach–Athlete Relationship Questionnaire (GrCART-Q): Scale construction and validation. *International Journal of Sport Psychology, 34*, 101–124.

Kenow, L. J., and Williams, J. M. (1993). Factor structure of the coaching behavior questionnaire and its relationship to anxiety and self-confidence. *Journal of Sport and Exercise Psychology (Supplement), 15*, S45.

Krane, V., Ecklund, R., and McDermott, M. (1991). Collaborative action research and behavioural coaching intervention: A case study. *Applied Research in Coaching and Athletics Annual, 12*, 119–147.

Lacy, A. C., and Darst, P. D. (1989). The Arizona State University Observation Instrument (ASUOI). In P. W. Darst, B. Zakrajsek, and V. H. Mancini (eds), *Analyzing physical education and sport instruction* (pp. 369–378). Champaign, IL: Human Kinetics.

Loehr, J. (2005). *Leadership: Full engagement for success.* In S. M. Murphy (ed.), *The sport psych handbook* (pp. 155–170). Champaign, IL: Human Kinetics.

Meier, S. T. (1994). *The chronic crisis in psychological measurement and assessment: A historical survey.* New York: Academic Press.

Nunnally, J. C., and Bernstein, I. H. (1994). *Psychometric theory.* New York: McGraw-Hill.

Patton, M. Q. (1990). *Qualitative Evaluation and Research Methods.* London: Sage.

Porter, L. W., and Lawler, E. E. (1968). *Managerial attitudes and performance.* Homewood, IL: Richard, D. Irwin.

Riemer, H. A., and Chelladurai, P. (1995). Leadership and satisfaction in athletics. *Journal of Sport and Exercise Psychology, 17*, 276–293.

Sarantakos, S. (1993). *Social research.* Basingstoke: Macmillan.

Seifriz, J. J., Duda, J. L., and Chi, L. (1992). The relationship of perceived motivational climate to intrinsic motivation and beliefs about success in basketball. *Journal of Sport and Exercise Psychology, 14*, 375–391.

Sherman M. A., and Hassan, J. S. (1986). Behavioral studies of youth sport coaches. In M. Pieron and G. Graham (eds), *The 1984 Olympic Scientific Congress proceedings: Vol. 6. Sport pedagogy* (pp. 103–108). Champaign, IL: Human Kinetics.

Smith, R. E., and Smoll, F. L. (1990). Self-esteem and children's reactions to youth sport coaching behaviors: A field study of self-enhancement processes. *Developmental Psychology*, 26(6), 987–993.

Smith, R. E., Smoll, F. L., and Hunt, E. B. (1977). A system for the behavioral assessment of coaches. *Research Quarterly*, 48, 401–407.

Smith, R. E., Zane, N. W. S., Smoll, F. L., and Coppel, D. B. (1983). Behavioral assessment in youth sports: Coaching behaviors and children's attitudes. *Medicine and Science in Sport and Exercise*, 15, 208–214.

Smoll, F. L., and Smith, R. E. (1989). Leadership behaviors in sport: A theoretical model and research paradigm. *Journal of Applied Social Psychology*, 78, 602–610.

Smoll, F. L., Smith, F. L., Curtis, B., and Hunt, E. (1978). Towards a mediational model of coach player relationships. *Research Quarterly*, 49, 528–541.

Summers, R. J. (1983). A study of leadership in a sport setting. Unpublished master's thesis. University of Waterloo, Canada.

Tharp, R. G., and Gallimore, R. (1976). What a coach can teach a teacher. *Psychology Today, 9*, 75–78.

Wałach-Biśta, Z. (2013). A Polish adaptation of Leadership Scale for Sports: A questionnaire examining coaching behavior. *Human Movement*, 14(3), 265–274.

Wandzilak, T., Ansorage, C. J., and Potter, G. (1988). Comparison between selected practice and game behaviors of youth sport soccer coaches. *Journal of Sport Behavior*, 11(2), 79–88.

Weiss, M. R., and Friedrichs, W. D. (1986). The influence of leader behaviors, coach attributes, and institutional variables on performance and satisfaction of collegiate basketball teams. *Journal of Sport Psychology*, 8, 332–346.

White, M. C., Crino, M. D., and Hatfield, J. D. (1985). An empirical examination of the parsimony of perceptual congruence scores. *Academy of Management Journal*, 28(3), 732–737.

Zhang, J., Jensen, B. E., and Mann, B. L. (1997). Modification and revision of the Leadership Scale for Sport. *Journal of Sport Behavior*, 20(1), 105–121.

Chapter 16

Sustainable performance with empathy

Tadhg MacIntyre

CHAPTER OBJECTIVES

Upon reviewing the material in this chapter you should be able to:

1   outline the traditional approaches to coach–athlete relationships;
2   discuss the construct of empathy and why it may be important;
3   describe the advantages of empathy for coach leaders;
4   give examples of where empathy can lead to extraordinary behaviour in the sporting context.

KEY TERMS

- emotional contagion
- emotional intelligence
- empathy
- mirror neurons
- pushing the envelope
- sustainable performance

INTRODUCTION

The professionalisation of elite performance sport in recent decades has led to a proliferation of incidents in which the questionable practices of leaders have been the subject of intense media attention. One could label this spectrum as *the good, the bad and the ugly* of leadership in sport (see also Chapter 6). High profile accounts of negative behaviours that have been reported in the media include the use of extreme techniques in team building sessions at Kamp Staaldraad for the South African rugby team in 1995 (Kremer and Moran, 2013). More recently, allegations of abusive and unethical practices by coaches have led to resignations and reprimand. For example, in 2013, Mike Rice was fired from his position as basketball coach at Rutgers for his harsh coaching style which included throwing basketballs at players (Eder, 2013). And in the NFL, the 'Bountygate' scandal revealed that the New Orleans Saints players were allegedly receiving bonuses for inflicting injuries on opposing players that forced them to leave games (Ford, 2014). Undoubtedly, elite sport has the capacity to challenge the mental and physical health of performers (Hughes and Leavey, 2012). Typically, coaches have been seen as part of the problem. For example, evidence has linked sport pressures from coaches with disorder eating among female athletes (Anderson *et al.*, 2012). Both sport coaches' criticisms or comments about weight/body size (Kerr *et al.*, 2006) and the belief held by coaches that a thin/small body improves performance (Bonogofski *et al.*, 1999) can have deleterious effects. The surprise is not that leadership in sport coaching has a potential dark side, one that can impact negatively upon players, athletes, other stakeholders (e.g. volunteer staff) and even coaches themselves, but that there remains a paucity of research on conflict in the coach–athlete relationship (Jowett and Poczwardowski, 2007). As stated in 2006, 'If we, sport and exercise psychologists, are to make a mark and a noticeable progress we need to consider the impact of relationship contexts on human behaviour' (Jowett and Wylleman, 2006, p. 121).

Arguably, researchers have avoided this topic until recently because of the limited paradigms that have been employed to understand coach–athlete relationships, in both their positive and negative instances, in the sport domain. Researchers have employed a variety of lenses including the expertise approach (Bloom and Salmela, 2000), dispositional accounts (Chelladurai, 1993), social psychological viewpoints (Jowett and Lavallee, 2007), motivational climate perspectives (Smoll *et al.*, 2007), a focus on coaching effectiveness (Côté and Gilbert, 2009), an emotional intelligence viewpoint (Lane *et al.*, 2009) and, more recently, a reflective practice has been used to illuminate coach–athlete relationships (Dixon *et al.*, 2013). The three Cs model is perhaps the most commonly used framework to explore the coach–athlete relationship (Jowett and Cockerill, 2002). It postulates that closeness (e.g. trust, respect), co-orientation (shared understanding), complementarity (e.g emotional support) underlie the relationship. The model has explanatory value but it may be more interesting to explore the underlying processes instead.

One of the limiting factors of the above approaches is that they are largely sport-specific accounts. This may facilitate an understanding of the distinctiveness of the sport context but it also maintains independence rather than an interdependence with movements in mainstream psychology (Walker *et al.*, 2006). As a result, innovations and paradigm shifts that occur in other realms of psychology including cognitive neuroscience can go largely untested in the

229

sport realm. For example, social cognitive neuroscience (see Decety and Sommerville, 2003) has emerged in the decade as an interdisciplinary domain concerned with eurobiological, epigenetic and psychological mechanisms underlying affective and social interpersonal processes, including empathy, perspective-taking, moral judgement and prosocial behaviour. This approach, which emerged from studying the representation of action and mental practice (MacIntyre, 2012), clearly resonates with recent attempts to develop links between neuroscience and sport psychology (Moran *et al.*, 2012a). We shall return to this issue momentarily, but first let us consider the construct of emotional intelligence, one of the constructs that has recently been employed to understand coach–athlete relationships (Lane *et al.*, 2010). Emotional intelligence has been defined as 'the ability to monitor one's own and others' feelings and emotion, to discriminate among them and to use this information to guide one's thinking and actions' (Salovey and Mayer, 1990, p. 189). The present challenge for researchers to consider is not just how emotional intelligence influences the formation, maintenance and development of relationships but to evaluate and explore the underlying processes. One such process, with a neural basis, is empathy and it's an objectively measureable construct unlike emotional intelligence (see Chapter 15). Next, we shall consider how this construct aligns with the research evidence in the coaching leadership literature.

THE WRITING IS ON THE WALL

Since the seminal paper by Ellen Berscheid more than two decades ago where she advocated for research on the impact of affect on 'cognition and research on the impact of relationships' exterior environments on their interior dynamics' (1999, p. 260), the development of a science of interpersonal relationships has emerged. Within the sport context, having good rapport with athletes is now considered a prerequisite for elite performance (Williams and Kendall, 2007). Effective relationships include factors such as empathic understanding, honesty, support, liking, acceptance, responsiveness, friendliness, cooperation, caring, respect and positive regard (e.g. Jowett and Cockerill, 2003; Jowett and Meek, 2000). In contrast, ineffective relationships are undermined by a lack of interest and emotion, remoteness, even antagonism, deceit, exploitation and physical or sexual abuse (e.g. Balague, 1999; Brackenridge, 2001). Evidently, the athlete–coach relationship in sport is too significant to neglect and its significance may stretch beyond the confines of sport. If this is the case, researchers should employ the most sophisticated approaches to understand these relationships and investigate the underlying processes to illuminate our understanding beyond mere descriptions and correlational research. Social cognitive neuroscience provides such a lens, one that may illuminate our understanding of coach–athlete relationships and the integral role of leaders in that context. Furthermore, given the physical and mental health challenges present in elite sport environments it is vital to develop an understanding of sustainable performance within a sports system. Sustainable performance is defined as the goal of superior consistent performance that is adaptive for the individual. The personal development, mental health and values of both coaches and athletes should not necessarily be undermined while engaged in their athletic pursuits.

MONKEY SEE, MONKEY DO!

Since the discovery of *mirror neurons* in macaque monkeys our understanding of our action observation system has been greatly advanced (Rizzolatti *et al.*, 1996). Mirror neurons are a set of neurons that are activated both when we perform an action and when we observe another performing that same action. In sum, we have a range of processes by which we can learn from watching another person perform a task (Moran *et al.*, 2012b). Since the work of Nobel prize winner Konrad Lorenz (Lorenz and Leyhausen, 1973), we have been familiar with the role of imitation in attachment – he was concerned with geese imitating him during the critical period of attachment. Subsequently, Albert Bandura (1986) proposed that we learn through learning enactively (by doing) and vicariously (by observing others). Thus, while social learning theory and action observation processes help us acquire skills and learn strategies, imitation is posited to be a less sophisticated but more automatic process. Thus the challenge as a coach and leader is to avoid simply *doing unto others what was done to you* and instead, choose to learn what is optimal for you. Peer observation is one such mechanism by which coaches can learn. Another is the capacity for reflection that is integral to the optimum practice of practitioners and coaches alike (Anderson *et al.*, 2002; Knowles, 2013). For instance, in 1998 Poczwardowski *et al.*, referring to practitioners, suggested that 'reflecting on each consulting experience is essential for maximal professional growth and development' (p. 201). Subsequent research has highlighted the role of reflective practice for coaches. Our mirror neuron system, emotional recognition system and empathy are fundamental to both of these aforementioned strategies. For example, emotional contagion can rapidly impact upon a team's performance and potentially lead to choking behaviours. 'Our survival relies on . . . our ability to interact with others. Such social transactions involve both an ability to identify with others, and also an ability to distinguish ourselves from others' (Decety and Sommerville, 2003, p. 527). Consequently, it is not surprising that imitation seems to be intrinsically coupled with empathy for others, broadly construed.

WHY EMPATHY?

> For me as a coach, I realize what I went through as an athlete. I realize the athletes are going to have problems making adjustments. As a coach, you have to understand where they are coming from.
>
> (Field hockey coach, Bloom and Salmela, 2000, p. 70)

Empathy, which means literally 'to feel for another', is an important aspect of social interaction and may be central to the effectiveness of coaches. 'Empathy denotes, at a phenomenological level of description, a sense of similarity between the feelings one experiences and those expressed by others' (Decety and Jackson, 2004, p. 71). Thus, from a social cognitive neuroscience perspective, empathy consists of both automatic affective experience and controlled cognitive processes (Decety and Sommerville, 2003). In essence, it requires the ability to recognise an emotion in others and subsequently, the intention to share or reciprocate that emotional state (see Table 16.1). Only tentative research has been conducted on this topic. Recent research has, for instance, focused on empathetic accuracy judgements among athletes and coaches (Jowett and Clark-Carter, 2006).

Table 16.1 Why is empathy important for coaches?

1 Empathy allows us to feel safe with our failures because we won't simply be blamed for them.

2 It encourages coaches to understand the root cause behind poor performance.

3 Being empathetic allows coaches to help struggling players improve and excel.

4 Empathy allows leaders to build and develop relationships and a shared vision with those they lead.

5 Coaches gain a greater awareness of the needs of your employees.

6 Empathy allows coaches to create an environment of open communication and more effective feedback.

7 It allows coaches to understand and explore problems players face and how to help them resolve them.

8 Being empathetic with players helps to validate what they're going through.

9 Empathy is a trainable attribute that can be developed by coaches over time.

10 Empathy is central to reflective practice.

CASE STUDY 1
'I KNOW EXACTLY HOW YOU FEEL!'

Emotional release by players and athletes, in tears of joy, for example, are so commonplace that award ceremonies are becoming more like the Oscars every year. What is more unusual is when sport has provided us with instances when players and managers from rival teams engage in empathetic behaviours (see Table 16.2).

One such example involves cousins Steven Gerrard (Liverpool) and Anthony Gerrard (Cardiff City) in the 2012 Carling Cup final. With the scoreline 2–2 after extra-time the match went to a penalty shootout. First player up to take a penalty was Liverpool captain Steven Gerrard who's strike was saved by the Cardiff City goal keeper. Four minutes later, after two misses by Cardiff and one by Liverpool, it was 3–2 in the shootout with Cardiff needing to score to prevent Liverpool from taking the silverware. Cardiff number six was the defender Anthony Gerrard. His strike could keep Cardiff in the game. Anthony put his spot-kick wide, bowed his head in disappointment and pulled his jersey over his face, while the Liverpool players celebrated their first trophy success since the FA cup in 2006 (BBC, 2012; Hunter, 2012). One Liverpool player didn't celebrate, but instead he walked over to embrace his cousin.

Steven Gerrard said:

> It was always going to be . . . one was going to be sad and one was going to be celebrating. You know, it happens, I've got mixed emotions. Obviously I'm delighted to win the cup for our supporters, but I feel for Anthony and Cardiff. . . . It doesn't matter what I say to him at this time you know he's going to be down. I'll be there for him and all the family will be behind him.

> (Bevan, 2012)

Ironically in this example, besides their family connection, they both missed their penalties and so shared the moment of performance failure, but Stephen Gerrard showed tremendous empathy given that they played for opposing teams. Another notable example has occurred in rugby and this one doesn't have family ties at the heart of it. Rivals Ronan O'Gara (Ireland) and Stephen Jones (Wales), former Lions Rugby team tourists from 2005, were their teams' respective out-halves in the Grand Slam showdown in 2009. That month O'Gara had become the top Six Nations point scorer ever and if Ireland won this match they would take their first grand slam title in 61 years. Wales were going for the Triple Crown title and with two minutes left on the clock O'Gara got a drop goal to take the score line to 17–15 to Ireland. As the game approached the final whistle, Ireland conceded a penalty near the half-way line. Having kicked four penalties and a drop goal in the match already, it was no surprise that Stephen Jones indicated he would attempt a penalty at goal, and if successful a one-point lead would give them the game. He struck it on target as the Irish players watched anxiously but it dropped just inches short of the target. At the final whistle, Ronan O'Gara, instead of celebrating with his team, walked straight up to Jones and embraced him. As he said in his own words:

> I went up to Stephen afterwards because I know how he'll feel – he'll be seen as the fella who missed the kick but that's not necessarily fair because it was a tough kick. I missed a kick to win a European Cup final against Northampton so I wanted to go up to him.

(*Guardian*, 22 March 2009)

Table 16.2 *Examples of players and managers from opposing teams engaging in empathy*

Date	Match	Characters
26 October 2014	Manchester United vs Chelsea Premier League match ends in 1–1 draw. Two managers had worked together previously	Respective managers Louis van Gaal (Man. U.) and Jose Mourinho embrace both prior to kick-off and after the final whistle
26 February 2012	Liverpool win Carling Cup final (3–2 AET) by Penalties against Cardiff City	Steven Gerrard (Capt.) embraces his cousin Anthony Gerrard, after his cousin's missed penalty handed Liverpool the victory
21 March 2009	A drop goal by Ronan O'Gara against Wales clinches a Triple Crown, Six Nations title and Grand Slam title for Ireland, despite a last ditch penalty attempt by Stephen Jones	Ronan O'Gara hugs rival kicker Stephen Jones after he missed the penalty to give Ireland the match

CASE STUDY 2
WALKING IN SOMEONE ELSE'S SHOES: A STEP TOWARDS EMPATHY

*The following case study highlights the role of empathy in leadership among professionals in high-pressure environments. It is based upon an interpretation of events and the interaction between three key individuals involved in the story documented online by Red Bull (www. redbullstratos.com).

Introduction

On 14 October 2012, in an attempt to freefall to earth, Felix Baumgartner jumped from a balloon capsule at 24 miles above earth, and in doing so he stepped into history. On his descent he broke the sound barrier, the unofficial record for the highest manned balloon flight and he also broke the record for the highest altitude jump set 50 years previously. This moment was the culmination of several years of planning, testing and development and Baumgartner's jump was 65 years to the day after 14 October 1947, when Chuck Yeager broke the sound barrier for the first time in a manned aircraft. In that tradition, the objective was literally to *push the envelope* and for Felix too to break the sound barrier. Pushing the envelope, a term derived from aeronautics where 'envelope' was a flight-test term referring to the limits of a particular aircraft's performance, colloquially means to push the boundaries of what is possible. However, the cast of characters involved and the demands of the tasks at the cusp of technological limits provided more than their fair share of setbacks to be overcome. This case study focuses on a snapshot of the interactions during that successful autumn day in New Mexico.

The characters

The project was built around the world record holder base jumper, 43-year-old Austrian Felix Baumgartner. Octogenerian Joe Kettinger, the team's flight operations, safety manager and capsule communicator was a retired USAF Colonel Joseph Kittinger. The former military Colonel and war veteran stated that 'I believe in what Felix is trying to do, test the next generation full pressure suit and I'm just delighted to be a member of the team.' The technical director was Art Thompson, who had responsibility for programme management and the handling of the mission's critical technology as well as assembly and oversight of the entire project team.

The setbacks

With such a great challenge the demands on personnel from both a technological and interpersonal perspective would be immense. Felix stated how he was up for the task: 'I love a challenge, and trying to become the first person to break the speed of sound in freefall is a challenge like no other.'

In the development phase, Felix expressed anxiety with the new generation flight suit which he described as 'swimming without feeling the water' as he could not feel the air to give him a sense of direction. His prior experiences and skill-set were as a parachutist in base-jumping not high altitude flight, so his ability to control his direction and velocity was now diminished. Interpersonal conflict also plagued the programme with Art Thompson being temporarily replaced in his project lead role. Psychological support was provided, not to the key players but just to Felix to help him cope with the anxiety he had expressed. Further setbacks occurred which only heightened the anxiety for Felix. On the launch date, there was a minor technical failure with the communications system and a subsequent postponement for several days due to adverse weather conditions.

The launch

The second attempt at a launch was successful and the discourse reflects the positive nature of relationship between Joe and Felix.

Joe: Keep it climbing Felix, you're on the way to space buddy!

Felix: Rock and Roll! Thank you so much guys.

Joe: And you're going up just great . . ..

And beyond 10,000 ft the positive dialogue continues:

Joe: Felix, you are going up at 1,200 ft per minute, right on track, everything's looking good, your doing great on the cabin, and everything's green.

Felix: The same here on my side. . . . Everything's stable and I'm trying to do my best.

Joe: We know you will Felix, we've got the confidence in you.

The ascent went smoothly until approximately 62,000 ft. when Felix expressed concerns that his visor heater was not functioning properly. A discussion unfolded between Joe and the ground crew.

Joe: Here's the problem. He thinks he doesn't have face plate, *it's his own perception* and if he doesn't trust it, that he doesn't have face plate, he's not a safe person, then he probably wants to abort.

Joe used *perspective taking*, a key component of empathy to reflect on the situation with Felix. The problem was dramatic as if Felix could not see the horizon or his instruments he couldn't jump safely. Joe and Art discuss the situation.

Joe: We have a choice to continue up a little bit to see if it gets better as you pass the cold or abort? Art, what do you think we should do?

Art: I think we are seeing face plate heating. I don't see it fogging up.

Above 105,000 ft the dilemma continues – abort or continue with the potential risk for Felix on the descent. Pay attention to the contrast in the following dialogue between Felix and

235

Art and the aforementioned discourse with Joe Kettinger.

> *Art:* He needs to hurry up and find out if it's going to work or not so we know if we are pressing on to 128 [thousand feet?] . . . Felix, are you good there?
>
> *Felix:* Let me disconnect my chest pack umbilical and see what's going on, ok.

Note how Art probed Felix's state rather than affirming it and not surprisingly Felix didn't respond to the question directly. Subsequently, Felix tries the back-up system, calls back to mission control and they test the heat shield again.

> *Art:* How you doing Felix? Hanging in their buddy?
>
> *Felix:* Ok I think we should continue and hopefully our chest pack face shield heating is working.

Again Felix focuses on the task, not his own emotional state despite Art's probing. It's not just about keeping Felix's face warm, it's also about the very real danger of not being able to see where he is in relation to the horizon. Without that vital visibility, going into a spin could be disastrous. A situation that ultimately *did* come to pass.

The descent

One of the predictable risks in the descent was the possibility of an uncontrolled spin. The spin started within the first minute of the jump which could have been fatal, but it ended at 01:23 when Baumgartner regained stability. Nine minutes after jumping from the capsule Felix landed back on earth. The empathetic interactions between Joe and Felix can partially be explained by Joe's vitae. In 1960, he had set the previous record of 102,800 ft.

Lessons learned

Several questions arise from the case study. First, was Felix the best candidate for the task, given his inexperience in high altitude flight? Second, should only Joe have been communicating with Felix, given that Art and Felix had interpersonal conflict? And finally, it is worth reflecting on the role of empathy in the high performance context. Should empathy be the core skill for the leaders of tomorrow? Felix aptly summed up the achievement of the Red Bull Stratos project: 'We put one foot in front of the other and after so many years finally reached our goal.' It may have been Joe's steps towards empathy that proved critical to this groundbreaking project.

SUMMARY

Relationships are central to our psychological experiences in the sporting context and they are fundamental to the coach–athlete dyad. To date, research has only recently attempted to employ social cognitive neuroscience perspectives to add theoretical rigour to our understanding of coach–athlete relationships. 'Theoretical diversity can shed light on relationship-related research questions from well-defined yet distinct angles' (Jowett and Wylleman, 2006, p. 121). The novel approach outline in this chapter can pay dividends in our understanding of leadership in the coaching context and move beyond the three Cs model (Jowett, 2005). Empathy is a measureable construct with a neural basis that can be employed readily in this domain to understand factors such as effective communication, peer observation, emotional contagion among others. Effective relationships, where empathy is central, can prove valuable in developing sustained performance that is adaptive for both coaches and athletes.

REVIEW QUESTIONS

1   Is empathy central to relationship development?

2   Do high performance teams need leaders who excel in empathy?

3   Can you think of examples of empathy between sporting rivals?

4   Is a lack of empathy a reason why many elite players don't make it in coaching?

REFERENCES

Anderson, A. G., Miles, A., Mahoney, C. and Robinson, P. (2002). Evaluating the effectiveness of applied sport psychology practice: Making the case for a case study approach. *The Sport Psychologist, 16*, 432–453.

Anderson, C. M., Petrie, T. A. and Neumann, C. S. (2012). Effects of sport pressures on female collegiate athletes: A preliminary longitudinal investigation. *Sport, Exercise and Performance Psychology, 1*, 120–134.

Balague, G. (1999). Understanding identity, value and meaning when working with elite athletes. *The Sport Psychologist, 13*, 89–98.

Bandura, A. (1986). *Social foundations of thought and action: A social cognitive theory.* Englewood Cliffs, NJ: Prentice Hall.

BBC (2012). Steven Gerrard has mixed emotions despite Carling Cup win. Retrieved 22 February 2015 from www.bbc.com/sport/0/football/17174043.

Berscheid, E. (1999). The greening of relationship science. *American Psychologist, 54*, 260–266.

Bevan, S. (2012). Football: Cardiff 2–2 Liverpool. Retrieved from www.guardian.com.

Bloom, G. A. and Salmela, J. H. (2000). Personal characteristics of expert team sport coaches. *Journal of Sport Pedagogy, 6* (2), 56–76.

Bonogofski, S. L., Beerman, K. A., Massey, L. K. and Houghton, M. (1999). A comparison of athletic achievement and eating disorder behaviors among female cross country runners. *Medicine and Science in Sports and Exercise, 31*, S65.
Brackenbridge C. (2001). *Spoilsports: Understanding and preventing sexual exploitation in sport.* New York: Routledge.
Chelladurai, P. (1993). Leadership. In R. N. Singer, M. Murphey and L. K. Tennant (eds) *Handbook on research on sport psychology* (pp. 647–671). New York: Macmillan.
Côté, J. and Gilbert, W. (2009). An integrative definition of coaching effectiveness and expertise. *International Journal of Sports Science and Coaching, 4*, 307–323.
Decety, J. and Sommerville, J. A. (2003). Shared representations between self and others: A social cognitive neuroscience view. *Trends in Cognitive Sciences, 7*, 527–533.
Decety, J. and Jackson, P. L. (2004). The functional architecture of human empathy. *Behavioral and Cognitive Neuroscience Review, 3*, 71–100.
Dixon, M., Lee, S. and Ghaye, T. (2013). Reflective practices for better sports coaches and coach education: Shifting from a pedagogy of scarcity to abundance in the run-up to Rio 2016. *Reflective Practice: International and Multidisciplinary Perspectives*, 14 (5), 585–599.
Eder, S. (2013). Rutgers officials long knew of coach's actions. *New York Times*, 6 April. Retrieved 22 February 2015 from www.nytimes.com/2013/04/07/sports/ncaabasketball/rutgers-officials-long-knew-of-coach-mike-rices-actions.html?pagewanted=all&_r=0.
Ford, M. L. (2014). *A history of NFL preseason and exhibition games:* 1986 to 2013. London: Rowman & Littlefield.
Guardian (2009). Cool-headed O'Gara hits back at his detractors. Retrieved 22 February 2015 from www.theguardian.com/sport/2009/mar/22/ronan-ogara-ireland-grand-slam-six-nations.
Hughes, L. and Leavey, G. (2012). Setting the bar: Athletes and vulnerability to mental illness. *British Journal of Psychiatry, 200*, 95–96.
Hunter, A. (2012). 'This is just the start', says Kenny Dalglish as Liverpool celebrate. *The Guardian* (online).Retrieved 22 February 2015 from www.theguardian.com/football/2012/feb/26/kenny-dalglish-liverpool.
Jowett, S. (2005). The coach–athlete partnership. *The Psychologist, 18* (7), 412–415.
Jowett, S. and Meek, G. A. (2000). The coach–athlete relationship in married couples: An exploratory content analysis. *The Sport Psychologist, 14*, 157–175.
Jowett, S. and Cockerill, I. M., (2002). Incompatibility in the coach–athlete relationship. In I. M. Cockerill (ed.) *Solutions in sport psychology* (pp. 16–31). London: Thomson Learning.
Jowett, S. and Cockerill, I. M. (2003). Olympic medallists' perspective of the athlete–coach relationship. *Psychology of Sport and Exercise, 4*, 313–331.
Jowett, S. and Clark-Carter, D. (2006). Perceptions of empathic accuracy and assumed similarity in the coach-athlete relationship. *British Journal of Social Psychology, 45* (3), 617–637.
Jowett, S. and Wylleman, P. (2006). Interpersonal relationships in sport and exercise: Crossing the chasm. *Psychology of Sport and Exercise, 7*, 119–123.
Jowett, S. and Lavallee, D. (2007). *Social psychology in sport.* Champaign, IL: Human Kinetics.
Jowett, S. and Poczwardowski, A. (2007). Understanding the coach–athlete relationship. In S. Jowett and D. Lavallee (eds), *Social psychology in sport* (pp. 3–14). Champaign, IL: Human Kinetics.
Kerr, G., Berman, E. and de Souza, M. J. (2006). Disordered eating in women's gymnastics: Perspectives of athletes, coaches, parents, and judges. *Journal of Applied Sport Psychology, 18*, 28–43.
Knowles, Z. R. (2013). Sports coaching: Reflecting on reflection – Exploring the practice of sports coaching graduates. In R. Neil, S. Hanton, S. Fleming and K. Wilson (eds), *The research process in sport, exercise and health: Case studies of active researchers.* Hove, East Sussex: Routledge.
Kremer, J. and Moran, A. P. (2013). *Pure sport* (2nd edn). Hove: Routledge.

238

Lane, A. M., Thelwell, R. C., Lowther, J. and Devonport, T. J. (2009). Emotional intelligence and psychological skills use among athletes. *Social Behavior and Personality: An International Journal, 37* (2), 195–201.

Lane, A. M., Devonport, T. J., Soos, I., Karsai, I., Leibinger, E. and Hamar, P. (2010). Emotional intelligence and emotions associated with optimal and dysfunctional athletic performance. *Journal of Sports Science and Medicine, 9*(3), 388–392.

Lorenz, K. and Leyhausen, P. (1973). *Motivation of human and animal behavior: An ethological view.* New York: D. Van Nostrand.

MacIntyre, T. (2012). What have the Romans ever done for us? The contribution of sport and exercise psychology to mainstream psychology. *The Psychologist, 25* (7), 2–3.

Moran, A., Guillot, A., MacIntyre, T. and Collet, C. (2012a). Re-imagining mental imagery: Building bridges between cognitive neuroscience and sport psychology. *British Journal of Psychology, 103*, 224–247.

Moran, A. P., Campbell, M., Holmes, P. and MacIntyre, T. (2012b). Mental imagery, action observation and skill learning. In N. Hodges and M. A. Williams (eds), *Skill acquisition in sport: Research, theory and practice* (2nd edn, pp. 94–111). Sussex: Routledge.

Poczwardowski, A., Sherman, C. P. and Henschen, K. P. (1998). A sport psychology service delivery heuristic: Building on theory and practice. *The Sport Psychologist, 12*, 191–207.

Rizzolatti, G., Fadiga, L., Gallese, V. and Fogassi, L. (1996) Premotor cortex and the recognition of motor actions. *Cognitive Brain Research, 3*, 131–141.

Salovey, P. and Mayer, J. D. (1990). Emotional intelligence. *Imagination, Cognition and Personality, 9*, 185–211.

Smoll, F. L., Smith, R. E. and Cumming, S. P. (2007). Effects of a motivational climate intervention for coaches on changes in young athletes' achievement goal orientations. *Journal of Clinical Sport Psychology, 1* (1), 23–46.

Walker, G., Kremer, J. and Moran, A. (2006). Coming of age in sport psychology. *Sport and Exercise Psychology Review, 2* (1), 43–49.

Williams, S. J. and Kendall, L. (2007). Perceptions of elite coaches and sports scientists of the research needs for elite coaching practice. *Journal of Sports Sciences, 25* (14), 1577–1586.

Chapter 17

The future

Trends and challenges in sport leadership

Nick Takos, Ian O'Boyle and Duncan Murray

CHAPTER OBJECTIVES

The main purpose of this chapter is to:

1   bring together topics and issues covered in the book and discuss the changing environment faced by the leaders of sport organisations;
2   explain the most recent developments of leadership theory and practice and consider the major future challenges sport leaders may face;
3   describe the keys for leadership success in sport organisations at the various levels: board, administration and coaching.

KEY TERMS

- digital era
- integrity
- shared leadership
- authenticity
- authentic relationships
- trust
- values
- emotional intelligence

INTRODUCTION

We generally accept that sport has now been subsumed under the moniker of 'big business' (Hoye *et al.*, 2012; Bradbury and O'Boyle, 2013). Still, while this may well apply to the big 'professional' sporting leagues around the globe, such as the American National Basketball Association (NBA), Australian Football League (AFL) or the English Premier League (EPL), increased professionalism has also resulted in changes in the non-profit sporting environment. Both professional and non-profit sport organisations now generally share a common imperative for high quality leadership in the modern era.

The landscape faced by sport leaders has changed, and so too have the skills and competencies required by leaders to be effective on this new playing field. So what is this new landscape, and what threats and opportunities will it provide leaders of sport organisations?

THE NEW ENVIRONMENT – TECHNOLOGY

As we saw in Chapter 2, influencing individuals is central to many definitions of leadership. In our global world, much of this influence may occur via non-traditional forms, and may occur in virtual or cyber environments. Therefore, understanding the impact of these new forms of technology by which leaders and followers communicate is critical when discussing the future trends and challenges facing leaders.

People now communicate directly to large networks, at greater speeds, and via multiple platforms, using technology that facilitates easy and instant transfer of information. As described in Chapter 8, sport fans consume sport, interacting with other fans and sport organisations on a 24/7 basis. Initially, Generation Y were the early adopters and at the forefront of using the latest communication tools (such as Facebook, Twitter, Instagram etc.). However, these platforms have now also been accepted by other mainstream consumers, with organisations, including sports organisations, understanding their potential as a professional business tool that can facilitate effective communication with their client base.

Instant communication is both a blessing and a curse for leaders of sports organisations. Sport engenders passionate emotions. Sports teams have fans that are emotionally and passionately connected; thus the consequences of the leader's actions are highly visible to the public; and the pressure to make popular decisions is fuelled by unprecedented levels of media interest. The emotional uniqueness of sport, coupled with the digital revolution, sees the actions of leaders such as coaches, managers, players and management of sport associations scrutinised more than ever before. For example, the recent drugs in sport scandal in Australia, involving AFL club Essendon and the NRL rugby club Cronulla, illustrates the magnitude to which the public interest can reach as a result of the combination of the new media and passionate sport followers' capacity to communicate with each other. Both of these clubs have been required to manage their way through a media storm. Also, other clubs in both codes have been indirectly associated and suffered from constant innuendo (in multiple media platforms) due to their previous liaisons with the sport scientist who is at the centre of investigations with Essendon and Cronulla. All of these clubs are faced with restless stakeholders who are looking to the club leaders for strong and positive leadership. The value of the brands of these clubs could be severely harmed, resulting in potential financial loss and jeopardising future relationships with key stakeholders. While technology has potentially escalated the damage caused by the issue, it also provides a vehicle for club leaders to mitigate the damage via communication with its followers.

In such a climate, leaders of sporting organisations will need to ensure their decision making and behaviours are well suited to this new environment if they are to optimise their chances of success.

LEADER INTEGRITY

Perhaps as an outcome of the growth in instant communication, there has been increased scrutiny on leaders in both the sporting as well as the wider business world. The global financial crisis led to the collapse of a number of iconic financial institutions, with questions being asked about how the leadership of these organisations could fail so badly. Likewise in the sporting world questions have been raised following issues such as systemic doping of athletes (such as Essendon and Cronulla, discussed previously) and other allegations of corruption and scandals within the industry. In both cases, business and sport, the integrity of the leaders comes under heavy scrutiny.

A leader's integrity centres on followers' perceptions of how closely a leader's behaviour aligns with their words; put simply, that their leader 'walks the talk'. The concept of behavioural integrity is linked to a leader's values and highlights the emerging import-ance placed on a leader's actions matching their deeply held beliefs. If a leader does display behavioural integrity, then they generally gain credibility in the eyes of their followers. For example, the words and actions of a club coach are likely to be judged by the players as a group.

Imagine a comment made by a coach to the eagerly awaiting media regarding the trading of a player to another club. The coach states it is due to the player's lack of work ethic. However, players at the club, knowing the player in question, may doubt how true the coach's comments are based on the fact they know the player and know their work ethic at training. Therefore, athletes' perceptions of the coach's integrity may be shaped and influenced, affecting their commitment levels to their leader.

SHARED LEADERSHIP

The relationship between the leader and follower has formed a part of leadership studies for many years; however, the emerging literature is placing the leader–follower relationship increasingly at the forefront of research. In sport, followers such as athletes, staff, volunteers, and fans have the capacity to exert influence on the organisation's formal leaders. People and organisations are complex and rely on ongoing social processes and therefore interest in the follower, and the role they play in leadership warrants a closer examination when considering the future of leadership in sport (Pearce et al., 2014).

With increased involvement of the followers in the practical setting, and the more recent interest by academics in the follower, shared leadership is remerging as a potentially effective approach within which to examine successful leadership. Avolio et al. (1996) rekindled the interest of scholars, having demonstrated a positive relationship exists between shared leadership and team performance. Pearce *et al.* (2014) agreed and suggested leadership has moved beyond the top-down approach. They argued contemporary leadership involves more than individuals leading the way, and that leadership should now be shared by others in order to improve organisational effectiveness.

Shared leadership occurs when two or more members engage in the leadership of a team in an effort to influence other members to maximise effectiveness (Carson *et al.*, 2007). Shared leadership can entail multiple official leaders, or the emergence of unofficial leaders who form a mutually influential leadership process (Yukl, 2010). This is not to say that shared leadership has only one form. There may be varying degrees where sometimes it is completely shared and in other contexts it may be shared only slightly. However, research has demonstrated that shared leadership delivers positive organisational outcomes and this has also been demonstrated within the sport management and coaching environments (Hoye and Cuskelly, 2007; Wang *et al.*, 2014). Within the practical setting of sport coaching for instance, there are many recent examples where players share leadership, sometimes formally as 'co-captains' and in other organisations more informally. Ric Charlesworth (Hockey Australia, 2014), coach of the Australian women's hockey team, highlights a shared leadership approach in practice:

> While much of the focus of any team is placed on the captain, our model is based firmly on developing leadership across the squad. It has been a change to the traditional role of the captain as figurehead to a model where the captain has an active role to mentor leadership qualities in all players.

The increased interest in the followers within shared leadership is also evident at the board level within sport organisations. For example, Hoye (2004) explored leadership from a relationship perspective, considering the relationships between paid staff and volunteers. He concluded high quality relationships are important for successful leadership. Hoye suggests the challenge is to better understand how these relationships are formed, developed and maintained in the varying levels within sport organisations (e.g. board, executive/staff, coach/athlete).

In the modern era where leadership is more likely to be undertaken by multiple persons within the organisation, it is important to understand what facilitates the success of this new 'leadership' paradigm. When leadership is shared, relationships are formed between multiple 'leaders' and these have been found to be important.

Linking back to the notion of integrity, a number of recent leadership theories argue that values (and sharing of values) are an important component for leaders to enhance their leadership capacity when developing relationships with followers (Lewicki *et al.*, 1998; Kouzes and Posner, 2012). The increased prominence of values-based leadership is due to organisational leadership suffering severe critique in the wake of many corporate and sport scandals and ethical lapses. Accordingly, the future sport leader can expect to be scrutinised more closely and face more pressure than ever before. The values of leaders are critical, as when an individual is performing under stress they will often make decisions based on their innermost beliefs (Yardley *et al.*, 2012).

TRUST

An important challenge for the sport leader who works with groups and teams is building trust with their followers (Creed and Miles, 1996; Dirks and Ferrin, 2001). Trust is the bedrock through which they can successfully engage more effectively with followers to strengthen the organisation's leadership capability. Trust can be described as the expectation that a person can rely on another person's actions or words to be positive towards them (Lewicki et al., 1998). In sport, groups and teams are the basic structure of many situations, boards, coaching groups, player teams and executive staff. These are the places where trust must be built. Bennis (1999) emphasises the role of trust, describing it as the strongest glue binding people together in groups and highlighting that trust is an outcome of a leader's accumulated actions and behaviours.

So how can leaders develop higher levels of trust throughout their organisation? As already discussed, having and knowing your values is becoming increasingly important in leadership. This is captured in a relatively new concept in the leadership genre; authentic leadership, which defines an authentic leader as genuine, real and committed to their core values (Luthans and Avolio, 2003; Hassan and Ahmed, 2011). This understanding of one's core values that drive a deeper sense of purpose assists the authentic sport leader to develop authentic relationships and build higher levels of trust with their followers. If, as mentioned earlier, followers' perceptions of a leader's credibility and integrity are based on the leader 'walking the talk', then to walk the talk, you have to know your own values and beliefs (Kouzes and Posner, 2012).

Building an authentic relationship is critical for leaders as they not only behave in congruence with their own values, but also show genuine interest in the values of their followers. This concept of relational leadership extends LMX theory to its next logical step (Brower et al., 2000). The challenge for the future sport leaders is to not lose themselves with a focus on the relationship. As Alegra and Lips-Wiersma (2012) recommend, they must develop their leadership skills so they can be true to their 'self-in-relationship'.

In order to build genuine authentic relationships, leaders will need to identify those factors that influence the establishment of authentic relationships such as negotiating shared values and achieving a level of reciprocal trust. This 'contested ground' of shared values between leaders and individual followers, or within teams and groups, is a process of negotiation (Eagly, 2005), as they seek to align values for the attainment of broad goals of the sport organisation. To date, however, how these relationships are developed is not well understood. While trust is considered to play an important role, a range of other factors may play a role, particularly since the relational context in sport organisations is multifaceted. For example, relationships may occur between:

- coach and athlete;
- coach and assistant coaches;
- CEO and executive staff;
- CEO and president/board directors;
- president and board directors;
- national sport boards and regional boards;
- functional team members and their leaders.

244

So who instigates these relationships? Is it the leader, the follower, or is it reciprocal? It has been suggested that the future sport leader should often be the one who initiates the development of such an authentic relationship. Kouzes and Posner (2012) advised a great leader is the one who steps forward first and learns about another's values. This relational recommendation for future leadership can be likened to a dance; both participants rely on each other, but someone must lead the way and make the first move. There needs to be some agreement on shared values, and a necessary skill required by the future sport leader is that of listening (Kouzes and Posner, 2012).

EMOTIONAL INTELLIGENCE

According to Goleman (1998), the authentic leader of the future will have the characteristics of self-awareness, empathy and social skill, which allows them to understand their own self, but also have the emotional intelligence to understand others as well. This is supported by Taylor *et al.* (2008) who advise future leaders to develop those behaviours associated with high levels of emotional intelligence, as they will be critical to their future success. In team settings, Zhou and George (2003) also endorse the importance of emotional intelligence. The future sport leader, situated in an often intense climate – fuelled by emotionally charged stakeholders such as athletes, fans, board members and coaches – is advised to understand their own emotions and, equally as important, understand those of others as well. This will be challenging in the 'arena' that sport organisations contest where a crisis is always nearby; a coach's sacking, an athlete's indiscretion or a spectator's emotional outburst. Leadership relationships will be tested as organisations are tempted to manage their image rather than see the crisis as an opportunity to trust the multiple leaders who must manage the situation (Brockner and James, 2008). As recommended in Chapter 8, the sport leader will require strong communications skills, and to be both task and relationship orientated.

SUMMARY

The professionalisation of sport has resulted in the formally appointed leader of a sport organisation often being the most highly remunerated person in the administration staff; however, we should be hesitant to place the entire responsibility of leadership on one person. Sport, with its heightened media and community interest, places enormous pressure on formal leaders, and in some cases looks to former athletes with a celebrity status to 'rescue' a struggling organisation, either as an executive, board director or coach. The sport organisation should be wary of this 'saviour' being a larger-than-life individual, and instead understand the modern sport leader is better positioned by utilising the concepts recommended in this chapter to develop leaders throughout the organisation. Great leaders achieve great results not by themselves, but through the assistance of willing followers who trust the leader and each other, and are willing to take on leadership responsibilities themselves when required to do so. The leader should be the curator of other leaders throughout the organisation.

Leadership is often referred to as a process, viewed from the leader and follower perspectives, an interaction whereby leadership is co-created (Uhl-Bien *et al.*, 2014) and not equated with one's hierarchical position in the organisation. For instance, at board level many of the board incumbents are leaders in their own organisations, or at the team coal face; an assistant coach leads athletes, however, may be a follower when interacting with the senior coach.

The building and maintenance of relationships is important in the leadership process, requiring an emotional intelligence and commitment by leaders. While this is arguably time consuming, it will generate better leaders throughout the organisation and a competitive advantage for the sport organisation trying to achieve success in an increasingly professional sport industry. The skill of relationship management is an important component of emotional intelligence, along with the behavioural competency of being able to develop others (Goleman, 2001), which are both seen as critical for successful organisational leadership. The future sport leader will be required to develop others, abandon their egos and know themselves and, importantly, listen to others so that they can embrace the leadership of those who 'follow'.

The leadership process at the coach and manager level requires a similar focus (to overall organisation leadership) on the follower and relationships. As stated in Chapter 12, effective coaching relies on interpersonal and social awareness, and the skill of emotional intelligence offers a valuable route for improving sport performers'/teams' learning and performance.

The physical aspect of working as an athlete requires coaches to have an additional care for the follower when compared to the administrative division of a sport organisation. In the coach/athlete relationship the leader requires an increased level of sensitivity to the health and well-being of athletes. In an environment with enormous pressure to win, the values and ethical behaviours of coaches can be considered even more important as direct physical harm could be inflicted upon athletes if leaders ignore legal and moral obligations to their followers. Examples of issues relating to the coach's values and ethics include fair selection, sportsmanship, being treated with respect in front of team mates, verbal abuse and creating an environment that develops the 'whole of person'.

REFERENCES

Algera, P. M., and Lips-Wiersma, M. (2012). Radical authentic leadership: Co-creating the conditions under which all members of the organisation can be authentic. *The Leadership Quarterly*, 23(1), 118–131.

Avolio, B. J., Jung, D., Murray, W., and Sivasubramaniam, N. (1996). Building highly developed teams: Focusing on shared leadership process, efficacy, trust, and performance. In Beyerlein, D. A., and Beyerlein, S. T. (eds), *Advances in interdisciplinary studies of work teams* (pp. 173–209). Greenwich, CT: JAI Press.

Bennis, W. (1999). The end of leadership: Exemplary leadership is impossible without full inclusion, initiatives, and cooperation of followers. *Organizational Dynamics*, 27(1), 71–79.

Bradbury, T., and O'Boyle, I. (2013). The future: Trends and challenges in sport governance. In O'Boyle, I., Bradbury, T. (eds), *Sport governance: International case studies* (pp. 277–288). Abingdon: Routledge.

Brockner, J., and James, E. H. (2008). Toward an understanding of when executives see crisis as opportunity. *The Journal of Applied Behavioral Science*, 44(1), 94–115.

Brower, H., Schoorman, F. D., and Tan, H. H. (2000). A model of relational leadership: The integration of trust and leader-member exchange. *Leadership Quarterly*, 11(2), 227–250.

Carson, J. B., Tesluk, P. E., and Marrone, J. A. (2007). Shared leadership in teams: An investigation of antecedent conditions and performance. *Academy of Management Journal*, 50, 1217–1234.

Creed, W. E., and Miles, R. E. (1996). Trust in organisations: A conceptual framework linking organisational forms, managerial philosophies, and the opportunity costs of controls. In Kramer, R. M., and Tyler, T. R. (eds), *Trust in organisations: Frontiers of theory and research* (pp. 16–38). London: Sage.

Dirks, K. T., and Ferrin, D. J. (2001). The role of trust in organizational settings. *Organization Science*, 12(4), 450–467.

Eagly, A. H. (2005). Achieving relational authenticity in leadership: Does gender matter? *The Leadership Quarterly*, 16(3), 459–474.

Goleman, D. (1998). What makes a leader? *Harvard Business Review*, 76, 93–102.

Goleman, D. (2001). Emotional intelligence: Perspectives on a theory of performance. In Chermiss, C., and Goleman, D. (eds), *The emotionally intelligent workplace* (pp. 13–26). San Francisco, CA: Jossey-Bass.

Hassan, A., and Ahmed, F. (2011). Authentic leadership, trust and work engagement. *International Journal of Human and Social Sciences*, 6(3), 164–170.

Hockey Australia. (2014). *Exclusive interview with Ric Charlesworth*. Retrieved 19 November 2014, from www.hockey.org.au/News/exclusive-interview-630.

Hoye, R. (2004). Leader-member exchanges and board performance of voluntary sport organizations. *Nonprofit Management and Leadership*, 15(1), 55–70.

Hoye, R., and Cuskelly, G. (2007). *Sport governance*. Oxford: Elsevier.

Hoye, R., Smith, A. C. T., Nicholson, M., Stewart, B., and Westerbeek, H. (2012). *Sport management: Principles and applications*, 3rd edn. Abington: Routledge.

Kouzes, J., and Posner, B. (2012). *The leadership challenge: How to make extraordinary things happen in organisations*, 5th edn. Somerset, NJ: John Wiley & Sons.

Lewicki, R. J., McAllister, D. J., and Bies, R. J. (1998). Trust and distrust: New relationships and realities. *The Academy of Management Review*, 23(3), 438–458.

Luthans, F., and Avolio, B. J. (2003). Authentic leadership: A positive developmental approach. In K. S. Cameron, J. E. Dutton, and R. E. Quinn (eds), *Positive organizational scholarship* (pp. 241–261), San Francisco, CA: Barrett-Koehler.

Pearce, C. L., Wassenaar, C. L., and Manz, C. C. (2014). Is shared leadership the key to responsible leadership? *The Academy of Management Perspectives*, 28(3), 275–288.

Taylor, C. A., Taylor, J. C., and Stoller, J. K. (2008). Exploring leadership competencies in established and aspiring leaders: An interview based study. *Journal of General Internal Medicine*, 23, 748–754.

Uhl-Bien, M., Riggio, R. E., Lowe, K. B., and Carsten, M. K. (2014). Followership theory: A review and research agenda. *The Leadership Quarterly*, 25, 83–104.

Wang, D., Waldman, D. A., and Zhang, Z. (2014). A meta-analysis of shared leadership and team effectiveness. *Journal of Applied Psychology*, 99(2), 181–198.

Yardley, I., Kakabadse, A., and Neal, D. (2012). *From battlefield to boardroom: Making a difference through value-based leadership*. Basingstoke: Palgrave Macmillan.

Yukl, G. A. (2010). *Leadership in Organizations*, 7th edn. Upper Saddle River, NJ: Prentice Hall.

Zhou, J., and George, J. M. (2003). Awakening employee creativity: The role of leader emotional intelligence. *Leadership Quarterly*, 14, 545–568.

Index